MAIN STREET   PETERSON IOWA.   5876

REFLECTING A PRAIRIE TOWN

THE AMERICAN LAND & LIFE SERIES   *Edited by Wayne Franklin*

REFLECTING A

Text & photographs by DRAKE HOKANSON

Foreword by Wayne Franklin

PRAIRIE TOWN

A Year in Peterson

UNIVERSITY OF IOWA PRESS Ψ *Iowa City*

University of Iowa Press, Iowa City 52242

Copyright © 1994 by Drake Hokanson

Printed in Canada

Design by Richard Hendel

Printed on acid-free paper

98 97 96 95 94 C 5 4 3 2 1

Page vi: Little Sioux River, circa 1900.   Page viii: Threshing on the E. C. Bertram farm near Peterson, circa 1920. Photograph courtesy of Ione Johnson.   Page xvi: Ora and Ernest C. Bertram are obviously proud of their rural Peterson farm in this photograph dated 1912. Photograph courtesy of Ione Johnson.   Page xviii: Art Johnson Implement Company, circa 1950. The author's grandfather, Henry Hokanson, is at center, with Evelyn Busby and Frank Mohror. In a fashion similar to general stores of earlier eras, implement dealers sought to carry everything a farmer might need from parts and tools to Coca-Cola and oil stoves.

Library of Congress Cataloging-in-Publication Data

Hokanson, Drake, 1951–

   Reflecting a prairie town: a year in Peterson / text and photographs by Drake Hokanson; foreword by Wayne Franklin.

     p.   cm.—(American land and life series)

   Includes bibliographical references and index.

   ISBN 0-87745-466-3

   1. Peterson (Iowa)—Description and travel.   2. Farm life—Iowa—Peterson.   3. Landscape—Iowa—Peterson.   I. Title.

II. Series.

F629.P47H65   1994

977.7'153—dc20   94-6369

                                        CIP

For my mother, Mona Beck, and my grandmother, Ione Johnson.

This book springs from love: their love of home, my mother's love of

the written word, my grandmother's love of history, and my love for them,

because they gave me the first three.

Little Sioux R.
Peterson, Ia.

Struve Photo.

Contents

Foreword *by Wayne Franklin*

Many readers of this book will never have visited or even heard of the small town of Peterson, Iowa. If they have, so much the better; if not, Drake Hokanson will give them the next best thing, and much, much more. Having lived in Peterson for a time in his youth, Hokanson returned there following a long ramble around the globe. After Cairo and Bangkok, Peterson must have seemed even smaller and simpler than youthful memories otherwise would have made it. But it must also have seemed even more deeply rooted there, in the Little Sioux valley, than Hokanson recalled, the lines of its modest buildings crisp under the insistent, silent prairie sun. A homecoming of unexpected intensity moved him to capture all he could of the physical shape and varied past and human spirit of Peterson.

He has been so successful that visitors to Peterson, however eagle-eyed, never would find on their own a fraction of what his book discovers. Even Peterson's regular inhabitants, fixtures there during Hokanson's own interrupted residence, have much to gain from his prose and his photographs. But Hokanson's small town is also uncannily large. In capturing the essence of this one place he helps us understand our own worlds better. With a singular combination of word and image, of both of which he is a master, Hokanson gives us a long and deeply moving meditation on our common rootedness in the earth. Whether we live in Peterson or St. Petersburg, we need to be called back to the earth, and Hokanson calls us back with gentle insight and insistent art.

In the process, he makes us appreciate how profound an invention human place is; how place, constructed from the raw expanse of natural space, contains and defines human life. It relates us both to the physical universe and to each other. We may misunderstand or resist him at first. Many Americans no longer believe in place. We live so much in a placeless web of electronic impulses that the ground beneath our feet seems to have lost its substance. If we venture out into the three-dimensional world, it is as commuters carried along a kind of electronic circuit ourselves, from node to node, terminal to terminal. Place appears to have very little power over us. It is compliant, recessive, always there but rarely visible. We do not need it.

Why, then, do we hunger in the midst of the city for some artful western "view," with its splendid sense of depth and contingency, forest above valley, mountain peak above forest, the deep blue sky above it all? Or seek out, if only in imagination, a stretch of farmland where the stone or wire or wood fences mark off but cannot contain the fruitful life of the fields? The answer is both simple and profound. We feel deeply the loss of such landscapes; we mourn the loss of the meaning they have had for us, the loss of the selves we might have been had we inhabited them.

The fundamental truth of experience on this continent has always lain in the challenges and opportunities of space. All of us came to this hemisphere recently—compared, that is, with how long our common ancestors have inhabited Africa or Eurasia. As a result, whether we entered the hemisphere via the Bering Strait or the Atlantic or the Pacific, we were always organizing a space too big for us. We constructed smaller, limited, contained places out of the heartless expanse of the land in order to shelter ourselves from the vastness beyond. Like a niche in the warm sandstone walls of Canyon de Chelly, such human places located us in the harsh, seemingly endless distances of this continent. Place mattered so much for so many of us for so long because we were so few before the immensity of the land. But place at the same time rooted us in that immensity. We lived *on* the land, not against it or in spite of it.

Perhaps we now devalue place because the continent no longer feels big to us. Most of us live not on the land but in the layered aggregations of a few desperate urban zones. We compete for increasingly rare and costly artificial room up and down a vertical axis that ignores the great horizons of the continent as well as the intimacies of human place. Place is redundant in this urban zone, piled on top of itself until too few of us touch the earth and no one really is located anywhere anymore. So situated, we devote ourselves to integrating the abstract structures of urban life, especially the urban economy, rather than the people with whom we share our crowded, smudged domains or the vistas that lie beyond. Most of America, in the phrase an Iowa farmer used for Hokanson, is for most Americans just "fly-over country." Our only possible relation to it might come, god forbid, when the engines that keep us adrift fail and we plummet to earth. We can imagine no gentler contact with the land than this.

Not that we do not need the real thing: we simply cannot handle it when it lies all about us. At most, we can cope with the simulacra that glut our urban eyes. An inner office in an Atlanta skyscraper, closed out from actual views, has its darkest wall covered with an enormous photographic mural of Muir Woods. A dentist's chair in upstate New York pits the patient, face-on, against a view of saguaros and mouth-drying dust. A beer sign in a smoky bar in Minnesota needlessly loops around, a Möbius band of landscape through which/on which flows an endless brook. It keeps flowing downstream until it tumbles over a fall and then flows on until, with another rotation, it has mysteriously risen back to the edge of the fall again. It tumbles into itself in the kind of circular logic that our inner dread of real landscape requires. The world as we might invent it has the self-absorption of our souls.

Over against that confected, self-enclosed world, place the real town of Hokanson's book. Peterson is no summary of all the other places it resembles even though, as Hokanson describes it, it becomes a kind of universal symbol. Anchored by the hills that rise behind it and before it and on either side, set off by the Little Sioux along its southern boundary, Peterson clings tenaciously to its own niche of North America. Yes, the economic realities of this town today, as of most others, link the townspeople with powerful forces that seem to pull Peterson out of its physical niche and into the placeless market of international trade. In that market (which is not really a market, either, not a concrete place of exchange but, again, a matter of electronic impulses), corn and beans are not the seeds of past and future growth but rather rootless commodities with no local character or history. No longer do the farmers of the Peterson area raise their own foodstuffs or those of the small tradespeople of the town. No longer can Peterson sustain and reproduce itself without running its produce, via those big trucks that pull up to the elevator, through a complex economic system of which Peterson is a virtually anonymous dependent.

Yet there is a better lesson in Hokanson's careful and caring vision. Peterson has been many things in its relatively short history. The earth it occupies—to the extent we can know that earth in the aeons before the European pioneers or the Lakota they displaced or the little-known "Mill Creek people" of a truly remote era—the earth endures, running below all human divisions, fertilizing not only the surface we tread but also our memories and dreams. That Hokanson can sense so much about so small a place, uncovering layer after layer in this ancient palimpsest of space, suggests how superficial are the systems by which we deny the power of natural space and the meaning of human place in our own lives. Peterson might become the home of all of us. To enter this book is to come back to a place we have never really seen before.

Acknowledgments

In writing this book I have climbed over several fences that separate one academic discipline from another; patient scholars have steadied those fences as I climbed them and have happily guided me around their green pastures. They have withstood my persistent questions and have read and corrected my words with care. These scholars include geologist Jean Prior, whose precision with words is equaled only by her precision in geology; archaeologist Joe Tiffany, whose excitement for Chan-ya-ta is undimmed despite his being two thousand miles away; State Climatologist of Iowa Harry Hillaker, who deepened my understanding of what I see above.

So too did the people of Peterson and the surrounding area open their pasture gates and doors for me, allowing me to snoop, photograph, and ask questions without end. Their cheerfulness, trust, and bottomless cups of coffee made working on this project a delight from beginning to end.

In specific, such businesses and organizations as the Farmers Co-op Association Elevator, Kirchner Memorial Library, Peterson Heritage, and Senior Citizen Center allowed me unlimited access to their property or archives. Individuals including Bill and Norma Althoff, Oma Rohrbaugh, Carroll and Elsie Tigges, and Wilbur and Marguerite Tigges allowed me unlimited access to their farms and even their homes while I sought the perfect photograph. My truck, person, and tripod became so familiar in the area that I soon found I had no need to seek permission to work on anyone's private land; everyone knew me and seemed to think "Oh, there's that Hokanson again; he's strange but harmless."

Many people stood or sat patiently for long periods of time for my tape recorder and camera or hauled me to out-of-the-way places to show me something I'd never have found on my own. Deep thanks go to Janet Anderson, Mona and Eddie Beck, Rod Burgeson, Clay County Engineer Roger Clark, Clint Fraley, Lyle Goettsch, Sue Goettsch, Jim and Sue Hass, Art and Ione Johnson, Bob Klinefelter, Boyd McGee, Mary Alice Plagman, Maudia Richard, Roger and Jane Stoner, Kelli Terrell, Dan Toft, Velma Walrath, and Bob White. I owe special thanks to Julia Heywood Booth, who not only sat for my questions but who opened her extensive archives on the Kirchner family and other early Euro-American settlers to my eager inquiries.

And last are three people who helped me shape this book: Wayne Franklin, Charlie Drum, and Carol Kratz. American Land and Life Series editor Wayne Franklin provided insight, sources, shaping, and encouragement; friend Charlie Drum provided the detailed scrutiny of a meticulous reader; and Carol, dear Carol, provided willing assistance at every moment, the first read of every word, the first look at every photograph, and enthusiastic support always. Just like last time, I could not have done it without you.

. . . they were in at the beginnings of things; and Time is every year writing supplements to their biographies—with foot-notes by you and me—with a pen of structural steel dipped in brick and stone and cement, with human beings for pigments, on a page of glacial drift.

—Herbert Quick, *The Hawkeye*, 1923

There is much confusion between land and country. Land is the place where corn, gullies, and mortgages grow. Country is the personality of land, the collective harmony of its soil, life, and weather.

—Aldo Leopold, *A Sand County Almanac*, 1949

In most American mythology . . . small towns have occupied something of the same place as Paris has to the French, or the green countryside to the English: they are central to the American experience.

—Peirce F. Lewis, "Small Town in Pennsylvania," 1972

REFLECTING A PRAIRIE TOWN

Introduction

This book is both about a particular place and, in a way, about all places.

The ostensible subject is Peterson, Iowa, and its surrounding farm community, and yet the broader topic has to do with how we might come to know *any* place. While I have discovered particular facts about Peterson, verities that apply to Peterson alone, the methods I've used to discover them might be applicable to the study of all places. For that reason, this work could almost as easily have been done in Peterson, Alabama, Peterson, Idaho, or on Pederson Street in Saint Paul, Minnesota.

What I have hoped to develop here is a sort of chart, a map of this town and surrounding countryside, and with it a near-universal set of cartographic symbols that can be used to draw other maps of other places.

This book is not a map in the usual sense. It is not simply a road map, or a historical map, a topographic map, or a survey map, but instead is a chart of the intersections of lives and places. It is a map of the associations among people and their points of geography. These bonds tying people to place are strong and many and suggest a cycle of influence that affects both. I have tried here to trace something of this cycle of causes and effects that operates between the inhabitants of this farm community and the land, the town, the woodlands, the river. How has this farmer understood his acres; how then has he molded that farm and in turn been molded by it? How does a woman in her nineties comprehend a century of change in Peterson? How has she contributed to that change and our perception of it?

Author and photographer Wright Morris shaped the term "inhabitant" in a poetic way that suggests this cycle of influence between places and those who live there. For Morris, an inhabitant is what you can't take away from an empty house; by extension, it may be what you can't take away from any place. Nor can you take a place away from an inhabitant; even when she is a long way from home, you can tell where the inhabitant is from. Morris knows that our home place affects even how we look:

"I guess a look is what a man gets not so much from inhabiting something, as from something that's inhabiting him. Maybe this is what it is that inhabits a house. In all my life I've never been in anything so crowded, so full of something, as the rooms of a vacant house. Sometimes I think only vacant houses are occupied. That's something I knew as a boy but I had nobody to tell me that that's what an Inhabitant is. An Inhabitant is what you can't take away from a house. You can take away everything else—in fact, the more you take away the better you can see what this thing is. That's how you know—that's how you can tell an Inhabitant."

People inhabit places; their places in turn inhabit them. The two are so intertwined as to be inseparable. While people today inhabit this place in northwest Iowa, Peterson also inhabits them and contributes immeasurably to who they are, their "look." And even when they move away or die, their imprint stays behind; they remain Inhabitants, silent participants in later lives in the place they shaped.

We carry that Inhabitant within us wherever we go and can never escape it. According to poet Maya Angelou, "Tom Wolfe said you can't go home again, but really you can never leave it; it gets under your fingernails and is always there in every wink and every gesture."

Writes Morris: ". . . the thing about Grandpa is that all you see is where he is from. No matter where he is all you see is where he is from. . . ."

Though Morris says it of Grandpa, he might say it of us all. The Inhabitant is what I find when I see sun-washed fields reflected in farmers' eyes and hear the sound of night winds in the voices of old people in town.

I chose this place for this project for two reasons. First, Peterson inhabits me fully; its soil is under my nails. This town has been my family home for several generations, and mine for some years off and on. I am an insider here. I know the place and people from the experience of long association and have a resident's access to barnyards, the back door of the café, private archives, and the top of the grain elevator.

Second, and almost paradoxically, I have something of the perspective of an outsider. Since I've lived elsewhere most of the time, I found I could bring a kind of fresh awareness to the study of this place. The view down Main Street, or through the winter trees along the river, is not dulled by long habit. Peterson is home, and always will be, but because I am usually elsewhere, for me the place will always remain somewhat novel, unexpected.

This book is a vernacular landscape study: a detailed, prolonged look at a common place in what I think of as an uncommon fashion. I have brought tools to bear on this task that aren't usually employed in the study of places and have used them to look at Peterson over especially long stretches of time. I've relied greatly on the methods and materials of history but have also employed those of other disciplines, other ways of knowing. To fully understand a place, history is not enough.

I encountered an example of the limits of a purely historical approach in a recent popular history of Iowa. Written by a fine scholar, this two hundred page volume has a thorough index that, like any good index, provides clues about the author's approach. The index lists many of the major players in Iowa history, significant events, numerous places—but there is no entry for "prairie."

Whatever an author's approach, it strikes me as a sharp limitation of the historical method, and perhaps the author's view of the subject, to attempt to write about Iowa's past without at least mentioning the tall-grass prairie. This pedological, biological, and psychological reality molded early peoples here, both Native and Euro-American, and was the first and most important factor in the agricultural and economic machine that prairie lands became. For what is Iowa, if not the manifestation of what the prairie made possible?

Hence, this study makes use of sundry tools, beginning with history and returning often to it but ranging through geography, direct observation and analysis, climatology, botany, oral history, archaeology, agricultural science, literature, geology, art, and even a bit of astronomy. And why not? If my intention is to take some measure of this place, I am obliged to study it in any way that helps reveal its nature.

Geographer Peirce Lewis provides a focal point for the concept of vernacular landscape:

"The basic principle is this: *that all human landscape has cultural meaning*, no matter how ordinary that landscape may be. It follows, as Mae Thielgaard Watts has remarked, that we can 'read the landscape' as we might read a book. Our human landscape is our unwitting autobiography, reflecting our tastes, our values, our aspirations, and even our fears, in tangible, visible form."

This book then, is about Inhabitants, about the past, about reading the landscape; it is a map, and in every sense, it is a reflection of a prairie town.

Chapter 1

Fly-over Country

New corn stands six inches tall this morning in Rod Burgeson's field two miles southwest of Peterson, Iowa. This day marks the forty-second since he planted it, since the beginning of his summer-long race with the frost of fall. The ankle-high seedlings—these are from De Kalb 547 hybrid seed—are the pale green of new plants. The stalks are soft like the tops of young green onions; they would be a succulent treat for any loose livestock. Day by day the plants will grow darker as they harden against sun, storms, and wind. In this field and others nearby, many leaves bear scarred brown edges; a few nights ago there was a light frost. Had the temperature dipped lower, it would have meant replanting thousands of acres. But no farmer will worry again about frost this season. June 11 is to be the first hot day this year, and so marks the turn from spring to summer, a turn from fretting about frost to worrying about drought and hail.

This ordinary field accounts for forty-four acres of the earth's surface, a plot defined by right angles and straight lines, a field that, seen from above, is shaped a bit like the state of Utah. This plot of corn has a precise but awkward legal description: it lies within the northeast quarter of the northwest quarter of Section 6, Township 93 North, Range 38 West. The township is Brooke Township, and it forms the far northwest corner of Buena Vista County. The point where four counties meet is only a quarter mile west. It is an average field, thick with good Iowa soil, marked by a gentle ridge and a series of controlling field terraces.

Despite the new corn, the field looks bare. Dark soil overwhelms narrow rows of sharp green plants. The image is one of fresh earth, of clods and heavy dirt, pinstriped in light green. On this warming morning these corn plants could fit in with house plants on some bay window ledge. In texture, scale, and shape, they would be at home in a row of pots among asparagus fern, coleus, philodendron, ornamental cacti. But each day now the stripes will grow more bold; each day the corn will shade a little more soil. During the 105- to 110-day growth season from planting to maturity, corn will transform the land—not just in this forty-four-acre field, but for two hundred miles in any direction—from a bare dirt plain to a jungle of bamboo-tall grass from whose floor even the sun is excluded. In only a couple of weeks, their hyper-growth would allow a few corn plants to shade out a whole parlor of house plants.

These corn rows are very straight, a fact most noticeable when the plants are small. The rows run east and west, parallel to the road and the slight ridge that runs the length of the field. They were planted by an expert, a steady hand on the wheel of a tractor; in only a few places can I detect slight kinks or wanderings, the occasional eight-row-wide blip where the hand or mind wavered and the machine went a tiny bit off track. These minute variations from the straight and true are like background noise on a seismograph or the tiny errors in a long stretch of straight railroad: straight, but not perfectly so.

This field has recently been cultivated; the soil between the rows has been tilled to root out upstart weeds, mostly foxtail, a persistent weedy grass. The broken dark soil is dotted with crop residue from previous years' crops: bits of yellow cornstalks, cobs, gnarled roots. Occasional field cobbles, stones hauled here by ancient glaciers, lie between the rows. They are chipped and scarred by a century's worth of collisions with plows, harrows, cultivators, disks.

Today the new crop, small as it is, bends hard over before a rising wind that sends the young leaves flailing with a dazzling stroboscopic effect. The hard wind pushes square out of the south, warming quickly with the climb of the sun above thin clouds and with the advent of air straight from the Gulf of Mexico. The sky carries a high, tattered overcast, moving out of the west-southwest, spitting an occasional cool raindrop.

A short distance north, across the county line in Clay County, the Little Sioux River valley cuts across the landscape. In the valley at a point about two miles northeast of the cornfield, just where Iowa Highway 10 and county road M27 intersect, lies the town of Peterson. Here below the valley rim the wind is diminished, but still brisk enough to swirl chaff from the loading alley of the grain elevator. The metal roof of the feed warehouse creaks in the wind, and the chatter of sparrows is as everpresent as the smell of fecund grain. A sharp cold draft rises from the basement of the tall silo. Inside the low office it is bitingly cool and very quiet on this late Monday morning. A few farmers come in from time to time, lean their elbows on the high counter, check morning grain prices on the computer terminal, buy cattle feed and pig starter, talk of the wet weather. Soybean planting, delayed by frequent but welcome rains after two years of drought, has just finished in this part of the farm belt. With the beans in the ground at last, things will be quiet at the elevator until a brief flurry of activity during oat harvest in July, then quiet again until the main harvest starts in September.

At noon up on Main Street, several vehicles, my own included, are angled against the curb in front of Sue's Diner. It's not a diner in the stainless-steel sense of the word; Sue's is a cafe that operates out of a small, old storefront. The chalkboard inside lists today's specials: roast beef plate (with beans, Jell-O, vegetable salad) and hot beef sandwich. Two fans stir the warm air, and the iced-tea glasses sweat. On the back wall a sign reads: "There may not be much to see in a small town but what you hear makes up for it." The booths and stools are occupied by a mix of customers: farmers, businesspeople and workers from town, and retired men and women. Work clothes are standard, and seed corn caps—Co-op, Funks G, Pioneer—are left on, probably to prevent forgetting them and probably because of what close-fitting caps do to hairstyles on warm days. As I sit and mop up roast beef gravy with white bread, I hear talk of livestock prices, of good moisture at last, of somebody's new pickup. At twelve-fifteen, the five tables and several counter stools are nearly full; by twelve-forty, as people go back to work, nearly empty.

On the counter near the cash register sits a fist-sized rock once found by somebody in a field. Shaped roughly like an ax head, it now holds down customer tickets against the indoor wind. It is dark from having been handled by many hands. I inquire about its origin.

"Somebody thought it was an Indian ax head," says Sue Goettsch, owner of the cafe, "but Jim Hass says it's a leaverite."

"Leaverite?"

"Leaverite where she lays," replies Sue.

At mid-afternoon on the bank of the Little Sioux River half a mile south of Main Street, soft river-snag maples reveal their silver under-leaves in the gusty wind. Here amid the river trees, the sky is only an opening overhead, framed by dense tangles of maples, cottonwoods, boxelders, and other native trees and occluded by the sides of the valley itself. Ragged stratocumulus clouds, pushed out of the southwest, cover about a third of the visible milky sky. Cottony airborne seeds gyrate past, northbound on the wind. The temperature has passed ninety degrees, and the hot wind drives all hint of cool from the deep riverside shade. No one fishes. At ground level in this deep valley the wind, diverted and mixed by the valley walls and the dense woodland, heaves and dies from time to time, but high in the trees the air moves loud and steady. The sighs of the trees mix with the sounds of mourning doves, red-winged blackbirds, and house wrens, noisy with territoriality and late-spring nest building.

Somewhere very close to this spot a hundred and thirty-four years ago, the sound of steel axes rang out against the valley walls as the first Euro-American settlers began to cut trees for a cabin. Somewhere close by, Sioux once camped and hunted and no doubt told stories about this river.

The water swells silently past, just as it did then. Today it is perhaps two-thirds bank full after recent rains; it is a busy springtime river, pushing around and over tangles of bleached tree skeletons choking the channel. There has been no scouring, river-cleaning flood in recent years, leaving old, barkless snags to litter the streambed. The moving water is like chocolate milk, opaque and still cool this early in the season.

By evening the wind diminishes, but not by much. I drive a few miles north of Peterson, where the land stretches dead flat, and when I stop and get out of the truck I hear the wind whine and howl in the electrical wires as if mimicking a blizzard. The unsettled sky has cleared itself some, leaving rumpled cumulus clouds in a sunset colored

Picture postcards, by N. J. Struve and others, were popular for many years with Peterson boosters. Copies of this one can be found in several collections in town. This view looks south and shows the old Kirchner woods beyond the river to be dense, mature forest. Photograph courtesy of Peterson Heritage.

orange by haze, dust, and moisture. To the south, under a darkening sky, the glow of lights at the baseball field in Peterson illuminates the turbid air. One by one blue farmyard lights flicker on all around, and the faint outline of an anvil cloud asserts itself on the western horizon.

On June 11, 1990, the very last of the lilacs were fading as the Queen Anne's lace along the roadsides came into full bloom. A half-dozen turkey vultures spent the day riding the uplift of air off the north side of the valley. The swimming pool in Peterson opened for the season. And just at dark on the ball field in Peterson, the home team, the Sioux Valley Soos, led the South Clay Spartans, nine to three.

Peterson, Clay County, northwest Iowa, lies near the center of the prairie and the Great Plains; a region that was once seamless grassland, it is now an agricultural planiform landscape extending over the horizon for endless miles in all directions. The distances to mountains, seacoast, or forest—either conifer or hardwood—are measured in days of driving. This place is too far west to feel the pulse of the industrial Northeast, too far east for sagebrush, too far south to see the aurora very often, and too far north to count on ever having an easy winter.

Peterson—the town and surrounding countryside—is a rural place, an agricultural place. Conversations in the bank, on the street, at a church smorgasbord may not always start on agricultural topics, but they are never far from the affairs of land, weather, machinery, and markets. The town hides along the river in a valley filled with trees, a protected place of woods and echoes and diminished winds. Many people will tell you that Peterson is safe from tornados, that a tornado can't dip down into such a pronounced valley. But up on the flatlands, where a tornado can take long aim at your house, the trees shrink back to hold only farmsteads and occasional ravines. Here farm groves stand as islands in an ocean of square fields, and the wind can blow to make souls lose their sanity.

Row crops, trees, and grasses cover every bit of soil around here: corn and soybeans where it is flat and square, trees throughout the valley, and grass everywhere else, filling in between all things. In miles of road ditches, in sidewalk cracks in town, holding sandbars in the river, in a pot of geraniums indoors, grasses are the predominant texture of this place. Native and imported grasses surround every field, follow every road, suffuse every neglected corner. By growing in the interstices and along the edges they make a mesh, a matrix; grasses provide the network which holds everything else in place.

A farmer remarked to me not long ago that this is "fly-over country": a part of the world which most Americans see—if they bother to lift the shade during the in-flight movie—only from 35,000 feet at 650 miles per hour. And it's true; the main routes of travel, except for a major east-west jet airway, pass elsewhere. A narrow and lightly used state highway goes through town east and west; a county blacktop runs north and south. The railroad pulled out in 1981. An out-of-state license plate, a rarity in town, usually means someone has come to visit family. Peterson sits near a point common to four counties, and not only are most license plates here the dark blue of Iowa tags, but most bear the name of one of the four counties: Clay, Buena Vista, Cherokee, O'Brien. Peterson is an out-of-the-way place in an out-of-the-way part of an out-of-the-way state, yet each day thousands of people pass high overhead in jet flagships following electronic paths, bound for Chicago, Seattle, San Francisco, or the Pacific Rim. Their presence is known only by the high rumble of the aircraft, heard only because of the relative silence. High above, passengers doze, sip their coffee, read in-flight magazines, and perhaps once in a while someone peers out to wonder what town that is along that river.

Space abounds here, room on the land to turn a twelve-row combine, room in the sky to see bad weather a long way off. There is distance between things here, between farmsteads, between towns, between houses in town, between trees, between people. There is space enough to extend a person's shadow half a mile and horizon enough to make anyone wonder about places beyond it.

In homes at night, via cable, satellite, and video cassette, people see stories about distant and very different places, but here, on the land itself, there is nothing to suggest that the entire planet is made of anything but farms and small towns. Where the farm landscape of Illinois might hide an occasional steel mill or manufacturing plant, here there are only soybeans, corn, and lightly traveled roads. In places many miles to the south and west, oil rigs dot the land, or a strip mine appears, or a pipeline terminal, but not here. There is no hint of urbanity over the horizon either; no high-tension power lines lope across fields, pointing to a distant city marked by a glow in the night sky, nor are there the shiny ribbons of the high iron leading freight cars to distant terminals. No hum and scent of traffic greet you when you step outdoors. The air smells of soil, of weather, and occasionally of livestock, but never of exhaust.

Peterson is a town along a small river—but not quite a river town—in a part of the state with few rivers deserving the name. The terrain of the four-county area is undulating former prairie, not really flat, except in a few places; it swells and dips beneath the wheels of cars crossing the broad landscape, revealing long views over each slight rise. Towns ten or more miles distant signal their presence with grain elevators rising white above fields and farm groves, but Peterson's elevator, no shorter than the others, isn't seen until a traveler is upon it; it stands in a valley which is just as deep as the elevator is high. The town itself is hidden from view, tucked into the valley and guarded by thick woodland.

The commercial part of Main Street is a block long and presents a scattering of businesses facing each other across the wide and quiet street. The deterioration is apparent here like in many small towns across the Midwest; empty stores and empty lots threaten to consume those businesses that hold on. According to the Iowa highway map, as of 1980, Peterson had 470 citizens; the 1990 census marked the decline to 390. An empty lot sold on Main Street recently, a lot in what would be a prime business location in a town that wasn't losing population. The owner of the adjacent plumbing and heating shop wants to add on. The cost of the lot: fifty dollars.

Peterson is interested in its past and concerned about its future. Peterson Heritage, the local historic preservation group, has restored and now maintains two fine old homes—including the first frame dwelling in the county—and the blockhouse to a frontier fort. Nearly every fall they sponsor a tour of homes which brings several hundred people to town. Looking to the future are the Peterson Betterment Council and a new organization, Peterson Promotion and Development. Both groups seek economic and social revitalization for this endangered small town.

There is natural beauty as well. Hunters, anglers, fall-color enthusiasts, and occasional long-distance bicyclists enjoy this wooded valley, and those seeking wildflowers often hike the hills of nearby Wanata State Preserve, which is part of a mile-and-a-half-long stretch of native timber along the river.

A motorist westbound on Iowa Highway 10 spends about eight minutes passing through the immediate area. Highway 10 runs east to west through Peterson, uninterrupted by either stop signs or stoplights; at the speed limit, it takes about a minute and forty-five seconds to drive from one city-limit sign to the other at the far end of town.

Approaching Peterson from the east on Highway 10, a traveler passes grain and livestock farms similar to those scattered everywhere across the agricultural Midwest. Some of the farmsteads are inhabited; some are vacant and the houses have been torn down; some are bereft of buildings altogether and betray their history only by a grove of tangled trees marking an old homestead.

Rather suddenly for prairie country, Highway 10 turns and drops into the Little Sioux River valley. The square farms and horizon are gone, replaced by scattered woodland, the valley sides, and cramped fields. If not in too big a hurry, the traveler can glance to the south and catch a view of a bend in the Little Sioux.

In a moment a sign announces the town limits, then comes a short curve, and the highway changes into a town street, speed limit thirty miles per hour. To either side are glimpses of common American domestic architecture—sometimes vacant, occasionally pretty, usually prosaic. A side glance at the right instant brings an end-on snapshot of Main Street, revealing little except that it resembles thousands of similar Main Streets in the United States and that, like the houses seen a moment ago, the storefronts run the gamut from the well-kept to the ready-to-fall-down.

A look out the opposite window at the same instant provides a view of the grain elevators at the foot of Main Street, but anybody driving the speed limit wouldn't have time to look both ways.

After passing the one operating gas station in town—the only fixture likely to elicit much interest on the part of a traveler—the highway rapidly reaches the west edge of town, makes a little turn where it used to cross the railroad (only the most observant would notice the little bump where the tracks once were), and soon crosses the river on a newish girder bridge with sides high enough that it is hard to get much view of the water.

In minutes the traveler has ascended from the valley and is back on the uplands, accelerating west, once again among farmsteads and fields spreading to distant horizons.

What would a traveler remember? Probably the unusually narrow highway. A generic small town. Maybe the impression of trees. But anyone in a hurry or listening to a ball game on the radio might have noticed little except that radio reception grew fuzzy in the valley and later remember nothing of the town, the valley, the farms.

The traveler's view is always limited, compressed; what is a truer measure of a small town and its farm neighborhood? Is it found in the firmness of the banker's handshake? The color of the river in the spring flood? The texture of mashed potatoes around family tables on Thanksgiving? The dollar offering at the Methodist church? The average corn yield per acre? Certain details can help.

Peterson has a library, a good one for a town this size, complete with fax machine and new computer. On the shelves is a copy of *Main Street*, but there is no listing for *Boy Life on the Prairie*. In town and in the country around, two out of three people wave as they pass you on the road. Farmers in the area seem to prefer Chevy pickups over Fords. The two churches in town are Congregational and Methodist. Residents subscribe to such publications as *Redbook*, *Capper's Weekly*, and the *New Yorker*. The local paper, the *Peterson Patriot*, is a weekly, circulation 650; many copies of each edition are mailed to expatriates living in California, Arizona, Wisconsin, Virginia, Nevada, Ohio. There are 160 mailboxes on the hundred-mile-long rural mail route; there are 258 postboxes in town; 225 are currently rented. Few people pay any attention to their street addresses. Mail is not delivered in town, and only the United Parcel Service driver seems to take any notice of the numbers on the houses.

People are neighborly here, neighborly to the point of noticing what time your lights go off at night and then telling you about it the next day. If you misdial and get a wrong number, the party who answers is certain to be someone you know. And at least a few people, when they get a new dog, pay a visit to Max Wetherell, town cop, town employee, in order to introduce him to the new mutt so that when the dog gets loose, Max will know where to bring it home.

This place—Peterson and the surrounding miles of river valley and farmland—is an ordinary place, as common, unscrutinized, and ubiquitous as the line of power poles running along Highway 10. The local area is a minute part of a continent crowded with ordinary places, places that stretch continuously, uninterrupted, from one ocean to the other. They have no boundaries; one place blends seamlessly into the next down the road. These common places are the streets, suburbs, towns, rural lands where we live our lives: Flatbush Avenue, New York, Flatwillow, Montana, or Peterson, Iowa. They are the places we come to know with dulled familiarity, the sort of accustomed neglect that makes it easy for us never to perceive our own surroundings.

As in any ordinary place, people do ordinary things here: they plant spring bulbs, take note of the television schedule, add on to their houses, misplace their glasses. The neighbor kids play football in our front yard while I talk with their father, an old classmate, of work and cars. Social intercourse and commerce move at regular, preset rates; a neighborly stop for coffee is expected to take forty-five minutes, and every afternoon at four-thirty the mail truck passes on Highway 10, heading for the post office to pick up the day's mail on its way to Sioux City.

Though common, though ordinary, Peterson—like any place—is unique. Though the elements and forces that have formed this town and its environs are the same as those which form most every place, they have interacted here in their ordinary ways to make a singular place with unique attributes.

Though at a glance the buildings of Main Street seem just like those of thousands of towns sprinkled across the Midwest, these storefronts, like all, are individuals. They are singular in detail and shape; some are well maintained and express the life within; others have caved in or soon will. Each has a distinctly expressed character, a personality, and taken together they make a specific place: Main Street, Peterson, Iowa.

What we see when we look closely at any place is the combined total of all the forces that act and have acted on that place, that landscape. Some forces, like water, have acted on the face of the land for countless centuries; others, like the gardener across the highway putting in onion sets, began only today. Whatever their duration, these agents of change engrave, erode, construct, excavate, shape, concentrate, and dissipate patterns and structures in and upon the land.

Glaciers once rumpled the land surface all across the upper Midwest; they have left particular marks of their passing here. Water leaches minerals from the soil, cuts streambeds, gnaws at the headlands, and daily sorts its work

Peterson fielded some heavy hitters for the 1904 season, including Archie Evans, far left, back row, who would later be editor and publisher of the Peterson Patriot. Evidently the druggist didn't want to miss any of the action. Photograph courtesy of Peterson Heritage.

by size: rocks, cobbles, pebbles, sand, silt. Though water follows a uniform code of hydrological conduct, its handiwork makes individual forms wherever it goes. Plant and animal communities—including those of human beings—have affected and continue to affect the shape and character of the land. Bur oaks flourish in a protected ravine; a badger mound in a pasture becomes a seedbed for a red cedar; during several thousand years, a vast and complex prairie ecosystem has evolved and created deep rich soils to which Euro-Americans have given elaborate names: Dickinson Fine Sandy Loam, Clarion-Storden Complex. Some of these soils are found here in this part of northwest Iowa and nowhere else.

With energy and available materials, people here have done their work and made their marks on the landscape, and with the intensity of agriculture in this region, perhaps few places anywhere show so clearly the hand of humankind on the land. It is the work of individuals we see so clearly. Their work is ordinary yet unique: farmers can drive past fields prepared for spring planting and often read the signature of the farmer who did the work. The land is layered with the works of human hands, the single and multiple acts of creativity that build cattle sheds, prune roses, scribe field patterns, thin woodlots for firewood, restore a historic home, put up a new sign on the hardware store, or survey section lines. Institutions are at work here as well, but even the work of grading a new highway embankment comes down to the flexing of levers on an earthmover, levers manipulated by a single person. It is the act of the individual, the woman or man who consciously shapes the environment, that is so evident to us, that makes a place so specific to those who know it or to anyone who cares to look closely.

These agents of formation and change all operate on the land as if it were a parchment, an expanse of vellum to be written upon and drawn upon time and time again: a palimpsest. Ancient Greeks and Romans left us palimpsests; forced by the scarcity of materials, they often reused parchment and papyrus for recording important documents. Prior writings were erased at each reuse, but erasure could not remove the imprint of an earlier writer's stylus; hence, after several recordings and erasures, a single sheet might yield several layered but incomplete pages of information.

Thus the forces that shape the landscape create a rich, overlaid parchment bearing the marks of the processes that created it and those that change it today. The landscape is a primary document, a document carrying multiple, and sometimes contradictory, messages. Its code is a direct but incomplete source to past events, lives, geography. Because this palimpsest is three-dimensional, the information recorded on it is found in a complex aggregate, sometimes stratified, sometimes jumbled. Layers are compressed, interrupted, occluded, upended, and sometimes missing altogether, but they still act to provide some glimpse of a place over time. The history and prehistory of this ordinary, this vernacular landscape, like that of any place, is a fragmented story full of questions and ellipses; yet within are concordances and revelations that lie hidden and lost like ancient stone ax heads among ordinary field cobbles, among "leaverites."

I believe much of my love of history was instilled in me by Grandfather Ker. He was a splendid old man, tall, with long white whiskers, and full of humor as are most Irish. He was well known in Peterson, being a "squatter" in O'Brien County. Neighbors were the Reaneys, McCrackens, the Sweeneys; the nearby neighbors—Fred Modings, Charley Tigges, whose popularity was proven in that although a Democrat, he made good as a supervisor at Primghar, the Tripletts, Mide and Minnie, and the Neguses—Bill and Grace and Orson and Roy, homey folks, all of them, a place where you felt like dropping in unexpectedly and sitting down to a real dinner, an evening of enjoyable harmless gossip, and a drive home at peace with the world.

—Archie Evans, editor, *Peterson Patriot*, August 23, 1928

Thanks to whoever found our hubcap and put it on a fence post by Gene Baier's place.
Earl Peterson.

—Card of thanks, *Peterson Patriot*, June 21, 1990

Chapter 2

The Meridians of Home

I think of Peterson as home. I was born here but have spent most of my years elsewhere; I have lived here only eight years scattered over some forty. Though I have departed this town as a child and as an adult, I have always returned: for summers as a schoolboy, for my last two years of high school, for holidays, and for a year after living abroad.

Peterson is the place where the meridians of my life converge. Like the earth's meridians which intersect at the North and South Poles, all my life lines cross here; they all pass through this single point on their way around the globe. No matter where I go or when, I seem to find myself on a line that, from any place, will eventually take me through Peterson.

I returned to Peterson again recently, this time after a year and a half teaching and traveling abroad, returned home to the familiar sounds of familiar birds, to the kitchens of my mother and grandmother, to the scent of lilacs and of bed linen dried in the Iowa sun. After wandering through places starkly unfamiliar, my wife, Carol Kratz, and I found ourselves emptying worn backpacks in my grandmother's guest house. We had been places where every sight, scent, and sound had been new; we had found that all our assumptions about how people live, about places, about food, transportation, and ordinary daily patterns were challenged, and soon suspended. Coming back to the familiar, I discovered my sensitivity to this accustomed place was keen and clear as if new.

My heightened sensitivity to home brought me the spirit of this place as expressed in the sounds of speech, the slope of the hills, the scent of spring grass, the edge of the winter wind. That the streets of Peterson are paved or that houses are made of wood—instead of thatch, or marble, or manure—could no longer be taken for granted. Having seen the color of tropical thunderstorms in Australia, I was better able to read the light of the prairie variety found around home; having squinted across the dusty horizons of India, I was better prepared to take in my own; having walked the narrow and crooked streets of a few Irish villages, I was better able to take the measure of Peterson's own broad, straight Main Street.

As it is for anyone who ever calls some place home, that place—or its memory—evokes certain unmeasurable, but unmistakable, responses. Not only does Peterson exert over me a gentle gravitational pull, it also imprinted my mind, long ago, with certain indelible images, images that accumulate into a portrait of this single place. For example, it seems to me that the hills here, though similar to other hills nearby and cousins to hills everywhere in Iowa, have a certain cut, a particular slope, shape, and texture caused by a specific thickness and composition of glacial drift overlaid by a cap of windblown loess soil, a crust of very particular thickness, eroded in a particular fashion. I do believe I can look at a photograph of a valley and hill and tell whether it is on the Little Sioux River, and if so, just how far upstream or down from Peterson. Is this my romantic perception? Or my desire to make what I know to be the home country look like the home country in my mind's eye?

My family roots run deep here, like those of prairie grass, and the anonymous works of my ancestors are visible in the angles of sturdy wood houses, in trees and lilacs they planted, in squares of prairie they first turned to the plow, and perhaps in faint initials marked in the wet cement of some town sidewalk poured years ago. My people weren't among the first settlers, but my great-great-grandfather as a young man broke prairie in the township to earn money to buy his own farm.

My earliest memories grew in and around this valley like cottonwoods. As a young child, I first knew snow here and the sounds that trucks make at night in the distance. There were bushy beards all over town for the centennial in 1956, and at about the same time, I noticed the first evolutionary budding of tailfins on cars, seen first on Bert Like's Kaiser. We had a circus once, all the neighborhood kids and I. It seemed huge and elaborate, with exotic acts and stands full of enthusiastic adults; the tiny black-and-white pictures give little hint of its glory, and none show the elephant I imagined so clearly.

Velma Walrath, the oldest person in Peterson and fast approaching a hundred years of age, took care of me during daytimes when I was quite small and before we moved away. She lives in a cluttered and warm house on Main Street surrounded by photographs, sewing projects, and a world-class collection of purple cows. She reminded me recently that as a kid of four I often laid my books end to end to make a road—a road to California, she recalled. When I was five, my mother remarried and we moved to California. After a few years in northern and then southern California (neither had snow, I was disappointed to find), we moved to Colorado, to suburban Denver, where there was snow once in a while, but much more common was a restless yellow topsoil that apparently never settled down after the dust bowl. Every time the wind blew, which was often, the sky turned brown and all horizontal surfaces indoors and out collected thick dust. My bedroom window faced east, and with my elbows on the gritty windowsill I could look across stony lawns and between the roofs of new tract homes and see a scrap of the Great Plains twenty miles east. I dreamt of green trees and black soil in Iowa, somewhere beyond the curve of the planet.

As a kid I was granted escape from the city during summers and, at my insistence, was put on the train for Iowa the very day school ended. At the end of summer, I always waited until the last minute to return to Denver; usually there was just enough time for my parents to buy me a few new clothes and send me off to school.

Summers in Iowa were a city kid's dream come true. My great-grandparents, Art and Edna Johnson, had retired to a farm two miles south of Peterson, and my grandparents, Henry and Ione Hokanson, ran a John Deere implement

Petersonites beam with pride in front of their new speed-limit sign, probably the first one the town ever had. With the new sign, motorists were encouraged to slow down and perhaps even stop in town, two things travelers seldom do today. Photograph courtesy of Peterson Heritage.

dealership in town. On the farm, vast pastures, woods, creeks, and fields awaited my exploring feet; and at the implement shop there was an endless parade of interesting customers, trucks to ride in, and mechanical mysteries to explore.

I felt elation at escaping suburbia with its excluding chain-link fences, elation at being where a kid counted for something, where people knew me. There was complete freedom to move through a landscape that I could comprehend, actually get my arms around and understand. Yards in town were never fenced, and any rural barbed wire fence could be crossed in a second, making northwest Iowa a land of uniform access where the only barrier was the river if it happened to be a wet summer and the water ran high.

It was a large world and it was a small world. Views were long across cornfields when the crop was new but quickly shrunk as the corn overtopped the fence and then me. From then on, I climbed the silo for perspective. The world could be as large as a wall of thunderstorms reaching up nine miles into the humid air or as cramped and dark as my great-grandparents' coal room where we waited for the worst of them to pass.

With friends and cousins, I explored the woods and river bottom—when the mosquitoes would allow—and we were always on the lookout for Indians, that last band of Sioux who somehow escaped the cavalry, settlers, and eight-row combines, and who now lived and hid out where nobody had ever seen them. We looked for Indian signs, imagined sites and arrangements for tepee villages, scoured for arrow points at all the wrong times and wrong places; we never found a thing, though we knew they had been here, once.

To me, a city kid accustomed to suburban lawns, shopping centers, and freeways, the world around Peterson seemed a wilderness. Though much of the land was under cultivation, once I got out of sight of buildings—always easy to do here—even farm fields with arrow-straight rows felt remote from human contact. I had the feeling that few people had ever walked where I went, had ever really explored that stand of trees, or had ever watched the sky from where I stood. There were mysteries—in the land, in the woods, among rocks in the field—if only I could see them and read them.

I knew nothing of prairie. Vaguely I understood the word to mean something about the grass that was here before the white settlers came and made farms. "There weren't trees to speak of when the white man came," said my great-grandmother, "almost everything was grass." I pondered that and imagined it must have been like a shaggy lawn or the rolling hills of the north pasture. Sometimes when I walked in the pasture I would descend into a grassy draw where I could see no cornfields. I could look in a circle and try to imagine what prairie must have been like. No one else knew much of prairie either; those who knew it firsthand were mostly gone, and it had been a long time since anybody cared enough to pay any attention.

My great-grandparents' farmstead stood deep in a grove of soft maples and pines on a slight rise between two unnamed creeks. As the crow flies, the farm was a mile and a half south of Peterson, just across the line in Buena Vista County. On summer nights, on a north wind, I would occasionally hear a train going through town. The mailbox sported a red cast-iron cardinal and hung over a dusty gravel road that saw few cars on any given day. The farm was off the beaten path by even rural standards; the phone line was party, and the REC power poles passed our place and ended at the next place east.

The square white buildings had gone up around 1920 during the second boom in Iowa farm building. The barn, corncrib, garage and shop, hog house, and cattle shed stood in a circle with a light pole at the center. It was about a hundred steps between buildings. The house was a great two-story cube with porches on three sides. Lush grass, flower beds, and ornamental shrubs filled out the house yard. On the gatepost near the front porch hung a bell rescued from a long-vanished schoolhouse. I was allowed to pull the chain once or twice from time to time; prolonged ringing was a signal for fire and was intended to summon any neighbors within earshot.

This farm of the mid-1960s was not the diverse, multiproduct unit like those of earlier decades. Being retired, my great-grandparents rented the land and feedlot to a neighbor, so there was no field work, no cows to milk, and no eggs to gather. And even though I baled hay for the neighboring farmers, sprayed thistles in pastures, and helped shell corn, most days remained idyllic and carefree.

Thus rural life took on special appealing qualities. Its virtue lay not only in a near absence of real work, something a farm kid of the 1930s would find impossible to believe, but also in the fact that there was time to listen and look and smell. There was little distraction from the sound of wind and the presence of the sky. There was time to notice how much the corn grew overnight.

Real events were few. A neighbor might drop by for coffee and change the character of an entire day. Every few weeks the road grader would go by, piling a ridge of gravel down the middle of the road; some hours later it would pass in the other direction, spreading the rock windrow across the other half of the road. While not a big event by any yardstick, the grader's passage was always subject for comment by my great-grandparents, and after it went by in one direction, I would cock my ear for its sound and try to predict when it would come back the other way. One morning a small red airplane appeared quite low over the farm. We all heard it and went out to look. It circled our farm twice and headed off to the southwest. We never found out who it was, but I thought about it for the rest of the summer.

Like farm people everywhere, Edna and Art were always conscious of the weather. They listened more closely to forecasts than even to farm prices, and what the next day eventually brought was carefully recorded by my great-grandmother. Her daybooks contain a nearly unbroken record of daily weather observations—wind, rain, temperature—stretching back further than I've been alive. She seemed to feel the personality of the day's conditions: the restless angst of a cool overcast day when the wind moves high through the trees or a still, hot day beneath a brassy sky—"we'll have storms tonight," she'd say. She always knew when heavy weather was on the way, even in the days before KICD radio in Spencer got weather radar—an apparatus that, for her, never lost its charm.

In those years—the early and middle 1960s—I knew only the summer sky of Iowa; other seasons were spent in Colorado. During those summers, the permutations, colors, shadows, and moods of the atmosphere held a good part of my attention. Whatever I was doing or thinking, indoors or out, a certain portion of my consciousness was always reserved for the qualities of the atmosphere.

In town, the silence of the land and the supremacy of the sky were replaced by larger, noisier distractions. In Peterson the sky disappeared behind the two-story false-front buildings of Main Street and the great elms, maples, and hackberries of residential blocks. Days in town teemed with the pulse of people going about their business: customers in and out of the John Deere shop, an errand to the variety store, gossip, a long walk along the railroad tracks looking for whatever a kid might find.

The John Deere shop stood on Main Street across from the bank. A single-story cinder-block building, it had been a Ford garage years earlier. The big windows faced west and were protected from the hot afternoon sun by two sagging green awnings. On any day it didn't look like rain, it was my job at noon to crank them down; at six, when the evening whistle blew at the elevator, I was under standing orders to crank them up again as we closed up and headed home for supper. Above the awnings was a yellow-and-green sign that announced, "Art Johnson Implement Company—John Deere." My great-grandfather had begun the business; his daughter and her husband—Ione Johnson and Henry Hokanson, my grandparents—had taken over when he retired to the farm.

The showroom of the shop was florid with John Deere green and yellow. From the new tractor always parked in the center of the green floor to the matchbooks on the counter, everything—the advertising banners strung from corner to corner, the accessories, the parts bins, even the shirts worn by the staff—radiated the singular colors of John Deere. The green clashed with the yellow, and both fought with any notion of appropriate color schemes for a store. Never restful, they were nonetheless familiar and were welcomed by the family as a sign of, well, money. The colors were eye-catching in the fields, and whenever we saw a John Deere machine at work, my grandparents and I felt a tiny delight knowing that they sold not only the most popular machinery but, by the accounts of most farmers, the best. For chromatic reasons we might all have preferred to sell International or Oliver, but where quality of product was concerned, and family loyalty, it was yellow and green all the way.

Shop customers always fascinated me, and anybody in the front room looked up when the door opened. Overalled, ruddy-faced, often muddy or worse, some farmers carried bellies made by years of mashed potatoes and gravy. You could tell a farmer by the broad, strong hands; they were always cut and bruised and bore not just dirt, but Iowa soil, and grease under the nails. Some, if not most, came minus a digit or two from attempting to unclog running cornpickers.

Farmers brought in tractors for repair, stopped by to dicker with my grandfather over a new combine, or came to grab a few parts after a field breakdown. Strong, honest, and familiar, some barely spoke, while others, whenever they opened their mouths, had such a galvanizing effect on the place that the hoots and guffaws of the front room staff could be heard far in the back room where the mechanics worked. "Hap Ness must be in," somebody would say.

Henry Hokanson, my grandfather, was the manager of the operation, and though he had an office in the corner of the store, I never saw him use it. He preferred instead to do all his business from behind the counter in small-town-merchant fashion, accessible to his customers and employees.

My grandmother, Ione, was known to all as the "straw boss" or "parts man" and ran the parts department, an unusual occupation for a woman, especially a grandmother, especially in those days. She was the one everyone asked when they couldn't find something; she knew parts, parts numbers, and locations of parts in the thousands of bins like nobody else. When I was older, I often spent evenings at the shop working on my car or those of friends. When I got stuck trying to find parts, I'd call her: "Grandma, can you tell me where I can cross-reference a Timken 38749 bearing to a John Deere number?" If she didn't know the number outright, she could easily tell me where to look.

Days in town brought a pattern of familiarity, of comfortable variety. There was plenty to do and plenty to watch. I knew most people I encountered—or at least recognized them—and people knew me as well. Out in the country, people are too dispersed to form much of an observable community, a community whose moment-to-moment activities could entertain a restless kid, and in urban and suburban places, most of life is too complex, too much in motion, too large to comprehend. Most of it goes on inside buildings, inside automobiles, or in backyards screened from view. But in a small town in those days, life happened where I could see it; much of the community's social intercourse took place on Main Street and at such a pace that the sidewalk, stores, cafe, and post office became stages for tiny dramas in which the characters were all familiar actors.

Once, just out of high school, I had an accident on Main Street with a John Deere shop truck. It happened in the middle of a summer weekday when I cut too close and sideswiped a parked truck with the protruding combine corn head that was on my truck. The bulky harvester attachment was torn from the flatbed and crashed to the pavement with enough noise to draw everyone from every shop on the street; the cafe evacuated onto the sidewalk, patrons with napkins in hand. I was sick at seeing what I had done, in part because of the damage to the machinery (there were no injuries), but mostly because I knew that the accident would be the subject of town talk for a month.

And in fact even several years later, when I was introduced to a man who had once spent some time in Peterson, the accident on Main Street somehow came up in conversation. On my mentioning it, he exclaimed, "*You* were the one! I thought it was a plane crash!"

During the summer of my junior year in high school, my mother, my brother, and I moved back to Iowa, back home, and I discovered that Iowa had seasons other than summer. That fall I gazed through the rain-streaked windows of the school bus at an alien landscape: miles and miles of withered yellow cornfields, all rattling stalks and leaves, an annual grass now gone dead, gone to seed. I'd not seen the land look this way; the corn was always still brilliant green when I returned to Denver. With fascination I watched the harvest that fall, and with barked knuckles and dirty fingernails I worked after school and on weekends at the John Deere shop to repair machinery and get it back into the field. I had worked on corn pickers and combines before; I had just never seen them in operation.

Iowa put on one of its best seasonal pageants that year. The winter of 1968–69 was a particularly snowy and bitterly cold one. My great-grandfather had died the spring before; my great-grandmother Edna had moved to a house

Both the Chicago and North Western and the Little Sioux River were busy on this day, circa 1900, when a local photographer planted a tripod a few hundred yards south of where the Kirchner family established their first home- stead. Rotting stumps of large trees in the foreground suggest woodcutting from the log-cabin days of Peterson history. The hills north and east of Peterson are giving up their grass to encroaching woodland. Today, this view is blocked by thick stands of trees on both sides of the river and by trees that fill and surround the town. Photo- graph courtesy of Peterson Heritage.

in town, and my mother and brother now lived on the farm. I split my time between the two places. That year the county had decided not to put up the snow fence to the north of the farm; after all, it hadn't snowed much in the prior half-dozen winters. But the snow came that year, and the lack of a barrier meant the wind had a free run across a hundred miles of open country before it hit the farm grove; it paused momentarily there and dropped trainloads of snow on the road. That winter I learned the delights of being snowed in, about frostbite, school closures, four-wheel-drive, about the many kinds of snow. Some storms that year brought a snow that hardened like limestone: solid enough to drive cars on, it could best be handled by cutting it into blocks with a straight spade.

And in the spring, the river swelled with all the snowmelt and spring rains, and I learned about submerged roads, why farmers are careful about going into wet fields with big equipment, more about four-wheel-drive and about lilacs.

I became a resident of Peterson during these two years, my last years of high school. I worked at the John Deere shop as an apprentice mechanic and truck driver and proudly wore the loud green-and-yellow jacket I earned; I have it yet.

Like many of my classmates, I left for college after graduation. For the next eighteen years I returned to Peterson only as a visitor—for holidays and family gatherings.

Then, in the first days of 1989, Carol and I left the States to teach and travel overseas. Our wanderings took us many places, but I remember standing on the balcony of a cheap hotel in Cairo looking across the sun-baked city and down at the astonishingly busy street and noisy traffic. I concluded that Cairo must certainly be the noisiest city in the world (we hadn't yet been to Bangkok) and found myself remembering how quiet it is in Peterson on a windless winter night; there is a muffled, almost disturbing silence, as if my hearing had suddenly failed as I stepped out of my mother's house into the snow.

Then, in the early summer of 1990, after twenty years away from Peterson, I returned, and Carol and I set up temporary housekeeping in my grandmother's guest house—she calls it the Ida House after the woman who lived there for many years—at the corner of Second and Ash. It was our home for a year.

A lot has changed since my two years of high school here. Both my great-grandparents are gone, and so is my grandfather. My grandmother Ione has remarried—to an Art Johnson, making her Ione Johnson Hokanson Johnson. My mother has remarried as well and is now Mona Beck; she and Eddie live in town. My great-grandparents' farm is still in the family (the house is rented, as is the land), but the John Deere shop on Main Street was sold soon after I left for college. Caught by the farm crisis of the 1980s, it has gone the way of many small town businesses; it is closed and forlorn, and the roof has fallen in. It pains me to walk past it.

As I look at this town today, I realize that I am often looking for a place that no longer exists. I still seek the Peterson I knew as a child where Main Street was busy, the trains still ran, and the Lions Club had fireworks and free watermelon on the Fourth of July. As accustomed as I now am to the view down the highway through town, I still draw a sharp breath each time I notice again that the elms that arched over the road like a tunnel are gone, long gone, killed by Dutch elm disease fifteen years ago. Perhaps it always happens to those who go away and later come back; each time I've been here or lived here I've made a snapshot impression, captured an instant, and now I can no longer correlate mental images of the town made at different times. My mind's eye cannot adjust to the sunlight glancing off the pavement where the shade of trees had been. Had I stayed, had I not come and gone so many times, the evolution would have been gradual, a granular change, like a river shifting its course pebble by pebble. But now so many of the landmarks are missing, and the change, though it has occurred over slow decades, seems abrupt to one who returns.

The seasons are not characterized by the frequent and sudden changes so common in latitudes further south. The temperature of the winters is somewhat lower than states eastward, but of other seasons it is higher. The atmosphere is dry and invigorating. The surface of the State being free at all seasons of the year from stagnant water, with good breezes at nearly all seasons, the miasmatic and pulmonary diseases are unknown. Mortuary statistics show this to be one of the most healthful states in the Union, being one death to every ninety-four persons. The Spring, Summer, and Fall months are delightful; indeed, the glory of Iowa is her Autumn, and nothing can transcend the splendor of her Indian Summer, which lasts for weeks, and finally blends, almost imperceptibly, into Winter.

—A.T. Andreas, *Illustrated Historical Atlas of the State of Iowa, 1875*

A moment more, and the solid sheets of water fall upon the landscape, shutting it from view, and the thunder crashes out, sharp and splitting, in the near distance, to go deepening and bellowing off down the illimitable spaces of the sky and plain, enlarging, as it goes, like the rumor of war.

—Hamlin Garland, *Boy Life on the Prairie*, 1899

Chapter 3

An Invigorating Atmosphere

JULY 4 AND 5

By now the corn in Rod Burgeson's field south of town is waist high and in the middle of its adolescent growth spurt. My great-grandfather always used to say that corn had to be knee-high by the Fourth of July in order to be mature by fall frost, but that was in the days before super-cross hybrids; farmers' expectations were lower. These stalks are as big around as a hickory ax handle, and almost as hard. The dark green leaves are two feet long, four inches wide, and fuzzed over on top with a thickening white stubble, like a teenage boy's nascent beard. Each plant has eight to ten mature leaves, with more ready to spiral up and out of the growing stalk. The field is a shag carpet of green; the rows are now indistinct as the thick leaves of adjacent plants overlap to block the view of the soil—unless you do as I do and crawl about on hands and knees beneath the leaves to see the moist earth, shaded foxtail grass, and a few sprigs of volunteer oats.

At ten in the morning, the sky shows classic conditions for the distant approach of heavy weather—veils of mare's-tail cirrus hold forth high in the atmosphere while fragmented altocumulus sneak in from the northwest at middle altitudes. Jet contrails persist, adding condensation to the high cirrus.

Along the north side of the cornfield runs a crushed-rock section line road with shallow ditches on each side. Both ditches are filled with a uniform stand of fully-headed smooth brome grass, a common introduced pasture grass. Along the fence on the north side of the road stands a broken line of giant eastern cottonwoods, native *Populus deltoides*, planted at field's edge longer ago than anyone can remember, no doubt as saplings dug along the river a mile or two north and taken up onto the prairie and planted in hopes of slowing the great winds. They are large and dignified trees, with bark the color, texture, and hardness of weathered stone—trees that have withstood legendary wind, snow, and ice storms and droughts that killed livestock, crops, and hope. These cottonwoods are survivors; natives, bearing all the scars and stunted limbs of trees left on their own, but graceful trees nonetheless, made of thick trunks, burls, knobs, and lofting branches. Today the gentle southerly breeze makes the cottonwood leaves shimmer as only those of cottonwoods, aspen, birch, and their ilk can.

By early afternoon, the coming weather is visible to the north and west; a long, low band of clouds advances slowly across the plain, with a darkening blue band on the underside and a horizontal stratus layer extending in front like the prow of a great ship.

At about four, family and friends gather at Mother and Eddie's house to barbecue chicken and boil sweet corn. The debate about eating outdoors versus indoors is brief; the approaching line of storms has turned a summer afternoon to premature twilight, and the radio in the house crackles with lightning-induced static. By six-thirty Eddie puts the chicken on the grill as Mother turns on lights inside. There is the feeling of an electrical charge in the air. By seven-thirty the ponderous cold front brings lightning, thunder, and cool, sweet rain, heavy at times, as we eat in the dining room.

The day has not been especially hot, but the breeze wafting through the windows is so moist and refreshed with silver rain that we all comment on the change. As rain splatters through the bushes outside, lightning freezes droplets in midair against the deep blue evening.

The thunder tells us that the lightning is not close, that the main cells of the storm system have passed to the north and south. There is a palpable delay between flash and sound, and by the time thunder reaches us at the table, it has been stripped of its high-frequency urgency, the sharp cracks and bangs, leaving only a more durable low-pitched boom and rumble. The rain dwindles off and ends during dessert, but a storm cell somewhere nearby continues to be very active. For a time the thunder is nearly constant out of the south, rattling that wall of the house, and occasionally, simultaneously with strokes of lightning, the lights flicker.

Public fireworks are a thing of the past in Peterson, a victim of liability concerns and cost. Now people drive to the county-seat towns—usually Storm Lake, Cherokee, or Spencer—for their fireworks and public Independence-Day events. So, except for the fireworks of the storm and a few scattered firecrackers about town, Peterson is dark and quiet tonight. Our own modest fireworks display—sparklers—begins about nine-fifteen in the driveway under a strange sky.

Most of the sky remains thick with clouds; the storms have moved off to the east and south where the sky is indigo, punctuated often by yellow lightning; above our heads is dense overcast. To the northwest, the sky is clear of clouds, a brilliant deepening blue, nearly dark enough to exhibit stars. The margin between the band of clear sky in the northwest and the remaining cloudy sphere is a distinct line, an edge as clear as the shore of a lake, running from the north to the west; thick, wooly cloud yields sharply to clear sky. Directly above our heads—high above—hang gray, leaden pouches of mammatiform, "breastlike," clouds. They mark the rearguard of the passing front. The pendant clouds glow with a ghastly storm light that makes them look like inverted jellyfish, or roving, disembodied spirits. We gape upward, and friend Dan Toft mutters, "My aunt Cec, whenever she saw the Parker House roll effect, would head for the basement."

Mammatiform clouds are often harbingers of bad weather, but these are at the rear edge of the front; the storm is finished here. All over town, the sound and light of small fireworks begin, as holiday picnics forced indoors by the rain trickle out into yards and streets. We learn later that to the southeast the fireworks are bigger and of a celestial variety; in Storm Lake holiday-makers huddle in their cars against the searing lightning and driving rain; the municipal display is delayed for some time and plainly outdone by nature's high-voltage pyrotechnics.

Late that night—after midnight—the clouds have cleared and Carol and I take a drive up out of the valley to look at the rain-washed sky. With the passing of the front and the advent of cooled air, dense fog is forming along the river as we start out. There is no breeze. The line between fog and clear air is as sharp as I've ever seen it. The stars are winter-bright overhead despite the thin moonlight, but the tendrils of fog that climb uphill from the river into the streets and yards of town are as opaque as snowbanks. Fog has reached Front Street on its way uphill to First as we plunge into it, heading down toward the river and the upland to the south. Our headlights find little ahead; the fog instead splatters the light back to the windshield. At twenty miles per hour the road is hard to follow, but as we climb the hill past Wanata State Forest Preserve, the fog vanishes, and an instant later we emerge onto the plain.

We get out of the car at a point along the rim road where ordinarily we would have a good view of the town in the valley, but in even the few minutes it has taken us to reach the top of the hill, the valley has filled with fog like a bathtub with water. Under clear skies the temperature has dropped, within a few minutes, below dew point in the cooler valley, and it is now rim to rim with a fog that would close any airport in the country.

Sound is amplified; somewhere in the vapor below a dog barks and a car slowly enters town from the west, feeling its way, tires slapping the joints of the concrete highway as it comes.

On the upland the air is still clear. A waning gibbous moon hangs in the southwest, illuminating the fields and the milky fog below in the valley. Moonlight also falls on the receding line of storms running from east to south, distant now, but as active as ever. The storms stand sharply etched between the ground and clear sky. Lightning fills the bulging cumulonimbus tops, flashing cloud to cloud, cloud to ground. We hear no thunder; the line is fifty or more miles away.

From the southwest over the flat fields comes a new player in this atmospheric drama: out of thin air resolves a silvery glacier of fog, forming across the upland fields, as dense as ice and growing deeper by the moment, as if eons worth of snow were being piled upon it as we watch. The backlight from the moon gives it the deep blue color of glacial ice, ice so compressed as to be free of air. The glacier comes toward us slowly, with thin fingers at the front, deepening to what seems a thousand feet in the unreliable light. I can all but hear it groan across the land.

Within silent minutes the ice swallows the moon, and farmyard lights around us fade out one by one as the glacier envelops all, smothering the landscape.

By the next morning, the fifth of July, the glacier has vanished. At the river, warming air evaporates dew from the grass as bank swallows do their summer aerobatics catching insects. In the café no one mentions the midnight glacier; it has melted away in the sun, as if it had never been. The sun is high; the atmosphere is again transparent, with low humidity and a temperature of eighty. In fact, by afternoon coffee time at Sue's, it is warm enough that no one orders coffee; iced tea is the drink of choice.

The concrete silos of the Farmers Co-op Association Elevator stand at the foot of Main Street and cast sharp shadows across the city scale and the adjacent office with its bay window. A bright Kenworth tractor truck marked "Tuet, Inc. Crete, NB" pulls a low grain trailer across the scale and stops. Inside, Janet Anderson waits for the scale to settle down; when the digital readout stabilizes, she presses a button to print the truck's empty weight on the scale ticket, then waves the driver on.

A minute later the driver has pulled up to a chute adjacent a concrete bin, and a dusty rush of last year's soybeans hurries to fill the 870-bushel trailer. Boyd McGee, whose clothes, hat, and eyebrows are thick with grain dust, monitors the flow into the truck and motions the driver ahead a few feet at a time as the front of the trailer fills. It does so quickly. I stand on the ladder of the trailer and run my hands through the rushing round soybeans; they are cool, full of energy and life.

Boyd shuts off the flow to the now-full trailer. The driver cranks a tarp across his load, swings into his cab, crosses the scale for a re-weigh, and within twenty-five minutes of his arrival in Peterson, upshifts out of town eastbound for Manning, Iowa, and a soybean processing plant there.

Harvest is at least two months away, yet the preparations have begun. The elevator is starting to empty bins for the coming inflow, and inside the elevator office, on the high counter, is a stack of programs for the upcoming Buena Vista County Fair. Day by day, the cycle of the seasons makes its revolution.

No one who has been around Peterson, or anywhere in the Midwest, very long, would deny that this climate is formed by great and dramatic weathers. Despite the partial truths and outright lies of land promoters and town boosters of the last century, the Midwest has, by most standards, a climate of extremes: heat, cold, rain and snow, drought and flood, sudden shifts from one season to the next, and wind.

The simplest climatic maps show the middle latitudes of the planet to have a "temperate" climate, a climate that is said to be "the variable climate between the extremes of tropical climate and polar climate." Peterson is at forty-three degrees north latitude, about halfway between the equator and the North Pole, in the center of the temperate zone. According to the overall averages, Peterson has a climate of moderation: the annual mean temperature is 45 degrees Fahrenheit; precipitation averages 29 inches per year; and at any given time, there is a wind of about 11 miles per hour turning the blades of the few windmills left in the county. These are temperate numbers, "characterized by moderation or restraint."

But for Iowa, these gentle figures are reached by averaging numbers that run to both ends of the scale; on average it is neither very hot nor very cold, but on any day chosen at random, the mercury could easily be pushing to the top of the scale or be cowering in the subarctic zone at the bottom.

The sky is a dome over the prairie and plains, and with few trees and structures to interrupt the view, anyone outdoors and outside the valley has a fine opportunity to observe one of the best sky shows in the country. While Peterson is off the beaten path in most ways, it is very much on the main line for invigorating weather, and anybody who has lived here long has been treated to snowfalls of extraordinary depth; tropical downpours; tornadic winds that tear at the very earth; the clear, deadly calm of midwinter when stars look more like close neighbors than celestial bodies; and a palette and architecture of cloudscape second to none.

The weather isn't always extreme here; it just seems like it. There are plenty of ordinary and forgettably dull days, days when the weather attracts little interest, but these slow periods are sufficiently punctuated by memorable atmospheric events that a year in the area will give a person a story or two to tell the grandchildren someday.

Like rural people everywhere, especially agricultural people, residents here talk about the weather. The common background chatter—in the café, on the phone, between pickups stopped on gravel roads—nearly always starts with the weather, no matter where it goes from there. Talk of ordinary weather happenings shifts fairly soon to other topics, but unusual weather events hold long attention as they are analyzed and cataloged. Iowans are justified in such preoccupation.

People's lives are regulated not only by the weather itself, but also by the pattern of forecasts on radio and television. Farmers like to make sure they're home or in the pickup a little after noon or 6 P.M. for the detailed forecasts on KICD radio or home at other times for the TV forecasts out of Sioux City. In kitchens, farm shops, pickups, the radio is usually on, and everyone falls to a hush whenever a forecast comes on. Around here, television forecasters know better than to resort to cute cutouts of clouds and raindrops in front of suns; we want fronts and radar depictions, percentage chances of how many inches of what kind of precipitation. Around here, forecasters routinely put their intuition to the test and their credibility on the line to predict events that will send combines into fields or the farmers to the café.

Anybody alive at the time remembers where he or she was during the great Armistice Day blizzard of November 11, 1940, a storm that came with such suddenness and ferocity that hunters froze in their duck blinds and the trunks of apple trees burst as the sap, not yet drawn back down to the roots, expanded as it froze. The storm killed most of the apple trees in the state. Or ask people about the blizzard of January 10, 1975, or the great windstorm of June 16, 1970. And how many generations will pass before people no longer tell stories of the colossal floods of 1993?

The lore and mythology of weather run deep in the conscious, subconscious, and collective memory of people here, and my family is no exception. Because of the stories I've heard through the years, I associate the year 1888 with two unrelated events: the birth of my great-grandfather Art Johnson and the blizzard of that year.

Who we are as people, especially in a place so tied to agricultural processes, is determined to some degree by the hemisphere of air above our heads. People look toward the low horizon here, not out of restlessness, but out of interest in the approaching and departing weather. The kinds of hats people wear, their attitudes about crop failure, their choices of recreational activities, all stem in part from adaptation to forces of weather and seasonal change.

Of course the climate has an enormous effect upon the land itself; it is one of the fundamental forming influences on a place. Long-standing weather patterns determine to a great degree not only the shape of the land—its streams, hill slopes, and vegetation—but also who lives there, what sorts of structures they build, and what they do to sustain themselves.

Bur oaks, and not coconut palms, grow here because of the climate. That the state was originally 85 percent prairie is in great part due to climate. Prairie is established and maintained by the high evaporation rate of soil moisture and by fire. While some of the fires that arrested tree growth were set by Native Americans, the majority were touched off by lightning.

Iowa excels in corn production because of the soil, which was produced by the prairie biome, and because of some factors in the present climate. First, the growing season—the time between the last killing frosts of spring and the first of fall—is long enough for hybrid corn, and second, most of the annual precipitation comes during that growing season. Plus, the summer days and nights are hot, essential to the process of corn maturation. If Iowa received the bulk of its moisture during the cool winter months as does the Central Valley of California, the value of Iowa farmland would be a fraction of what it is.

More precise than "temperate," the region actually has a "midcontinental" climate: one not closely affected by the stabilizing effects of large bodies of water. Peterson lies close to the center of North America, in the middle of a wrestling mat for aggressive masses of air riding in from several points of the compass. Here great pools of air, some cool and dry, others warm and wet, push across the landscape, producing not only much of our ordinary precipitation, but making for great spectator sport as well.

The usual combatants in the battles of air masses around here are what meteorologists call the "continental polar" air mass, or "cP" for short, and "maritime tropical," or "mT." As their names suggest, they come from opposite directions and have little in common. Continental polar air is cold and dry. It is not exactly polar in origin, though it certainly feels like it in January when an "Alberta Clipper" hurtles out of the north bringing frightfully low temperatures on howling winds. It usually originates somewhere in the subpolar region of Canada, which at certain times of the year is plenty cold enough.

Maritime tropical air lives up to its name; it is warm and usually heavy with the moisture it has absorbed over the warm Gulf of Mexico. These tropical air masses, borne across Iowa on strong southerly winds, used to send my great-grandmother Edna around the house closing windows before eight on June mornings. She could keep the house cool for the entire day if she closed it up early to exclude the heat and humidity.

There are other players in the climate of the region. A continental tropical air mass ("cT") sometimes brings hot and dry weather out of the southwest U.S., but only under unusual summer conditions. Bubbles of cold and wet maritime polar air ("mP") sometimes stretch their way in from the Pacific Ocean off the British Columbia coast, but by the time they reach the Midwest, they have been considerably warmed and wrung out by crossing two-thirds of a continent and several mountain ranges.

At times these air masses blend one into another gradually with no distinct line separating them, but more often the boundary is sharp. This line of meeting is the classic weather front: warm front, cold front, or occluded, depending upon what air mass is on the advance. When a front stalls, it becomes a stationary front. The character of the interaction at these fronts is based on which is overtaking which, the temperature and moisture of one air mass relative to the other, the temperature of the ground below them, and the speed at which one overtakes the other.

Continental topography plays an important role in setting the stage for confrontations among air masses. The general north-to-south orientation of the Rockies to the west and the Appalachians to the east acts in part to guide air masses from the north and south to a collision in the Midwest. Most other continents have mountain barriers running east to west that impede the free mixing of polar and tropical air. The lack of obstacles—from mountain ranges to mailboxes—contributes to wind speed and the severity of certain kinds of weather. Central North America endures many more tornadoes than any other place in the world.

Bob White lives and farms on the flat ground north of Peterson, where the wind and coming weather are most evident. Years of habit make him tie down anything the wind might take, or move it inside, and each night he closes

and latches the big doors to the machine shed. There is an old swing set next to the house; Bob has wrapped the swings around the poles to keep them from banging in the wind.

Says Bob: "Boy, the wind does blow sometimes! This flat, open ground runs clear to Winnipeg, and god only knows where it ends after that. It lets the cold wind come down on us, and that's when we get the damned windchills. There's nothing to block it off—there's no mountain range, nothing. Of my farm I've always said that the only thing I've got for a windbreak is a three-wire fence a mile west, and it needs stretching!"

Iowa's most dramatic weather is usually associated with fast-moving late-spring or early-summer cold fronts. They sweep in from the northwest and can generate great solid lines of thunderstorms that often reach 45,000 feet, obliterating the sky and obstructing even high-altitude jet routes. Southerly winds in the region ahead of the front feed maritime tropical air into the advancing storm system. The oncoming cold air, being denser, forms a wedge of sorts and pushes beneath the warm, moist air. As it is pushed upward, moisture in the tropical air mass condenses into clouds, beginning a process that leads to thunderstorms.

The presence and passage of these fronts are often obvious. Ahead of the front, within the mass of maritime tropical air, the wind is southerly and conditions are usually muggy. Water vapor in the air is seen as a milky haze, sometimes limiting visibility to a few miles or less. As the cold front and associated storms draw close, the south wind dies, and just prior to the onset of the rain, the air may be very calm: the proverbial calm before the storm. Commonly the passage of a fast cold front brings a sudden wind change, a gust of cold air—from the north, the west, or even from above—air that may be twenty degrees colder than that of just a few seconds earlier.

Fast-moving, late-spring cold fronts usually have a squall line, an advance detachment of low, ragged clouds that actually turn like a rolling pin as they approach. At times, as this squall line passes, I have seen the actual intersection of the air masses, expressed as a slanting plane of purple underclouds stretching upward and back toward the northwest.

Fast-traveling cold fronts usually pass through quickly, leaving cooler temperatures, northwest winds, and bright, clear skies where, just a couple of hours earlier, enormous storms raged. Warm fronts tend to move more slowly, bringing extensive areas of storms and clouds. The frontal boundary is seldom visible, and there may be cloudy, stormy weather for days, unlike the often sharp, short-duration storms of a cold front.

Occluded fronts are hard to follow without weather maps. They occur when a faster cold front sweeps up behind a slower warm front. In its clearest presentation, ground observers note the passage first of the warm front, followed in a few hours by the cold, but quite often an observer without a weather map at hand will experience little more than a confusing welter of cloud and rain, wind and temperature changes. Seldom do occluded fronts produce severe weather.

Stationary fronts, on the other hand, may produce considerable severe weather, especially during the summer. Coupled with an upper air disturbance and fed moisture and heat from the south, they can produce days of poor weather, severe storms, and astonishing quantities of rain.

As a light-plane pilot, I have often flown through the boundaries of drier, weaker fronts. Flying from warm to cold air, the atmospheric visibility suddenly improves; usually any turbulence ends, the temperature drops, and I can easily see the shift in winds in the change of my drift over the landscape. But like any other pilot who would prefer to live another day, I avoid strong fronts and associated thunderstorms at all cost.

The best weather show often occurs during summer afternoons when there is no frontal system involved. Fairly often during the summer, an unstable weather condition evolves where there is a strong northward flow of warm, moist, maritime tropical air across even warmer earth beneath it. If the tropical air is saturated with moisture, the warm ground may impart enough additional heat to trigger the initial uplift required to create memorable thunderstorms. These "air mass" thunderstorms usually arise in the afternoon, after the sun has had sufficient time to impart maximum heat energy to the soil and thence into the air above it.

Since they are not associated with discrete frontal boundaries, it is very hard for even professionals to predict the exact location, timing, and severity of air-mass thunderstorms, and yet they produce some of the most spectacular weather in the Midwest. So when the forecasters talk about "an unstable atmosphere," "a strong flow of southerly air," and wave their hands in front of the map in vague circles as they talk of thunderstorms, and especially if the severe-storm people in Kansas City start laying out their rectangles for "a severe storm watch . . . thirty miles either side of a line from Worthington, Minnesota, to . . . ," I pay close attention, and if I happen to be in the right place at the right time, things will get interesting.

I've been lucky at times. I drove north of town one afternoon and parked my truck on the gravel road a mile or so east of Bob White's place where the land is flat and the sky is unobstructed by trees, wires, or hills. I sat on the tailgate and in a couple hours watched the sky evolve from summer-fair to one filled with severe storms.

The predictions were for severe thunderstorms in the area, but as I pulled to the side of the road, the sky was open and bright, about one-third filled with innocuous-looking cumulus. As I sat and watched over the next half-hour or so, the earth heated the already warm and moist air, and the cumulus grew larger and thicker, more energetic; meteorologists call these "swelling cumulus." Higher clouds began to appear, and the sky took on a ragged, unsettled appearance.

Suddenly—at least by cloud-formation standards—one of these clouds billowed upward; it had absorbed enough heat to become unstable and explode through the stratified air around it. It rose for a few minutes as a narrow column, but its small diameter prevented it from sustaining and feeding the rise. The uplift died out, leaving a wispy column of exhausted cloud.

Meanwhile, around me, the sum mass of cloud had grown thicker, now covering half the sky (much more than this and it would hinder the solar heating of the ground, vital to the job of starting this storm engine). I looked around for clouds with better chances of success.

The point of change was easy to spot. Some miles to the north, a cloud seemed to thicken, draw in a bit, and shove upward in concentrated fashion. Once the uplift was triggered, new clouds quickly formed around the first and were pulled into the updraft, their domes joining the leader in a rising cauliflower bubble of creamy blue. The flat underside, meanwhile, grew dark. This heat engine, primed now with energy from the ground, surged to life, generating its own power through the heat released by condensing water as it rose. As they climbed into colder, drier atmosphere, the cloud tops grew more distinct, more sharp. At a glance, this mass didn't appear to move upward very fast, but the very scale of the cloud hides its motion. With binoculars held on the truck's roof, I watched the slow explosion rise through my field of view as vapor steamed upward into the atmosphere, clawing over itself for altitude as the storm cell grew in diameter and strength. Cumulus tops can rise at a rate of several thousand feet per minute, exceeding the climb rates of everything but high-performance jet fighters.

Other clouds exploded upward to join ranks with the first, forming a wall or a group of cells, I couldn't tell which from my position. Soon the entire northern and western sectors of the sky were filled with darkening purple clouds sprouting dense shafts of rain and frequent lightning. I abandoned my observation spot and went home to close the windows.

If my position had been a bit more distant from the action, I might have seen the storms reach the tropopause, that boundary at about 45,000 feet in the summer Midwest, beyond which only the most severe storms can sustain development. Somewhere near this altitude, upward swelling slows, and as the cloud enters the jet stream, great masses of it are shredded and carried downwind, forming the characteristic "anvil" cloud, or cirrus densus, of a mature thunderstorm. Some storms top out at lower altitudes, some at higher. The weather maps used by pilots always note the heights of the tops of all thunderstorms; not only do these data tell pilots whether they have the climb capability to fly over the thunderstorms, but the information gives all pilots a sense of the severity of a given storm. All else being equal, the higher a storm top, the more severe the storm will be.

Seeing a giant prairie thunderstorm always reminds me of the name given to their clouds: cumulonimbus. "Cumulo" means heaped or massed; "nimbus" refers to "clouds of the gods," and the cumulonimbus of the Middle West bring the great gods of wind, hail, lightning, thunder, and the beneficence of sweet restoring rain.

It astonishes me, each time I see one, to remember that a thunderstorm is made of nothing more solid than air and water vapor. If you cut a gymnasium-sized piece out of a storm's center, subtracted out the heavy rain and hail, and released it into that gymnasium, you'd find only a gauzy mist making the ceiling lights indistinct. A hot shower in a closed bathroom creates much more in the way of an intense micro-atmosphere. It is only on the grand scale, over the span of cubic miles, that a storm generates its power; a small storm—three miles in diameter—can occupy more than fifty cubic miles of air and will contain something like 170 *million* gallons of water.

The most intemperate events in this temperate climate are tornadoes. While theoretically they can occur in many parts of the world, they are most common here, in the interior of the North American continent; "tornado alley" runs from Texas northeast through Oklahoma, Kansas, Nebraska, Iowa, and Illinois. Nobody who has experienced one ever forgets it.

In 1879 Gertrude Tolley and her husband, Wilson, arrived with their two small children in the Peterson area and bought a farm four miles north of town; Bob White farms the land today. Wilson was from Kentucky, and Gertrude from England and probably unaccustomed to the potential threat of midwestern weather. Sometime that very first year a tornado struck their farm with enough violence to destroy their house and tear out the newly planted grove. Where the family rode out the storm is not known, but they all survived.

The experience affected Gertrude deeply. Instead of rebuilding on the same spot, she insisted the family move a half mile north and build a new place.

Meanwhile, Sam and Jennie Tillinghast bought the eighty-acre farm where the Tolleys had lost their home. About 1900, a full twenty years or more after the storm, the young Tillinghast daughter, Velma, who would later marry to become Velma Walrath, would walk the half mile north to visit the Tolley family on Sunday afternoons. Velma was young, perhaps six or seven. She remembers her visits there.

"Mrs. Tolley would tell me stories about England, about thatched roofs and things people did there. Of course I hadn't gone to school much as yet, so I didn't know anything about England. Mrs. Tolley served me tea and store-bought cookies, which were a real treat, since the cookies at our house were homemade."

Even as a small child, and even after the passage of twenty years, Velma could see the angst in Gertrude Tolley.

"She was always so afraid of storms. They had a cave, a storm cellar, and every time a cloud came up, she would go down there and stay. She kept a lantern down there, and bedding, so I guess she spent half her time down there in the summer, especially at night when she couldn't see the storms coming.

"She never went anywhere; she never was in my mother's house nor any of the neighbors' houses. People made fun of her because she was so afraid, but she was always good to me."

Tornadoes—past, predicted, or imagined—are an inescapable part of spring and summer existence here. No one listens to a weather forecast predicting thunderstorms without thinking of them. Their concentrated malevolence outstrips any other atmospheric phenomenon. Unpredictable as to their appearance in some storms and not others, and altogether unpredictable once on the ground and heading toward your farm, they are notoriously fickle in choosing some objects to destroy and others to leave untouched.

Tornadoes have scoured the land around Peterson on numerous occasions, though none in recorded history have carried the destructive charge of some experienced elsewhere. Around here they have demolished farmsteads and homes but have apparently never killed anyone.

The other great immoderations in Iowa weather are the occasional blizzards that push their way through the region, leaving behind record low temperatures and snowfalls. The best of them come as a result of both strong frontal movement and a deep low-pressure system. While local wags talk of blizzard conditions, or "white out," the true blizzard is unforgettable. The real thing comes in two stages: first, a snowfall of average or greater depth pushed by winds of ordinary velocity, followed by the onrush of staggering and frigid winds as a continental polar air mass roars down express-train fashion from the northwest. The winds may exceed fifty miles per hour on the open land, whirling every flake of snow into an atmospheric soup so dense as to make even the surface of the planet disappear in a hissing mass of white. The winds may persist for days, piling up drifts of astonishing proportions among farm buildings, in road cuts, in the lee of any obstruction to the wind.

Someone who knew firsthand the power of winter storms was author Herbert Quick. Born in 1861 on a farm in Grundy County, Iowa, Quick spent his boyhood growing up with the country. In his novel about early pioneer life in Iowa, *Vandemark's Folly*, Quick wrote of the experiences of early farm life in a prairie township, experiences that ring with the veracity of someone who lived them. His protagonist, Cow Vandemark, endures the hardships of the climate as he makes a farm out of prairie in fictional Vandemark Township, Monterey County:

". . . At noon the northwestern sky, a third of the way to a point overhead, was of an indigo-blue color; but it still seemed to be clear sky—though I looked at it with suspicion, it was such an unusual thing in January. . . .

". . . The bright sun was blotted out as it touched the edge of that rising belt of indigo blue. . . . It was a fearful thing to see, the blue-black cloud hurrying up the sky, over the sky, and far down until there was no bright spot except a narrowing oval near the southeastern horizon; and not a breath of wind. The storm was like a leaning wall, that bent far over us while its foot dragged along the ground, miles and miles behind its top. Everything had a tinge of strange, ghastly greenish blue like the face of a corpse, and it was growing suddenly dark as if the day had all at once shut down into dusk.

"I knew what it meant, though I had never seen the change from calm warmth to cold wind come with such marked symptoms of suddenness and violence. It meant a blizzard—though we never heard or adopted the word until in the late 'seventies. . . .

". . . Suddenly the house staggered as if it had been cuffed by a great hand. I peeped out of the window, and against the dark sky I could see the young grove of trees bowing before the great gusts which had struck them from the northwest. The wall of wind and frost and death had moved against them. . . .

"I wonder if the people who have been born in or moved to Iowa in the past thirty to forty years can be made to understand that we can not possibly have such winter storms of this sort as we had then. The groves themselves prevent it. The standing corn-stalks prevent it. Every object that civilization and development have placed in the way of the wind prevents it. Then, the snow, once lifted on the wings of the blast, became a part of the air, and remained in it. The atmosphere for hundreds of feet, for thousands of feet from the grassy surface of the prairie, was a moving cloud of snow, which fell only as the very tempest itself became over-burdened with it. As the storm continued, it always grew cold; for it was the North emptying itself into the South. . . .

"Even to the strongest man, there was terror in this storm, the breath of which came with a roar and struck with a shiver, as the trees creaked and groaned, and the paths and roads were obliterated. As the tumult grows hills are leveled, and hollows rise into hills. Every shed-roof is the edge of an oblique Niagara of snow; every angle the center of a whirlpool."

While other parts of the world experience blizzards, often more severe even than those here, it's no surprise that Iowa claims some of the best of them; the world's first blizzard was born here, and only forty miles from Peterson. The word had been around for a while and had been used in wartime to describe particularly violent volleys of fire, but it had never been used to describe a great, wind-driven snowstorm until around 1870, and probably after a storm on March 14, 1870, when the now-forgotten editor of the *Estherville Northern Vindicator* described the storm that went through his town as a "blizzard."

The south side of this Township, except the bottom land is very broken or rather a series of precipices on each side of the river pointing to the stream. North of the river on the high Prairie is good farming land. there are [two] cabins in this township, one on the S.W. 1/4 of section 34 the other on the S.E 1/4 [of] 32, No rocks except a few boulders.

—George Temple, U.S. government surveyor, field note description of Township 94N, Range 38w, later Peterson Township

Chapter 4

Alioth and Polaris

The most prominent marks on the local area, and perhaps the most enduring, were initiated by a man about whom we know almost nothing. His effect here was monumental, yet he was armed with nothing more powerful than a compass, was assisted by only four men, and completed his job in only a few weeks. The change he wrought on the landscape was complete and revolutionary, and the marks he made on the land will remain as long as human beings are the measure of this place.

George Temple arrived here in September 1856 and immediately began the pivotal work in transforming the postglacial landscape in what would become Peterson Township. His title was deputy surveyor, and his work was to

Rod Burgeson's forty-four-acre cornfield, October

There were days when ragged gray masses of cloud
swept down on the powerful northern wind, when there
was a sorrowful, lonesome moan among the corn rows,
when the cranes, no longer soaring at ease, drove
straight into the south, sprawling low-hung in the blast,
or lost to sight above the flying scud, their necks out-
thrust, desperately eager to catch a glimpse of their
shining Mexican seas.

—Hamlin Garland, Boy Life on the Prairie, *1899*

Corn harvest, Burgeson farm, October

Burgeson disk harrow, May

Section corner, sections 5, 6, 7, and 8, Peterson Township, September

There are some fifteen hundred townships in Iowa; and each of them had its history like this; and so had every township in all the great, wonderful West of the prairie. . . . Every one of these townships has a history beginning in the East, or in Scandinavia, or Germany, or the South. We are a result of lines of effect which draw together into our story; and we are a cause of a future of which no man can form a conjecture.
—*Herbert Quick,* Vandemark's Folly, *1922*

Corn, bluegrass, and brome, May

Bob White's new corn, May

*May fourteen, nineteen-
ninety-one; that's all she wrote;
God willing and the dike don't
break, we'll pick some corn this
fall!*
—*Bob White,*
on finishing corn planting

Peterson Township, August

   As I looked back at the results of my day's work, my spirits rose; for in the East, a man might have worked all

summer long to clear as much land as I had prepared for a crop on that first day. This morning it had been wilderness;

now it was a field—a field in which Magnus Thorkelson had planted corn, by the simple process of cutting through

the sods with an ax, and dropping in each opening thus made three kernels of corn. Surely this was a new world!

—Herbert Quick, Vandemark's Folly, *1922*

Carroll Tigges farm, June

Peterson Township, April

Swelling cumulus, Peterson Township, June

Bob White,
Peterson Township

Peterson Township, March

Soybeans, Brooke Township,
May

Prior to this time I had been courting the country; now I was to be united with it in that holy wedlock which binds the farmer to the soil he tills. Out of this black loam was to come my own flesh and blood, and the bodies, and I believe, in some measure, the souls of my children. Some dim conception of this made me draw in a deep, deep breath of the fresh prairie air.
—Herbert Quick,
  Vandemark's Folly, 1922

Burgeson cottonwoods at the corner of Clay, Buena Vista, Cherokee, and O'Brien counties, September

For I am writing of the Ancient Greek period of midwestern life, when communities were set out as our farmers

planted trees, by thrusting the twigs of cottonwood or willow or Lombardy poplar into the soil, and watching them as

they shot up to tempt the forest birds and check the blizzards. . . .

—*Herbert Quick,* The Hawkeye, *1923*

Section 15, Peterson Township, July

    It was a changed world, a land of lanes and fields and houses hid in groves of trees which he had seen set out. No one rode horseback any more. Where the cattle had roamed and the boys had raced the prairie wolves, fields of corn and oats waved. No open prairie could be found. Every quarter section, every acre, was ploughed. The wild flowers

were gone. Tumbleweed, smartweed, pigweed, mayflower, and all the other plants of semi-civilization had taken the place of the wild asters, pea-vines, crow's-foot, sunflowers, snake-weed, sweet-williams, and tiger-lilies. The very air seemed tamed and set to work at the windmills which rose high above every barn, like great sunflowers.

—*Hamlin Garland,* Boy Life on the Prairie, *1899*

*Bob Klinefelter
shelling corn, July*

Grain distributor, Farmers Co-op Association
Elevator, Peterson

Iowa is peculiarly an agricultural State.
Whatever inducements she may at present, or in
the future, offer to the manufacturer, the miner,
or persons engaged in the various other pursuits
of life, the essential fact remains, that the true
source of her rising greatness and prospective
grandeur lies in the capacity of her soil to supply
those staples absolutely necessary for the
sustenance of man.
—Iowa: The Home for Immigrants, *1870*

Peterson, August

Where do you go except back where you came from?

I can't tell you how many people have lost track of where they were going—how many people are not too sure of where they are from.

But I can tell you that it's a farm or a little town—and that little towns are mighty big places to be from. The smaller they are the bigger they are to be from—

—Wright Morris, The Inhabitants, *1972*

Peterson, April

West side of Main Street, August

    Nothing gives ye editor more of a feeling of having been "born thirty years too late" than to hear some of the older men tell about things they did in the Horse and Buggy Days. There is no desire on my part to go back and fight with old Chief Inkpadutah about whether I should wear my scalp on top of my head or he wear it on his belt. But when the 1940 type of life begins to wear your nerves to a thin edge, just sit on the bench in front of the Fastenow store and listen to a few old timers tell about the '90s and the early 1900s and you're pretty sure to feel that they really had something.

    —Peterson Patriot, *January 11, 1940*

make square miles out of unsurveyed prairie, to take land that had heretofore been without limit or precise boundary, and enmesh it in a net of points, lines, and numbers. Temple—along with thousands of other U.S. government contract surveyors—engraved a grid of square miles onto the landscape of much of the United States, creating uniform parcels of land for quick sale and linear farming. His lines engendered the geography of this place, and their effects are as pronounced today in southwest Clay County as those of any other lines, either natural or human-made. No single event has had greater effect on this place, and if we are to understand the landscape here, all events both before and since must be seen in its light.

Early on the morning of September 18, 1856, George Temple and his four assistants rolled up their bedding, ate their breakfast, and made ready for another day of work. Temple began by adjusting his large brass compass for magnetic variation: the angular difference between magnetic north and true north. As was the practice in those days, Temple had used Polaris—the North Star—to determine true north. He would have made his observations during the night before, and now, perhaps while his men had their last smoke around a dying campfire, he compared his nighttime observations with the needle of his instrument.

Temple may have been tired, for on this date his stellar observation would have to have been made in the small hours of the morning. Polaris does not hang motionless at true north but over a twenty-four-hour period describes a small circle, crossing the meridian of true north twice. On September 18, Polaris would have crossed the meridian at a few minutes after one in the morning. Temple knew that when Polaris and Alioth, the third star in the handle of the Big Dipper, rotated into a vertical line, Polaris would be at exactly true north. Using a crude but straightforward arrangement of stakes, boards, a candle, and a plumb bob dangled in a bucket of water (to prevent wind oscillation), Temple had carefully made his observation of the North Star and Alioth, and when they both disappeared behind the string attached to the plumb bob, he had marked his sighting. Leaving his apparatus fixed until day's light, Temple could then compare the meridian of the North Star with that defined by his compass, and could adjust the latter. Now, in daylight, Temple calculated the variation, and in his field notebook wrote 11 degrees, 30 minutes east.

Exactly where Temple's camp was situated is not recorded; it may have been near the river, maybe close to one of two newly built cabins in the area, possibly on the upland prairie. But two things are certain: it was a simple, primitive camp, and it was a considerable distance from what Temple and his men would have called civilization. In 1856, the closest settlement consisting of more than scattered cabins was the village of Fort Dodge, seventy miles southeast across prairie and slough as high as a horse's back. That these surveyors lived simply and at great distance from home comforts was made clear by Ira Cook, a government surveyor who did identical work in counties just to the south: "Except immediately along the Mississippi and in a few localities on some of the larger streams, these surveys preceded the settlement of the country, so that the deputy surveyor who had a contract to survey a given district generally found himself beyond any settlement, and, as a consequence, must carry with him his house (tent) and his supplies of provisions and complete outfit for a trip extending, in some cases, over many months. It followed, of course, that he was obliged to restrict himself and his men to the simplest necessities of food and clothing. A barrel or two of salt pork, flour in barrels, navy beans, with sugar, coffee, salt and pepper, made up the sum of our larder. For bedding we had rubber blankets, buffalo robes and heavy woolen blankets. With these we could keep both warm and dry."

The days were long and filled with tedious, plodding work, the labor of measuring across nearly featureless country that by now, in September, was deep with tangled prairie grass that impeded every step. But it was adventure as well. The days were filled with sky and space, and distant views over country new to Euro-American eyes. The work was like that of explorers: the long strides of white men taking the measure of new land. Certainly the surveyors had heard of Lewis and Clark, of Zebulon Pike. Secretly many may have wished to see an Indian—if only from a distance—so they could spellbind those back home in the dull towns of Burlington and Dubuque with stories of these mysterious people. And there was male camaraderie, too; stories told around a campfire miles from any woman's ear.

As they broke camp that morning, Temple and his crew no doubt worked as men accustomed to certain tasks, for these men formed a qualified crew; they had been in the field surveying for more than two weeks, and their swift progress across the landscape indicated efficiency. Temple himself was an experienced surveyor, having surveyed and subdivided eight six-by-six-mile townships in the previous two years. His party packed their few personal possessions, cook pots, bedrolls, provisions, shovels and axes, a sixty-six-foot measuring chain, flags, and tally pins. Probably they loaded their gear onto horses; by this time they were surveying an average of twelve miles per day, so it is likely that they traveled without the encumbrance of wagons. Temple would have shouldered the delicate sighting compass and its monopod "Jacob's staff," and in his coat pocket would have carried his field notebook and ink quills.

Temple's job as a federal contract surveyor was simply described, yet it required great effort and care. He and his crew were subdividing this township—a square of six by six miles—into thirty-six one-mile-square parcels. The township boundaries here and in most of this part of the state had been surveyed the year before by another contract surveyor and were to act as the reference lines for the work of subdivision. Temple and his men were to mark out each square mile—each "section"—by measuring north and south, east and west, on foot, across prairie and through wetlands, walking each mile twice to accomplish the task. Then they were to build monuments at each point where the section lines crossed. In addition, they were to place lesser markers at half-mile intervals. When finished with this township, they would have surveyed a total distance of 120 miles and walked a good many more.

The instructions Temple carried were issued by the Surveyor General of the United States and made clear that he was to keep detailed notes as to "the precise length of every line run, noting all necessary offsets therefrom, with the reason and mode thereof," and to record something of the character of the landscape: land surface, soil, timber, prairie, marshes. He was to describe all streams, springs, lakes and ponds, and any mineral concentrations, list the presence of any Indian villages or white settlements, and identify all "roads and trails, with their directions, whence and whither." For Euro-Americans, this was new and uncharted country.

First proposed by Thomas Jefferson, the rectangular land survey was designed as a simple system by which the vast lands of the country could be quickly measured, divided, described—in a legal sense—and sold. First applied in 1785 in what came to be called the Seven Ranges of eastern Ohio, the system was a vast improvement over the traditional "metes and bounds" arrangement whereby irregularly shaped parcels of land were identified, measured, and described by elaborate written descriptions of the parcel's perimeter.

By 1856, the rectangular survey system had been perfected and was quickly becoming the measure of the new states and territories of the United States. By the time the rest of the lands that would become the lower forty-eight states had been surveyed, 69 percent of the land area would be bound by it: some two million square miles. Governmental motivation stemmed in part from the Jeffersonian notion of the landed farmer, but more to the point, the sale of such vast lands—some not yet vacated by Indian peoples—would bring considerable money to a chronically anemic federal treasury.

The native population was not ignored in this effort; it was simply disenfranchised. In the age-old story, the Siouan-speaking tribes and groups that hunted in northwest Iowa at the time of Euro-American settlement were given no option but to cede their lands to the U.S. government and were pushed west with little thought save the occasional diatribe of a government official. Characteristic are the words of Surveyor General George W. Jones of Dubuque who wrote earlier of Iowa lands to the east:

The "unsurveyed parts of this Territory are nearly surrounded by Indian tribes . . . the Chippewas, Ottawas, and Pottawatomies upon the southwest and west, the Sioux upon the northwest, and the Winnebagoes upon the north and northeast. Of the lands thus occupied, the 'neutral ground' offers the best and strongest arguments in favor of immediate treaty and cession. No Indian country approaches the heavy settlements of the Territory so nearly as the rich and beautiful section in question, and nothing has prevented its settlement for several past years but the circumstances of its present improper possession and occupancy. Besides, the contiguity of a densely settled frontier with one of the lowest and most abandoned of Indian tribes, has the effect of holding the white man in constant fear and jeopardy, while it is every day sinking the wretched Indian far below the ordinary miseries of savage life. I regard it as among the plainest of my duties to urge that the effort to treat for these lands upon some plan better calculated to succeed than any formerly tried, should be attempted at the earliest day possible."

Not that Native Americans didn't convey their unhappiness to the surveyors. In 1855, the year before George Temple and his crew came to this area, another U.S. contract surveyor, one J. L. Ingalsby, was employed to stake out township lines at six-mile intervals near present-day Sioux Rapids, ten miles east of Peterson:

"We were pushing on north and west entirely beyond any communication with civilization . . . [when] a solitary Indian came to me as I was swinging on ahead of my chainmen at what was called the 'Surveyor's lope' and partly in mixed English and Indian and partly by expressive pantomime he endeavored to turn me back. He would point eastward 'Good-Good-Much Good,' pointing west 'Bad-Bad-Big Bad' making motions as if to push me back. Failing to arrest our advance he finally sat down by one of our monuments and remained motionless as the post by which he sat until we lost sight of him in the distance.

"I will here state that an Indian hates a surveyor worse than he does a settler or even a soldier. When the surveyor has passed over the land measuring it off into parcels guided by his shining instruments, setting his monuments at the intersections of his trails the Indian feels a superstitious dread to step inside those bounds."

Considering the reaction Native Americans often got from both settlers and soldiers, they can hardly be blamed for being reluctant to cross the lines.

The U.S. land survey system was simple in concept. At intervals across the country, surveyors, using equipment more sophisticated and accurate than the simple magnetic compass operated by Temple, established meridians and baselines as reference lines for the surveys. In Iowa nearly all surveys were measured and counted from the Fifth Principal Meridian, which ran north-south at longitude 90 degrees and 58 minutes west and passed through the "nose" of eastern Iowa, and with reference to an east-west baseline in Arkansas, which passed through the middle of that state. From these two reference lines, townships in the better parts of six states—Arkansas, Missouri, Iowa, Minnesota, and South and North Dakota—were indexed and surveyed, a series of columns of 164 townships stacked on the baseline from Arkansas to the Canadian border. Each township had a number that identified it by virtue of its position in relation to the two lines; the yet-unnamed township where Temple and his crew were working on September 18, 1856, was already known as Township 94 North, Range 38 West of the Fifth Principal Meridian. This township was ninety-four townships north of the Arkansas baseline and thirty-eight townships, or "ranges," west of the Fifth Principal Meridian.

As surveyors did their work of subdividing townships into square miles, each of the thirty-six sections was given a number, starting with 1 at the northeast corner of the township and proceeding west to number 6, dropping south to the next row, and then east to the east side of the township, dropping south again, west again, back and forth like plowing oxen, to number 36 at the southeast corner of the township.

The survey system was arbitrary. It took into account neither natural geographic boundaries nor existing cultural landmarks. The square grid was merely etched onto the topography, and settlers were expected to operate within its confines. Such a system as this would have serious flaws later in the arid and rugged west, but here, in the undulating prairies where landmarks and possible geographical conflicts were few, this pattern that looked as though it were applied to the landscape with a rolling pin was an appropriate expedient.

According to his field notes, Temple had four assistants: two chainmen and two axmen. The chainmen conducted the "chaining," the actual measuring across the ground; for axmen, the title was less appropriate. On the broad Iowa prairies, men expert in wielding axes were needed no more than grave diggers on board ship. Forty or fifty years earlier, Ohio axmen earned their pay and name clearing paths through dense forest ahead of the surveyors' chainmen, cutting trees that stood astride survey lines and blazing trees for markers at section corners. In Ohio a tree was often close enough to a section corner to serve as the marker; in Iowa there were often no trees in sight. But in those days jobs and titles were flexible; it is likely that one axman took care of the horses while the other acted as flagman.

Temple and his crew began this day's work at a section corner on the south township boundary, a point and a line established the previous year by another surveyor, one who had prepared the way by surveying the larger grid of six-mile-square townships. This section corner stood partway down the south slope of the Little Sioux River valley. From this marker they would work their way due north between what would, by the end of the day, become sections 33 and 34 of Township 94 North, Range 38 West of the Fifth Principal Meridian.

The survey crew set out to follow a line of true north from the section corner into the unsurveyed landscape. Even though they were working generally downhill into the valley, their northbound course first took them over the crest of a slight rise. It is likely that an axman-now-flagman strode to the top of the short rise with flag in hand as Temple steadied his compass at the section corner marker and directed the flagman into position on an exact north-south line via its sights.

Here were the first yards of a new line on the earth.

Taking up this cardinal line, the chainmen began their work. The rear chainman held one end of the chain to the previously surveyed section corner post as the advance chainman took the opposite end and started northward. On the sloping ground that September day they probably shortened the chain to half its length in order to keep it dead level for close measurement, an unusual task for men so used to chaining across miles of level prairie. As they worked, the men made a series of steps, repeated actions with a rhythm almost like that of dance.

At the first measure the chain was pulled taut and held level so the advance chainman could set his first tally pin. Once the pin was set, both chainmen moved ahead to measure the next length, and after doing so, the rear chainman took up the tally pin and moved ahead for the next measurement. Measure, set pin, pull rear pin, walk forward, measure, set pin, pull rear pin, walk forward, and so on, they moved quickly over the rise and down into the river valley.

At the point where the advance chainman set his tenth tally pin, he called "tally," and the call was repeated by the rear man. The rear chainman then brought the pins forward where both men counted them to ensure that no pins had been missed and that the number of chain lengths measured would be counted correctly. Both men then marked the count of ten tally pins—or ten chain lengths—by placing a ring onto a thong of leather worn on the belt, or by some similar marker. In usual surveying, each ring meant 660 feet; when eight tallies had been done and eight rings had been placed on the thong, the crew had surveyed 5,280 feet, or one mile, one side of a new section.

As the chainmen advanced, Temple would take new positions along the line and send the flagman further into unsurveyed territory, always directing the flagman to place the flag exactly on the line by peering through his compass sights and waving his arms right or left until the flagman assumed the correct position.

The men surveyed quickly; it is said that these government surveyors, who were paid by the mile, seldom looked back. Chain by chain, they marked this boundary onto the landscape as their feet trampled prairie grass into a line far more straight than any this valley had ever seen. While accuracy was important, speed was essential, because settlers were pouring across the Mississippi and flowing west to take up homesteads in the new state.

As George Temple and his men measured their way downhill into the Little Sioux valley, he recorded prominent landscape features in his notes. At three chains, or 198 feet, from the point of beginning, he noted that their line entered timber. At last axmen could work according to their name, for this was good, thick timber, unusual in this country. Soon the steep descent ended as the crew reached flat river-bottom land. For a time they had easy work as they crossed the broad river floodplain.

Less than a quarter-mile later, the line crossed the Little Sioux River for the first time; the river meandered at this point, looping across the new section line three times in a few hundred feet.

Quickly they left the valley's floor and began climbing its north side—steep enough that the chainmen may again have been forced to measure in half-chain lengths. And here Temple recorded no timber; they were back in prairie again after only a few chains of real forest in some hundred square miles of their contracted area of survey. Within a short time Temple and the crew climbed to the top of the valley side and could, if they paused to catch their breath after the climb, turn around and look back whence they had come.

If they paused to look back, they must have beheld a fine spectacle spread before them, one of the best views in many miles of surveying. The valley was about a mile wide, 180 feet deep, and it lay before them in a great curve. Back and forth across the width of the valley meandered the Little Sioux, shallow and clear, its course fringed with scattered trees. A prairie river, it ran gentle and clear between bare soil banks, tranquil in September. Like any free river in a bed of soil, the Little Sioux never ran straight. It turned back on itself, a twist of whorls, loops, bends, and sandbars.

Though they had surveyed through a third of a mile of woodland on this section line, what they would have seen from the valley rim was a universe of grass. Their eyes must have been full with the texture and color of tall-grass prairie: a matted carpet of coarse, uneven grasses and forbs, various greens, yellows, browns, and reds, now flushed with the dots of fall prairie flowers. It was prairie as far as the eye could see: deep, tangled big bluestem and dark prairie cord grass in the valley bottom, broad acres of little bluestem climbing the north slopes, with myriad fall prairie flowers in yellow, purple, red, and white.

But prairie probably wouldn't much interest the surveyors; they had seen and would continue to see so much prairie and so little else in their days of surveying that they must have seen it in their sleep: great masses of waving grass.

What would have interested Temple and his men was the dark area of timber off to the southwest, perhaps by this time beginning to show a little yellow in its green. There, in the valley, pinched between the river on the north and the valley rim to the south, stood mature red oak, bur oak, a few walnut, soft maple, cottonwood. This was dense, inviting, cool, green woodland like some of the men might have known back in New England, fine shelter from the prairie sun. It was narrow—probably a quarter of a mile or less on average—and extended for about a mile and a half in a crescent along the outer side of a bend in the river. This was the timber they had surveyed through a short time earlier; their line cut through its eastern end.

Certainly there were other trees within sight of the survey crew: scattered trees along the river, perhaps denser clumps in protected river loops, an occasional thicket of brush in a side ravine overlooked by prairie fires; but no forested area within many miles was as splendid as this one off to the southwest.

In all that sweep of prairie and river and fragment of woodland there were probably but two clear reminders of human presence. One was the newly surveyed section line standing out as a straight path of flattened grass; it dropped down the valley side opposite, ran across the bottomland toward them and up the near side, passed right through them, and pointed at the North Star.

The other was a small new cabin near the edge of the thick woods on the far side of the river. This log structure was the home of Ambrose Meade and his family and was one of two cabins in Clay County. In 1858, this cabin would be the site of the first election in the county, the election that organized the county itself. The other cabin stood out of sight a mile and a half west along the Little Sioux, at the other end of the grove of timber, and belonged to a large family named Kirchner.

There may well have been Indian trails in the valley as well; this was not uninhabited country, but the difference between a trail used occasionally by a moving group of Sioux and a trail frequented by deer and bison is difficult to ascertain.

But what these men would have beheld was not so much something as the lack of something; what they could see had much more to do with space and distance than with prairie grasses, trees, or idyllic rivers. This view, so typical of those seen by other government surveyors and by army engineers, squatting settlers, and railroad speculators in the 1850s, was one of broad, nearly treeless lands as yet without enduring human marks. Temple and his men were experiencing firsthand what the rest of the nation was only slowly beginning to grasp: the scale of the continental interior—vast, unfenced, and, to them, unsettled.

They were seeing a small bit of the sort of landscape that was increasingly to be absorbed into the American fabric, the American psyche—open planiform land: sometimes grass, sometimes desert, sage, table rock, or dry lake bed. Since emerging from the oak openings at forest's edge in Illinois, Euro-America had been trying to fit these distant horizons into the collective consciousness, and the adjustment was not always easy.

As white settlement spread westward, this new landscape, a world where foreground and horizon melted together in a single sweep of the eye, would become common—even ubiquitous. How different this sunburned wilderness was, compared to the gloomy forest wilds of a generation past! Certainly there had been space and horizons in Kentucky and Ohio, but nothing like this. The absorption of such distance, the act of focusing a horizon at infinity on the retina of the collective eye, prepared the mind for comprehending spaces to be accounted for later, further west—places larger, harder, less friendly.

And as they stood at the brow of the valley—if they stopped at all—they stood at the very point of change, for they were the agents of that change. In Kansas, in Oregon, in Wisconsin, and in townships and counties all around in Iowa, hundreds of other contract survey crews were taking the measure of a land new to Euro-American eyes, a land that by virtue of the survey was already beginning a great revolution.

These men couldn't have paused long to view their work spanning the valley nor to view this quiet river; they still had many miles to survey on foot that day, many tallies to make. They continued their work northbound for a few tallies, now on the flat plain, a prairie that swelled uninterrupted for some thirty miles to the Okoboji lakes. They could work faster here, with no climbing, no timber, merely thick prairie. At eighty chains, one mile from where they had begun that morning, they stopped to build a section corner marker.

And here is a curiosity, a logistical and spiritual dilemma for the crew: what do you use in such a trackless place to mark so microscopic and yet so monumental a point on the land as this section corner? Temple's instruction book was explicit on the importance of properly erecting these section corner markers:

"To procure the faithful execution of this portion of a surveyor's duty is a matter of the utmost importance. After a true coursing, and most exact measurements, the corner boundary is the consummation of the work, for which all the previous pains and expenditures have been incurred. If, therefore, the corner boundary be not perpetuated in a permanent and workmanlike manner, the *great aim* of the surveying service will not have been attained."

There were marks of other peoples here, but they were faint, ephemeral, and not so precisely regulated to the heavens as this marker was to be. There were old Indian village sites nearby, hidden by grass, and narrow foot trails, but they never required this sort of precision in their establishment. On such an open and nearly trackless landscape, what does one use to establish so small and so arbitrary a place as the common point among sections 27, 28, 33, and 34? What material lay at hand that would not only mark this junction but sanctify it?

This was a place made of grass and sky; grass was everywhere at their feet and the sky inescapable above. Mere grass could not make the marker; it could not provide the needed distinction from itself. The timber was too far away in the valley to provide a large pole, a log. There were stones about, but the crew could not see them; they rested within the soil and would emerge only after people cut the roots of the prairie with steel plows.

Temple and his crew knew their job; they had made dozens of such corner markers and doubtless without discussion fell to work digging trenches and building a pyramidal mound of the soft earth. Here was a guidon, a guide post: a marker built of the soil itself, the very resource that would soon bring thousands of men and women to the region. How much more appropriate than a staff of gold or a royal pennant was the idea of using the thing itself to mark this new point on the land.

If they followed their instructions, the mound they built had a square perimeter, about five feet on a side, and was two and a half feet high. The soil came from a trench that surrounded the heap of soil and from pits that were dug at a greater distance on all four sides. Tamped into and protruding from the apex of the pyramid was a squared-off stake. The corners of the stake faced toward the cardinal directions and were notched to indicate the number of miles in each direction to the township boundary; hence, the south corner of the stake carried one notch, since this marker was one mile from the township line to the south. The flat sides of the stake, which faced southwest, northwest, etc., were carved with the number of the section toward which they faced. The mound was covered with sod to stabilize and protect it from erosion.

When it was finished, Temple and his crew surveyed on, now east a mile to tie in with a marker they'd placed two days earlier, then back west to this marker, then on north again a mile into new, unsurveyed territory, to make more lines, to build more markers. As if performing a complex dance, they moved across the prairie, creating, chain by chain, tally by tally, marker by marker, a new world. And at the same time they set in motion the erasure of another.

See your Garst dealer for a square deal on seed corn for next spring.

—Radio commercial, Spencer

Chapter 5

Plain Geometry

Today no section corner markers stand where George Temple and his assistants built them. There are no mounds, no trenches, no notched stakes; instead, at almost every point where four sections come together is another sort of monument: a cross where two yellow-gravel section line roads intersect. Where the view ahead is clear and there is no oncoming traffic, rural drivers drive down the center of a gravel road. Doing so allows traffic in either direction to pack two smooth paths for a vehicle's wheels and works the loose gravel toward the sides. At almost any crossing of two section line roads, these packed wheel paths meet at right angles and form a tic-tac-toe grid at the center of the intersection. At the center of that grid, right where the starting "O" might be, Temple and his chainmen and axmen once built their mounds and set their stakes.

Section line roads are just that: roads that run astride the section lines marked by the federal surveyors of the last century. Nearly all of them follow section lines precisely, whether the surveying work was conducted accurately or not, and today they stand as clear evidence to the quality of work done by early surveyors. Even as they worked, the surveyors knew their lines would become roads; the law stipulated that a half a chain width on either side of the section line—sixty-six feet total—was to be left unsold and was to be considered the public right-of-way.

These roads today carry light and local traffic: dusty pickups and cars, combines, chisel plows and field cultivators (some big enough to hang over the ditches on both sides), feed salespeople and livestock buyers, grain trucks, and, once a day until he retired recently after twenty-six years, Jim Brown, the Peterson rural mail carrier who could always be spotted at some distance because he drove sitting in the center of the front seat so he could reach his mailboxes on the right-hand side of the car.

Most people slow down for these intersections—especially when the corn is high and a driver can't see intersecting traffic until nearly at the crossroads. There are stories of lifelong neighbors, accustomed to untrafficked rural section line roads, who have for years ignored the intersections and have at last, against long odds, smashed together at high speed and right angles, maybe as two of only half a dozen vehicles to cross the intersection that day.

Section line roads, perhaps unlike any other rural roads, have no destination; they never directly connect any place with any other, except by chance. They form a grid, a graph complete with X and Y axes—"His place is four miles north and, let me see, two miles west." Like city streets, section line roads are used predominantly by those who live along them. Rural residents almost always recognize and wave at vehicles passing their farms. Travelers, unfamiliar with the lay of the local land, avoid them for better mapped, numbered highways. In areas of Iowa free of large streams, section line roads form a nearly uniform system of routes passing across landscape that can look all the same to unaccustomed urban dwellers, leaving them turned around and lost in a square maze of open right angles with no informational signs, and no clues about where they have been or ought to turn next—"Honey, isn't that the same barn we saw a few miles ago?"

To local residents, each road and each mile is a distinct individual, a bit of the home country where farm buildings, crops, livestock, and fences add up to a familiar picture. Section line roads are a net, a mesh that holds rural land and life together.

A map of Iowa that shows the entire network of roads, the section line roads and highways, looks very much like a piece of window screen. Section roads, which account for the least amount of traffic, add up to by far the greatest mileage. Peterson Township, for example, contains less than seven miles of state highway (Iowa Highway 10) and no federal highway at all, but a full sixty-five miles of paved and unpaved section line roads.

Clay County, like the others in the region, is beginning to abandon little-used section roads. With continued and long-term rural population loss and the abandonment of farmsteads, many miles of roads now pass only empty houses and carry only farm implements to adjacent fields and an occasional misplaced salesperson. Many miles of such roads are now posted with signs that state, "Caution: Level B Maintenance Ahead" or "Road Closed Snow Season." A good many have been allowed to deteriorate so far that "B Maintenance" means the likelihood of getting stuck after any rain or thaw.

And some are being closed altogether. With fences on either side pulled down, the embankment graded back into the ditches, topsoil smoothed over the top, a farmer can grow soybeans where only a few weeks ago the Co-op feed truck passed.

The application of the land survey here has resulted in a certain "square-mindedness" on the part of residents. There is an inevitability to it since all the major lines—of travel, of communication, of land ownership, of agriculture, of daily life—are beholden to the grid. Garst Seed Company advertises "a square deal." People here are born and live their lives according to it, build their houses, park their cars, and plant their trees by it; when they die, they are laid to rest in accord with the cardinal directions. While certain religions dictate that the dead must be laid to rest with their feet pointing to the rising sun or toward some holy place, Americans—Iowans—go to their rest obeying the law of the square. Virtually everything—compost piles, outdoor Christmas displays, chicken houses, abandoned cars, flatware on the table at my grandmother's house, stacked firewood—conforms to the cardinal directions.

Even in Peterson, in the valley where the river exerts its meandering influence, life goes on with reference to the grid. Because there was no immediate topographic reason not to, Peterson was laid out according to the cardinal directions. Although the angle is off by maybe four degrees, all but one of the streets (the exception is Front Street, which paralleled the railroad) abide by the grid. All but two or three houses in town have the rising sun come squarely in their east windows on the vernal or autumnal equinoxes.

The only real exceptions to the rule of the square in this area occur close to the river itself or in steep side valleys.

Gravel roads that had followed section lines on the uplands will sometimes abandon the pattern to slant and turn as they submit to the force of topography in a ravine or around a side hill. Line fences, nonetheless, hold to the grid, and march with unswerving alignment to the four points of the compass despite the river or uneven terrain.

Viewed from 30,000 feet, the most prominent patterns on this landscape are those made by section line roads and right-angled fields; from 3,000 feet, fences, crop rows, farm groves, individual buildings, power lines all come into view and speak their part for the square. This is a square landscape, perhaps as square as any on the planet.

And why shouldn't it be a square place? In town, on crop land, among farm buildings, the grid is really the most logical and simple way to organize two-dimensional space. Such regularity is especially important for cropland, where the advantages of right-angled fields are obvious in these days of large machinery. Iowa farmers have always staunchly fought the construction of diagonal highways; to this day there are only a handful in the state outside of river valleys that cross flat farmland for any distance.

But while the square is the rule, some squares are more square than others. The original land survey was not perfect; it was never intended to be, and any close observer of the land or reader of maps can see where compromises and errors were made.

People who have traveled very often on gravel or paved section line roads may have observed that they aren't altogether straight, that they tend to angle back and forth slightly as they make their way; they seem to "hunt" like a car with loose steering. Though these roads usually run arrow-straight between intersections, at almost every crossing with another section line road there will be a tiny kink, a perturbation left or right from the vector of the mile just driven. It may be a degree or two, or even less, but it is noticeable, and great enough that engineers laying out paving projects must often engineer into them a gentle curve smoothing the bend over a few hundred feet.

Farmers, who are among the few who ever notice them, usually attribute these jogs to the corrections necessary in surveying a two-dimensional pattern onto a spherical planet, but such corrections were handled in other ways. These jogs amount to errors—sometimes quite laughable ones—in the original survey, errors usually caused not by mistallying a chain measure or by misadjusting the survey compass, but by the limitations of equipment and by a limited understanding of magnetic variation.

By the time George Temple took up his outfit and headed to the prairie of northwest Iowa, surveyors and scientists already knew a good bit about the unpredictable nature of magnetic variation. Surveyors knew they had to take into account the difference in position of the pole of true north versus that of magnetic north, and they knew that the position of the magnetic pole varied in cycles—over decades, seasons of the year, and, most problematic for surveyors in the field, on an hourly basis. In field tests, surveyors had noticed that their compass needles changed over the course of a day and that section lines surveyed in the morning, if checked with the same compass in the afternoon, would be found to be slightly askew.

They didn't know why their needles flickered, and they had no reliable way of adjusting for changes that might amount to half a degree over the course of seven hours. Surveyors noticed that the daily variation was greater in the summer than in the winter. The General Land Office, source of instructions to the deputy surveyors, boasted of solving the problem in 1855 when it announced, "It has been found by observation, that heat and cold sensibly affect the magnetic needle, and that the same needle will, at the same place, indicate different lines at different hours of the day."

Logical enough, but within a few years the bugbear was back; it wasn't merely heat and cold, it had something to do with the sun. Elaborate compensation tables were established and published in instructions to surveyors charting the wanderings of the magnetic variation hour by hour, but they weren't of much use. Finally, by 1881, scientists had determined that the annoying diurnal wandering of the needle was caused by the effect of solar magnetism on the earth's magnetic fields, that it was strongest during summer and during years of greatest sunspot activity, and that there really wasn't much to be done about it since the amount of effect on a compass needle at any given time was impossible to predict.

But by the time scientists figured it out, varying variation had nearly ceased to be a problem; most surveys on new land were being done with solar compasses. A solar compass makes use of the sun's daily arc across the sky to establish a much more accurate meridian of true north, with no need of Polaris, plumb bobs, midnight observations, or magnetic needles at all. The solar compass was in use elsewhere even as Temple was surveying parts of Clay County in 1856; surveyors were using them on state border and major baseline surveys. The Surveyor General knew of their superior accuracy, but in 1856 there were relatively few of them, and few surveyors were trained in their use. Quite simply, the errors of the magnetic needle were known and accepted; the need to survey great swaths of land expeditiously outweighed the need for exactitude.

George Temple did a good job taking his sightings of Polaris and Alioth and translating them to his instrument; he made the best of the clumsy compass and its inherent limitations, and his men pulled and marked their chain lengths with care. The square miles he scribed are reasonably square, and the jogs in his section lines are minor. The river valley along the south side of Peterson Township apparently did cause some trouble; the sections in the western tier are slightly rhomboid.

During Temple's short time in northwest Iowa, he subdivided three adjacent townships: Brooke, Peterson, and Clay, aligned north to south like three blocks amid hundreds of others in the state, thousands in the nation. He and his men built some seventy-five section corner markers in the course of their work. Brooke Township is in Buena Vista County, Peterson and Clay in Clay County, and all three are about as square as a magnetic compass could make them.

Other surveyors weren't so skilled—or lucky. At the northeast corner of Clay County, in the corner opposite to Peterson Township, is Lake Township, and as the name might suggest, there were certain obstacles to making a clean, square survey. But just what happened in this thirty-six-square-mile area isn't clear. Was it the especially swampy ground, chainmen who couldn't count or a surveyor who couldn't properly adjust his compass, or, as a survey examiner called in to make sense of the mess suggested, was it some sort of local iron-bearing rock that threw off the needle? Whatever the case, today the entire township has but a half-dozen miles of cardinal section line roads and hardly a right angle where any two of them meet. Many section line roads are so far offset as to have twenty degree bends in them in order to make them line up with the roads of the adjoining townships.

All of the surveyors made errors, but usually they were quite small. Considering the difficulty of the work, the small magnitude of the resulting errors, the wanderings, is surprising. Directing a flagman with an instrument having only a monopod, doing it in wind, rain, and tall grass, dragging a sixty-six-foot chain across rough landscape, trying to keep it both level and taut, and keeping count of the chains and tallies, are tasks that could breed inaccuracy like wet ground does willows.

Though sections were numbered with number 1 at the northeast corner of a township and number 36 at the southeast, they were not surveyed in numerical order. Temple's instructions, and those of all the government surveyors of the time, made clear that he was to start his surveying in the southeast corner—in what would become section 36—and finish in the northwest corner in what would become section 6. Beginning at the southeast corner of the township, he surveyed the lines to make section 36, then moved immediately north to establish section 25, north again to the next section, number 24, and so on, until he had reached the north boundary of the township and had lined out a six-mile north-to-south block of sections.

He then checked his work by surveying six miles straight south to the south boundary of the township, then measured west one mile along that boundary, and began the next south-to-north block of sections by working generally northbound again, lining out sections 35, 26, 23, etc., to the top boundary of the township. He stacked new sections one on top of another in a column of six, and then stepped over a mile west to build the next column of six, and so on until he finished in the northwest corner of the township in section 6.

By this method, by working generally from the southeast to the northwest, any measurement errors accumulated against the already established north and west boundaries of the township at the northwest corner of the township in section 6. And many farmers can confirm the fact. The ideal square mile should contain 640 acres; most contain a few more or a few less. In most townships, the biggest variations are in section 6. Farmers who own or rent land in section 6 of a standard township know that fence lines are often crooked here and that field sizes vary a great deal more than they do elsewhere.

Across Iowa and much of the agricultural regions of the United States, the square mile, though it is sometimes irregular, is the common unit of reference. Section lines enclose them, pickup truck odometers count them, distances between towns are measured by the lengths of their sides. As George Temple and thousands of other federal contract surveyors measured them, the sections could later be divided into fourths by means of the smaller half-mile markers placed midway between the section markers. This subdivision produced the "quarter," a square parcel of 160 acres which would soon become the basic unit for a farm. Later, as the land was settled and surveyed in greater detail, further subdivisions were possible and practiced. Thus a pioneer could buy half of a quarter, or an "eighty" as it came to be called, or even a quarter of a quarter, known as a "forty." A parcel of land could thus be described as the "SW quarter of the NW quarter of Section 12, Township 94 North, Range 38 West of the Fifth Principal Meridian" and leave no dispute about just what 40-acre postage stamp of blowing grass was under discussion.

Quite apart from the errors made in surveying are the adjustments in the survey made necessary by the curve of the earth. After all, the surveyors were attempting to inscribe a two-dimensional grid onto a sphere. Meridians, which form the eastern and western boundaries of townships, converge as they go north—they meet at the North Pole—and either townships would shrink in width as they were created northward or a system of adjustment must be implemented. Even in Iowa, more than three thousand miles from the Pole, the convergence in a sixty-mile stretch is about 450 feet, a substantial adjustment.

The need to account for convergence was not lost on the surveyors or on the Surveyor General. After clumsy errors accumulated on lands surveyed earlier in Ohio, the General Land Office built into the Iowa surveys two correction lines, each running east and west, and each being the baseline for the measurement of the width of sections to the north of it. As its name implies, the town of Correctionville, some forty miles southwest of Peterson, sits astride one of these correction lines; north-south streets in town are offset where they cross the line, and the sign at the edge of town encourages travelers to "Jog Down Our Main Street."

Section line roads or highways run on these correction lines most of the way across Iowa. It is an odd change from the near-universal pattern to drive on one and to observe the patterns of intersecting roads. Very few roads intersect and continue straight across a correction line; nearly all are offset by some distance where they cross it.

Between Correctionville and Early, U.S. Highway 20 runs on a correction line; driving down the road gives one the impression that the road runs on some sort of geologic fault and that somehow the land has slipped in some fashion. Neither fence lines nor section roads, nor even power lines on one side of the road, align across the correction. Even the county boundaries are skewed. Any map showing county lines clearly marks the westerly offset through the middles of some twenty counties.

In Iowa the counties, too, are part of this great system of squares. And though they are the largest expression of the square on the Iowa landscape, the odd fact is that they were already here in a sense years before anybody surveyed a single mile of northwest Iowa; they were named and drawn on maps a full five and a half years before George Temple first placed his staff in the region.

On January 15, 1851, 576 square miles of prairie suddenly became Clay County. Certainly no one in the new county registered the change; the last of the elk browsed through the snow as usual, and any Sioux in the region would have greeted the sunrise in the customary manner of worship.

The change was registered at the opposite corner of the state, in Iowa City. Legislators could look out of the big windows of the new stone capitol toward the bare trees along the Iowa River and imagine what the land was like far to the west and north. It is likely that none of them had ever been to Clay County, and they must have had very little idea of what lay in the northwest regions of the state. But in another of the thousands of legislative acts performed by states across the country, acts so imbued with frontier optimism, acts to tame the wilderness, to bring farms, churches, towns, and law and order to the howling prairie, the Iowa State legislature created at once, and on paper, fifty new counties out of thin air, half the counties in the state.

The Iowa legislature was eager to finish its state. While the actual surveying of the land into townships and square miles was a federal matter, county-making fell within the purview of state governments, and here Iowa was far ahead of the federal surveyors. There were as yet no survey stakes for the new counties; the counties were an artifice of the mapmakers who knew the rough dimensions of the state and knew approximately how many more counties of a particular size would fill it. The exact boundaries would be established—and the necessary adjustments made—when the federal surveyors completed their work in the next few years.

Most of the counties that were drawn are as rectilinear and uniform as surveyed lines and right angles could make them; none but those on the western border of the state, formed by the Missouri and Big Sioux Rivers, took into account any topographic considerations, and all of the new counties were piled one on another like a stack of packing crates on a depot platform. The ideal county was a square twenty-four miles on a side, to accommodate sixteen townships in a total of 576 square miles. Clay County fits the ideal; so do the other three counties around Peterson: O'Brien, Cherokee, Buena Vista. Because of state boundaries, correction lines, and the need to align with counties established earlier, some counties varied from the ideal, and several underwent later adjustment.

Names were as arbitrary as the boundaries. Many had names of American patriots: Franklin, Adams, Harrison, Hancock; others were given Indian names with no consideration to where these tribes had lived: Cherokee, Winnebago, Pottawattamie. Only Sioux County, in far northwest Iowa, names a place where the tribe existed. And Clay County was named for Lieutenant Colonel Henry Clay, son of Henry Clay of Kentucky, killed in the battle of Buena Vista in the recent Mexican War, a man who likely never set foot in Iowa. Whether the soil of Clay County contained any clay was not an issue.

These counties, like those across the country, were to become the binding unit of frontier government and would owe their allegiance to the state capital. They were drawn and given names but left unchartered until future white settlers had homesteaded and found sufficient time away from sod breaking to organize a county government. In northwest Iowa, that would be a good while. For at least the next seven years, there would be no courthouses or jails, stove salesmen, or nail kegs, much less any bridges or candidates for sheriff. But the boundaries had been drawn, and, in a political sense at least, the landscape was made ready.

The men of the Iowa legislature and the hundreds of federal contract surveyors drew the opening lines for what would become a landscape of unprecedented regularity. For the legislators it was a map of place names that were not yet places; for the surveyors, it was a land of unbroken grass; and for everyone it was, on paper, a land of squares: counties, townships, square miles, quarter sections. No doubt in the days before cities and towns appeared on the maps, a land agent or hopeful farmer could easily mix up the maps of counties, townships, and sections; all were square, all were themselves subdivided into squares; and all were equally blank.

You always hear about the births, the deaths, and the marriages, the weather, how the farmers are doing—what will happen if we get too much rain, or not enough. You hear about the implement companies, the elevators, what they're doing, your fertilizer companies, what the prices are, who's getting too much, who's not getting enough . . .

—Sue Goettsch, owner of Sue's Diner, Peterson

Chapter  6

Café Society

AUGUST 14

At a few minutes after six in the morning, five vehicles huddle on Main Street, all of them pulled up in front of Sue's Diner, the only place showing any signs of life at this hour. One vehicle is a pickup truck, three are cars, and the last is a cement mixer left idling in the center of the broad street, its drum turning slowly to keep the fresh concrete mixed. The seven street lights that illuminate Main Street are still lighted, but the silver light of summer dawn is rising to overcome them. The street is quiet save the grumble of the mixer, the morning song of a single robin, and the gossip of a handful of crows starting their day.

The light is brighter inside the café and the sound level a good deal higher as regulars at two or three tables drink coffee and carry on conversations of various degrees of seriousness and animation. Nobody but me looks as though they just got out of bed. Sue's is an early-morning place, a noisy place at a time when the rest of the town is just getting up.

This morning the talk is of canning sweet corn, making pickles, a license plate for a trailer that somebody found on the highway. Sue has been up late, canning. She pours a round of coffee and settles on a stool at the end of the counter.

Sue Goettsch is a large woman with a scowl that could boil water. To the uninitiated she seems formidable—and when crossed, she is—but her demeanor belies the fact that she laughs easily and often. A believer in small towns, homegrown produce, and honesty, she is not afraid to tell you what she thinks; the customer is right about half the time. She enjoys her work, the people, and would defend her customers against all comers. Nevertheless, only those with bullet-proof skin tease her about her cooking.

"You have your special people that you're glad to see," she told me once with a laugh, "and some I've tried to get rid of for fourteen years.

"I have a habit of saying what I think. The preacher who was here before, he used to tell me: 'Sue, don't say it to my face, say it behind my back; it hurts my feelings less.' I'd rather say it to someone's face, that way they know how I feel. But I get in a little trouble once in a while.

"Reverend Wooge—did you know him?—he was a great guy. He came in every morning. He hated grape jelly so I made sure he got grape jelly every day."

Sue's would be familiar to anyone who frequents small town cafés. The coffeepot stands within easy reach of customers, and the morning *Sioux City Journal,* already well shuffled, waits in an untidy pile nearby. The decor is basic café premodern, with paneled walls and Formica tabletops with some sort of pattern that looks like amoebas or boomerangs. Sue has a table reserved for nonsmokers, but no one pays much attention.

And like cafés across the country, this one is a transfer point for news both earthshaking and trivial. Whenever something big happens around the area, which is seldom, the café becomes the main exchange point for information. Whenever I plant the legs of my camera tripod anywhere within six miles, the fact is often reported at Sue's before I can make my exposures and get to the café for coffee.

"I hear you were taking pictures of Donna's place," Sue said to me once with that all-knowing, don't-try-to-pull-anything-on-me look as I banged through the door with my camera bag—a mere ten minutes after I had first arrived on Donna's sidewalk and unpacked my equipment to take the pictures.

Sue says that, running the café, "you get to know people. I'll bet you nine out of ten times when somebody comes through the door, I can tell you what they're going to order before they sit down. You know them, you know what they eat. Now Chris Vierow, he likes polish sausages, pork chops. He'll come out to the kitchen and he'll say, 'What are we having today, Sue?' and I'll say, 'You're having your pork chops.' 'All right,' he says, and sits down. You just know your people.

"Running a café in a small town brings long hours, hard work, but if you enjoy people, they make it worth it. There are so many who used to come in when I opened up fourteen years ago—and now they're gone. Rollie Kline-felter, Harold Johnson . . ." She paused in thought. "Rollie was in every day; Harold ate almost every meal with me—he had breakfast and dinner with me five days a week—Saturday was his church day. And I miss Ruth Baier. We harassed her; we always teased her about liking Irv Steffen and she'd get so mad. Some days she'd take it, and some days she wouldn't, but she always came back. And we still tease Irv about liking every woman who comes in."

Irv Steffen is a fixture at Sue's. He's not exactly a customer, nor is he an employee. He comes in before six most mornings and makes coffee and gets things going for the morning crowd.

"He came in off the street one morning and started helping. I didn't even know the man. He just wandered in, and he's been here for—what is it now, six, seven years?"

On his eightieth birthday, Sue and her customers passed the hat and bought him a microwave. And as best as she can recollect, it was Irv's eightieth that started the birthday coffee tradition at Sue's. Any weekday when you find more than the usual number of cars in front of the café from about 8 A.M. on, you can just about guarantee that it is somebody's birthday. The celebrant will hire Sue to bake cakes and make extra coffee so that all comers—complete strangers included—will get free cake and coffee. One fall day not long ago somebody had a birthday, and a couple of the attendees, people who had had an especially good squash crop, brought bags of them to the party and handed them out to everybody. Arriving on Main Street to get the mail, I was mystified to find each person on the street carrying an acorn squash.

While Sue disappears into the kitchen to fry somebody some eggs, Irv makes the rounds with the coffeepot, collects money, receives and returns—with dividend—most of the jibes that customers throw his way.

From time to time commuters on the way to jobs in Spencer, Storm Lake, or Cherokee drop in to fill their travel coffee cups. Usually they join the chatter for a moment or two; sometimes they stand and talk long enough that they will surely be late for work. Mavis Stoner stands with cup in hand and talks of the need for a new Methodist church; I overhear fragments of other conversations, "Dad had an old John Deere A—," "—got a buck a day . . ."

Even in a town as small as Peterson, there is no place that is common to all who live here. People fill the bleachers and root for the high school football team on fall Friday nights, but the experience is not shared by all. The swimming pool draws all ages during the summer, but it, too, is limited as a place of universal contact. A church congregation leaves out those of the other church, and any bar crowd will leave out a number of the church groups.

Perhaps a café comes closest to being the democratic heart of any small town. Certainly there are people in Peterson who have never set foot in Sue's Diner and who wouldn't feel any part of that small community, but still somehow it is the best place to take the pulse of the town.

At Sue's, conversation is often served as a main dish with coffee on the side. Most customers are well acquainted with one another but don't necessarily socialize outside their encounters—regular or occasional—at the café. Many interactions are intended merely to pass the time of day, an enduring small town tradition; some share gossip. Others, though it might be hard to tell with only a casually tuned ear, exchange real information and reinforce bonds of friendship and respect.

"Well Eddie, I bought me one of them Simmental bulls yesterday."

Silence.

"Fifteen hundred?"

"Nope, thousand."

"Must be a yearling."

"Yeah, he is."

Somebody bangs through the door; both glance to see who it is. Each takes two or three deliberate sips of coffee.

"All registered, papers and all?"

"Yep."

Gilbert's Grocery Store, October 1946. The war had been over for a while, and customers were again accustomed to full shelves. The occasion for the photograph is not recorded. Photograph courtesy of Peterson Heritage.

Silence.

"Semen tested?"

"Yep."

Silence.

"Disposition?"

"Quiet. Real quiet."

Silence.

"Measured?"

"Measured?"

Long silence. A couple of minutes pass. The only sounds from the table are the slurp of hot coffee and the chewing of food.

"How big are his gonads. In cubic centimeters?"

Silence.

"He's not measured."

Silence.

The talk turns to where so-and-so's farm is out southwest of town "A mile west of my mother's—" "Then where is it from Howard's?" "A mile north and two miles west." "Hell, I get out in there and always get lost."

Silence.

"So when is it we're going to turn our new bull out with the cows?"

Especially in rural agricultural areas, cafés have certain daily, seasonal, and climatic rhythms. Sue's is a morning place, and each weekday she has two morning crowds. The first is the steady and punctual bunch that comes in right when the place opens—sometimes they are waiting at the door when she or Irv unlocks it. With Irv's help she feeds them and pours gallons of coffee.

"The early risers like their sausage sandwiches," says Sue. "Later we have the women invade." Farm women, town women, retired women, they come in for midmorning coffee before some people are even out of bed.

"They'll get ten, fifteen women all around one table, and it's terrible to get coffee into their cups. They've been getting earlier and earlier these days. They were hitting about nine; now they're here by eight-thirty. I don't know if they think they'll miss something or what."

In a town as small as Peterson, the lunch rush—or "dinner" as it is properly called here—can hardly be considered a rush. It is rare that all booths and tables will be full, despite the sandwich menu and daily specials.

"We have a noon special every day. I don't think there have been two days in fourteen years that I haven't had hot beef and that sort of thing. The men like their meat and potatoes; sure, they'll eat macaroni salad and coleslaw, but it's a meat-and-potatoes crowd."

After dinner the place gets pretty quiet, especially in the winter, when most people stay close to home. The television above the counter usually comes on, and a game show will often compete with the conversation of coffee drinkers. Sue likes to close about three or four in the afternoon—at one on Saturdays in the summer so she can go to the stock-car races—but never before her last and most regular customer, Jean Saunders, stops by to finish the pot of coffee. Whatever the weather, Jean will be there, and Sue doesn't consider closing until she has come and gone.

There are other patterns. If it rains at any time when farmers are doing field work, Sue will have a full house. During planting and harvest times, and when the weather is good for field work, the crowd will dwindle to only retired people as everyone else seems to have pressing work to do.

By 8 A.M. this August day, the early risers are long gone, and the next crowd has yet to arrive. Sue tidies up and makes a fresh pot of coffee. Out on the street, the grocery store has opened, and the lights and ceiling fan are on at Peterson Mercantile, a small hardware store across the street. The flag is up at the post office, and the bank down at the corner will open soon. There are half a dozen cars in sight. Full sunlight flashes squarely on the uneven row of storefronts on the west side of Main Street, making the empty lots look all the emptier.

The only apparent sound comes from the foot of Main Street, from the elevator, where a roofing crew begin their work on the elevator and scale office. As they bend to the task, a handful of farm trucks and tractor-pulled wagons cross the city scale on their way to and from unloading grain. Inside the office, dust filters slowly from the ceiling as the roof crew tear and hammer at the old sheathing. It sounds like a thunderstorm close overhead.

Mid-August is an in-between time. Farmers are less busy now, since crops are well on their way and need little attention, only the occasional rain. They turn their hands to livestock, fences, and machinery repair for the coming harvest. Some take off for the several county fairs now going on. A few take their campers to South Dakota to fish. Many unseal their storage bins, full of corn and soybeans from last year's crop, and begin hauling it to the elevator in town to make space for grain from the upcoming harvest.

The cornstalks in Rod's forty-four-acre field out south of town—like the corn elsewhere—are beanpoles seven and a half feet tall, every stalk topped by a foot-long beige tassel. The gravel section line roads seem to have sunk into canyons of corn. So extensive and so uniform are the cornfields that, from the air, the entire landscape seems to be the beige of corn tassels. In this field, pollination is over; the tassels on top have cast off their genetic material. Pollen lies thick like dust on the leaves and on the ground.

The success of the crop rests on this critical event. Before any corn plant can produce a single kernel, the pollen from the tassel must fall onto the silk protruding from the nascent ear, and the genetic material must be transferred to the ear. Each silk attaches to a point on the cob that, when fertilized, will become a kernel of grain.

These silks have finished their job and have turned brown and stiff. The ears contain the life now; they are soft, green, as big around as my wrist, and growing quickly. Stripping the husk off an ear, I find milky kernels like baby fingertips forming on the soft cob.

Only a few flakes of sunlight make it through the layered overstory of corn leaves to reach the bare soil. Scattered weeds lie here, pale, light-starved, and salted with pollen. Around the base of each corn plant are prop roots: a dozen or so bent fingers that brace the tall stalk against wind and storm. They are the flying buttresses of the church of agriculture.

North of town, the Clay County road grader passes on a gravel road. Going east at a fast walk, it smooths and redistributes the gravel on the road, grading off high spots and filling in potholes. The machine works on well-traveled material. Created and hauled to the county by a glacier, sorted by water, brought here by a truck, today it is bladed across ten feet of road and piled in a windrow of sorts in the middle. Mixed in with the gravel are clumps of brome and native grasses, pulled out of the soil at the road shoulder for trying to colonize the roadway itself. In a few hours the grader will go the other direction; the ridge of gravel down the center of the road will finish the day on the opposite side of the road from where it started.

The river has changed in the last weeks. The water is down some two feet now that the rains have ended. Earlier in the season it was chocolate with suspended sediment; the water is still cloudy, but clearing, and low enough that tan sandbars hint at their underwater presence. The low river has made the banks look all that much higher and has revealed numerous additional snags: great naked trees, all with their crowns pointing downstream. Today water striders skate on the sluggish water.

Around the region, the native warm-season prairie grasses, hiding in road ditches and field corners, are blooming, though few would recognize their inflorescences as flowers. Local sweet corn has been available for a couple of weeks, and there seem to be two prices: either $1.25 a dozen or free, depending on the level of mutual goodwill. Most of it seems to change hands with only a thank-you. Meanwhile, the big crop in town is tomatoes, but they are slow in ripening. All over town plants sag with heavy green fruit. People say it's been just too cool this year for tomatoes.

… We have miles of upland perfectly level, at length cut by erosion channels so deep and with walls so precipitous as fitly to receive the name of canyons; from the sides of the canyons issue springs giving rise to clear perennial streams; we have hill-country, high, irregular, tossed about with no reference at all to present drainage; we have fine rolling prairie where the drainage is perfect, the slopes long and gentle and every thing contributes to fortunate husbandry.

—Thomas H. Macbride, "The Geology of Clay and O'Brien Counties," 1900

Chapter 7

Horizon Line

The character of any place is in part determined by the shape of the land itself. Leadville and Limon, Colorado, are what they are in great part because the former is deep in the mountains and the latter is in the heart of the Great Plains. While an extreme case, the example does suggest that places are indeed molded by their shape; Peterson wouldn't be what it is and where it is without this valley surrounded by flat uplands.

Most people around Peterson recognize the fact that glaciers have had a major effect on landforms and soils here; any farmer who gets off a tractor to pick up a rock knows to curse the ancient ice for importing it. Less obvious is why the land on Bob White's place north of Peterson is so flat while the fields just five miles south on Rod Burgeson's farm have a definite swell, a roll, or why the valley sidehills would be so steep as to make building pasture fence in places nearly impossible.

Bob White, who farms Velma's farm and his own, knows flat land; his place is north of Peterson on some of the flattest land in the four-county area. "One of the first things people who live in the hills do when they get out here is to look around and count all the farmsteads they can see—go see for yourself!"

It's spring, before the corn is up, and from Bob's pickup stopped on the road north of his place we can see farm groves and farmsteads six or more miles away, and the grain elevators at Sutherland and Royal.

Circling the horizon with his arm, Bob makes a count of farmsteads owned or rented by people he knows. He names them one by one, pointing and elaborating, sometimes backing up to catch one he missed. In a full circle he identifies, and I count, thirty-four farmsteads; when I add in groves that are now bereft of buildings, lone corncribs that mark former farmsteads, silos and barns at the very edge of the planet, I come up with seventy-five farmsteads or former farmsteads within sight of one spot.

This flat area north of Peterson is as intensely farmed as any land in the state. Few acres around here lie idle; farmers plant right up to the road ditches, and close around their farmsteads. There are occasional strips of government set-aside acres—usually planted in oats or grass—but right around here, where a farmer can plant every square foot to row crops, hay fields and pasture are uncommon. This former prairie is uniformly gridded according to George Temple's survey lines of 1856, and his line-of-sight work was easy here; the elevation varies barely ten feet in a mile and no more than twenty feet across good parts of northern Peterson Township away from the Little Sioux valley.

Bob White raises corn, soybeans, and hogs, and in any given year has some 400 acres under cultivation. Farming here since 1958, he lives with his wife, Marilyn, along county blacktop M27 three miles north of Peterson. Bob talks of soil conservation, their five grown children, the importance of planting trees—"By god, people, we've all got to breathe!"—market prices, farm safety, and everything else that crosses his active mind.

"Hell," he once told me, "when you sit out here on a tractor all day pulling a planter, going back and forth, up and down the rows, staring at the ground, you've got time to *think*!"

Conversations with Bob are a zigzag of topics, ideas, observations, and exclamations, all punctuated with the broad gestures of his strong hands, laughter, and occasional squirts of tobacco juice. Riding on his corn planter one spring, we talked of the pitfalls of getting the crop in the ground and a thousand other things, but the conversation kept coming back to his trying to remember the words to "Now Is the Hour," a song about American servicemen leaving their girlfriends in New Zealand at the end of World War II. From time to time, and in the middle of any sentence, he would proclaim, "Now, I'm no singer—" and lift his hands from the steering wheel of the tractor and belt out a couple more lines that had come to him as we talked of other things. Bob White plants a straight row, as straight as any farmer around, but I'll bet there were wanderings in the corn rows where Bob sang with his hands and the tractor planted on its own.

At one point that day he exclaimed, "Just look at this topsoil here, will you?" as if he'd just noticed it for the first time. "It's rich and deep, and there's not a rock in it. This dirt is nothing like you have around there in Lake Township and Freeman Township, oh heavens. You get over there east of Highway 71 and you really get into the rocks."

The topsoil on Bob's place is as rich as any I've ever seen, as dark and smooth as wet coffee grounds. Thanks to the prairie, it is rich; thanks to the windy side effects of glacial activity that came before it, there is hardly a handful of pebbles in an acre, much less any rocks. Occasionally he turns up an old cobble or two, but these usually appear where the field tilers have dug their ditches to install drainage tiles. Because the area is so flat, precipitation will pool in any low spots, and because the soil is so fine-grained, the water will drain away slowly. Until the railroad came to the area in 1882, bringing carloads of clay drainage tile, this immediate area had few settlers, and those who were here had to farm around the innumerable small and shallow wet spots that dotted northern Peterson Township.

Bob has several former wet spots on the farm and knows the location and shape of each. With a kidney-shaped one east of the house he is especially familiar.

"You can't see it most of the time, but you can sure feel it when you hit it with the plow—zoom!—you jump right through it. It's just powder, no aggregate whatsoever, and terrible to drain. Now it has tile up to the gumstump."

Farmers, geomorphologists, and landscape painters are perhaps the only people who pay much attention to the actual shape and character of the land. Bob White, like most farmers, knows his farm well and can, from his tractor in the field, find the indistinct ridges and low spots. He knows which way the slight slopes run on his flat farm ground, even though they may be invisible to anyone else without survey instruments. In some thirty-five years of farming the place, of going back and forth across every inch and squinting at these acres from nearly every angle, he understands the planes and textures of the place as well as anyone ever could.

When I look at land with Bob and other farmers, they often point to and describe features invisible to me: a subtle change in soil type, a point on a slope where water gathers sufficiently to begin gully erosion, a line or area where rocks tend to appear over the years.

The need that farmers have to understand their land springs from operational necessity and economics; that of the geomorphologist springs from the impulse of science. While both are often engaged by the beauty of the land, neither has much need to consider its aesthetic qualities. The artful curve of a horizon line or the appealing texture of smooth soil on a gentle slope is not one of their operational necessities.

Landscape artists, on the other hand, care little for soil types and past glaciation but instead seek the clear light that reveals dramatic shape in the landscape, and are generally intent on the striking and more obvious forms: rugged coastlines, pastoral valleys; hence western Kansas sees few painters set up their easels to paint the spirit of the flat horizon.

In much of the Midwest, where the horizon line is at rest as a gentle curve, the shape of the land and its appeal are overlooked. The earth's surface is merely a baseline to life's activities: is the yard flat enough for volleyball? Will the sprayer truck be able to negotiate the ravine? Interest in the land is not with the quality or beauty of its surface; it is merely the line of reference for the depth of soybean planting in the spring, the slope of sledding hills, the frost depth for water pipes, new building foundations, cloud altitudes, the height setting on the lawn mower. We measure vertical distances with reference to the surface of the earth and cause things to grow or be built above and beneath it, but the quality of the line, its curve and shape, seldom concerns us.

Nor do most of us think much about how any particular landform, obvious or subtle, came to exist. We seldom give thought to why the land rolls gently here and is flat there, or why some creeks run in knife-sharp valleys, while others have gentle slopes.

For years I had taken for granted certain characteristics of the land around Peterson. I knew that north of town it is flat, and that the sides of the Little Sioux valley are particularly steep around Peterson, steeper than places both upstream and downstream, and I knew that to the east and from the air, the land looks like a dog's attempt to paw a throw rug into a bed; it lies in restless folds of choppy ridges and undrained hollows.

But not until recently did I learn much about why it looks as it does. The answers lie in glaciers, running water, and wind. The combined effects of these agents are wide, varied, and sometimes puzzling, but invariably leave landforms that arouse the practical interest of farmers, the scientific interest of geomorphologists, and the aesthetic interest of landscape artists who like the challenge of more subtle terrain.

This part of the Midwest has been worked by glaciers at different times in the past. The planet has gone through several big-league freeze-and-thaw cycles during the last two million years; geologists, ever taking the long view, say we are now in an interglacial period and that more ice may be on the way in a few thousand years.

The most recent episode of glaciation—and the one that created most of the landforms around Peterson—carries the name Wisconsinan, after the state where it accomplished its most characteristic terrain building. The Wisconsinan ice advanced and melted back several times over 60,000 years and melted away for good only about 12,000 years ago.

The basic idea of a glacier is fairly simple. All that it requires is that the snow of one winter not melt entirely during the next summer and that it be added to by snows of the next winter, accumulating a little more snow that won't melt the following summer, and so on. Do this enough times and a glacier will result. What is hard to imagine is how a few inches of snow that fell on the polar ice cap ever coalesced with enough other snow that it could form a mile-thick, 2,000-mile-wide mass of dense blue ice that could grind south across 3,000 miles of intervening territory to gouge at the dirt of Clay County, Iowa. It took a very long time; it took a lot of snow.

Simply put, over the eons snow accumulated sufficiently at the top of the planet that it became packed into dense blue ice and began to squeeze outward and southward on all sides (Asia and Europe had their Ice Age at the same time as North America). This continental glacier accumulated so much snow that sea levels dropped several hundred feet during the Wisconsinan glaciation.

The Wisconsinan glacier inched its way out of the north, across what is now southern Canada and into the northern tier of the United States from the Dakotas eastward. Along its irregular margins, active lobes lengthened southward and melted back partway several times. One such advance, some 20,000 to 30,000 years ago, had the ice covering much of central Iowa and all of Clay County; geologists call the deposits it left behind the Sheldon Creek Formation. The glacier melted back for a few thousand years and then, by 14,000 years ago, had surged forward again, this time as far south as the present site of Des Moines. The tongue of glacier that pushed its way across Iowa this time formed a great peninsula of ice that covered about the middle third of the state. The deposits this advance left are referred to as the Dows Formation, and the region it covered is called the Des Moines Lobe. During this, the last advance of the Wisconsinan glacier into Iowa, the ice covered the eastern half of Clay County but did not come as far west as Peterson.

Like those that came in the prior great glacial ages, the advances of the Wisconsinan glacier erased existing landforms. Earlier glacial episodes had shaped the land and melted back, yielding to long interglacial periods when streams cut valleys and plant and animal communities developed and flourished. But each time ice came from the north, the slate was wiped clean as the new glacier pushed through the leavings of the prior ice ages.

"Melt-back" is a better term than the more commonly used "retreat." Glaciers, unlike armies, never retreat in the usual sense of the word; they cannot pull back in some sort of reverse gear. Instead, they stop advancing as the melting at the margins exceeds snow accumulation at the source; as the climate warms, they stagnate and melt in place, just like a pile of snow and gravel pushed up by a snowplow in a parking lot.

Glaciers are untidy things and are in the habit of grinding and mixing most everything beneath them into a conglomeration of boulders, gravel, sand, and rock flour. They make it by gouging at the soil and bedrock beneath them; they push it ahead of themselves and move it around in ways more inventive than those of kids in a sandbox. And, like kids, they get thoroughly mixed up with it. Far from being expanses of pure blue ice, glaciers are usually choked with debris; soil material was so thick on parts of the stagnant Des Moines Lobe ice that it bore meadows and forests on its back.

Geologists call the accumulation of loose material that melting glaciers leave behind "glacial drift"; in this region, it lies thick over the bedrock. Around Bob White's place, well drillers bore through 260 to 360 feet of it before hitting bedrock. At the surface, there is no bedrock exposed for fifty miles in any direction from Peterson. In most places here, the drift is an uneven mix of everything from boulders to silt, left by the ice where it melted. But where flowing meltwater played a role in the deposition of drift, accumulations of material are sorted and deposited according to size. On Iowa landscapes distant from rivers or streams, the appearance of a sand or gravel pit is a near-certain indicator that glacial meltwater flowed there once.

A continental glacier does much of its characteristic terrain building at its edges, where there is plenty of accumulated material to work with, and it does it by merely melting in place. As the ice decays, rock and soil material mixed within it settle and wash out unevenly. Great torrents of water flow off and out of the ice, building alluvial fans of sand and gravel, slashing huge sluiceways into the land to carry the outflow. As the glacier disappears, enormous blocks of ice become buried in the mud and rock. When they melt, the vanished ice leaves behind kettle holes and lakes. When the glacial mass finally disappears, it often leaves behind landscapes composed of humps and ridges, low wet areas, imported rocks, and no sign of the terrain that existed before. Low areas dot the new terrain to become marshes, lakes, ponds. This is classic glaciated terrain.

Over the course of several weeks one spring some years ago, I watched a big snow pile melt away and leave somewhat similar features on a miniature scale in a grocery store parking lot. Each time I went for milk or bread, I paused to see how things were coming. Plows had pushed and piled the snow up through the winter and had mixed in a lot of sand and dirt as they did so. For a while the heap was fairly white, but as soon as March came and it began to melt in earnest, its ice-and-dirt nature became daily more obvious as the snow ebbed and soil material concentrated. When the ice finally disappeared, it left behind on the asphalt familiar-looking irregular accumulations of material—humps, fans, ridges, and spots of bare pavement. It looked a lot like parts of the Des Moines Lobe I'd seen from the air.

But glaciers have other tricks. Sometimes they leave behind landscapes that are far different from the classic kettle-and-knob sorts that form parts of the upper Midwest. Some glaciated places, like Bob White's farm, do not so obviously bear the marks of the ice.

Because the land has been exposed to 10,000 years of rain and wind since the glacier melted here, nobody knows exactly what sort of landforms the Wisconsinan ice left north of Peterson, but it is fair to suppose that the land was reasonably flat. Some geologists think that the more level landscapes reflect a more uniform pattern of melting along a more energetic ice front. As water and its load of silt, sand, and rocks were released from the dying ice, this slurry may have covered the area like cake batter, oozing and filling the low spots to leave a nearly level plain. There would have been irregularities, but the best guess is that they were small compared with those elsewhere along more sluggish margins.

And the ice did leave rocks: all the usual sizes ranging from pebbles to boulders, in the loose accumulations for which glaciers are justly famous. But the reason Bob White never has to grub them out is found in what happened shortly after the ice disappeared from what became his farm.

While during any glacial age it is generally colder than at other times, there are still seasonal variations that include summers. The summers of glacial epochs never got as warm as summers do here now; nonetheless, they were warm enough that even advancing glaciers underwent considerable melting. The Missouri River was a major outflow river and ran valley-wide and deep during glacial summers of the Wisconsinan; south of Sioux City, some seventy miles southwest, the valley is twelve miles across and would have been a brown torrent without island or foothold. In the winter, melting ceased, water flow slackened, and vast quantities of alluvial material—mostly silt—lay exposed on the valley floors of the Missouri River and other outwash streams.

Great windstorms arose during those winters, perhaps because of the unbalancing effect on the atmosphere caused by the nearby mass of continental ice. The wind lifted and transported this unprotected silt in clouds of flying dirt that were to ordinary dust storms as glaciers are to snow piles in parking lots. This wind-borne alluvium was carried many miles downwind, to the east usually, and deposited in a blanket that varied in thickness from over a hundred feet close to its source to just a few inches in places half way across the state. Geologists refer to this fine-grained deposit as loess. Just east of the Missouri River, and for much of the length of the western border of Iowa, the wind left the deep loess that now makes up the Loess Hills; on Bob White's farm, the wind laid it four or more feet thick, apparently further smoothing and leveling the landscape, but most important to Bob, burying all his rocks and cobbles far enough beneath the surface that his implements never disturb them.

Despite what unobservant tourists say, Iowa, South Dakota, and Ohio are not really very flat. Extremely flat and level land, like the salt flats of Utah, is unusual and is most often a former lake bed. Other, only slightly less flat, places are sometimes expanses of land that have been thoroughly eroded down to base level. Some flat places, like the northern portion of Peterson Township, were left smooth by glaciers and are level enough that surface water has little place to go except to puddle in low spots and percolate downward through the topsoil.

And in fact, on flat terrain like that north of Peterson, water has a tendency to actually enhance flatness. Water seeks the low spots and will always carry with it what soil it can. Rainfall over the centuries has tended to brush at the high spots to fill in the swales, maintaining and enhancing a level landscape.

But water doesn't leave the landscape alone for long; change is on the horizon, or closer. Although the northern part of Peterson Township has remained flat and nearly unchanged for several thousand years, the agents of change are visible in the beginnings of little valleys, the tongues of stream headwaters, off to the northwest and to the south, nibbling their way into the flat landscape. If the glaciers stay away and nothing else interrupts the processes now in action, the view here will one day be of hills and creeks and valleys, more like that south of Peterson.

The flat land north of Peterson is really quite like a plateau. Though it is difficult to see on a casual drive across the area, this flat place stands a good ways above the Little Sioux and the energetic creeks that feed into it, and the slopes between the valley floor and the upland are sharp and unusually steep for the region. And unlike water pooled in flat cornfields, water flowing steeply downhill has considerable erosive power.

For the land in this area, the Little Sioux River is at what geologists call base level: the level below which erosion cannot continue because it is so close to that of sea level or a regulating stream. All smaller streams in the area debouch into the Little Sioux, meaning the elevation of that river channel, in relation to the elevation of the surrounding area, regulates the behavior and energy of all minor streams. Simply put, the greater the difference between the elevation of the uplands and that of the river, the steeper and more energetic will be any given rill or brook. The crop furrows of Bob White's farm stand a full two hundred feet higher than the river surface. This difference in height amounts to considerable potential energy and teams water with gravity to provide both the medium and the impulse for the erosional work of remodeling his farm.

The Little Sioux River at Peterson is new as rivers go, and its valley is deep; most of the creeks that flow into the Little Sioux are new as well and are working to cut their headwaters into the surrounding terrain. Unlike many creeks in northwest Iowa that are old streams meandering for miles in wide, gently sloping valleys, many that debouch into the Little Sioux around Peterson are steep, energetic, and flow in V-shaped valleys. On topographic maps these short, branching stream systems look like the multibarbed thorns of a honey locust tree.

I went with Bob one spring day after a good rain to check the outlets of his field tiles. We drove into a neighbor's place half a mile northwest of his own and bumped down a lane toward a slight downward crease in the land where the grass grows greener and thicker for being a bit lower, a bit wetter. We parked the pickup and followed the deflection downhill a few dozen feet to a point where the land surface suddenly breaks. Maybe a foot deep and a foot wide, a tiny stream begins, complete with black soil banks bearing a fringe of undercut grass roots. Downhill, the tiny valley widens a little, makes a bend to the right, and accepts the water of half a dozen cropland drainage tiles, including Bob's, all gurgling contentedly that day.

Farther downstream the little valley grows deeper and wider and combines its waters with those of other miniature valleys; soon it picks up a name, Henry Creek, and then tiny bars of gravel and sand; then there are minnows. Two miles downstream from its beginning, Henry Creek flows through a real valley, fringed by cottonwood and soft maple.

The top end of this tiny valley, the distinct point at which the grassy swale breaks and the cleft begins, is the sharp point of terrain change here; this is the very head of one of the fingers of Henry Creek, the scalpel of landform change. Crumb by crumb, it nibbles upstream into the flat landscape; year by year, it works into the flat uplands of Peterson Township. This spot marks a point of concentration, the place where the downhill flow of water gathers enough power to overcome the resistance of grass and soil to begin carving water's favorite terrestrial environment: a valley. Even though the entire gamut of erosional forces operates across the area, the arrow points of this creek and others in the township, these sharp breaks between flatland and valley, are the messengers of landforms to come.

Just south of the White place, where the water from the south side of the farm flows, the story is similar, but humankind has taken an antagonistic role. Like any good farmer, Bob wants to protect the soil. At the request of his neighbor a few years back, Bob filled in the head of a creek there. He filled and smoothed the encroaching gully and planted it to brome and orchard grass, and the curving grass waterway was left to grow for several years; then the stabilized land was reincorporated into cropland. What Bob did was shove the head of this creek backward, downhill, several hundred feet.

"It's planted in crops now, but I'm saying right now that we might have to come back and work at it again if we get into the summers again when we get those gully washers every June night. Sometimes we'd get two or three or four inches of rain all at once—why, that sucker will wash—that's quite a little watershed."

The matter of time scale is important here. Bob's work to prevent soil erosion—and that of every other conscientious farmer anywhere—is not futile. For Bob to give up on preventing soil erosion because of the intrusion of new valleys is akin to deciding not to paint the house because astronomers predict the demise of the sun in a few billion years. While the advance of these tiny valleys is, in a sense, inevitable, it is comparatively slow. Fighting soil erosion is a long-term agricultural consideration, one measured in decades and perhaps hundreds of years; the change in creek watersheds is best measured in thousands.

South of Peterson, on the far side of the Little Sioux valley, around the Burgeson place, the story is similar, but the interactions among ice, water, and wind are somewhat different. The Sheldon Creek deposits are here, and so is the loess, but the role played by water since glacial times has been more dramatic, more pronounced.

Twenty to thirty thousand years ago, during the episode of the Wisconsinan glaciation that deposited the Sheldon Creek drift, the ice covered this area as well, just like it did the flat land north of town, but for reasons that aren't altogether clear, it melted away to leave a lumpier landscape, probably one of broad humps and low spots that provided starting places for infant streams. Thus these streams got an early start and are older than the energetic and steep creeks associated with the Little Sioux valley. There are several newer streams energetically working their way into this landscape from the river, but most streams here are older and demonstrate their leisurely and longer-term work by cutting valleys with slow gradients and less steep valley sides. They seldom carry much water but form a gentle pattern of coalescent creases, rills, and shallow valleys.

The character of the land is very different from that north of town as well; the flatness is gone. The surface swells and dips over the miles, gently, with broad ridges lifting the horizon line. The horizon is never level here like that surrounding the White place; there is no precise plane into which the streams have cut. A sweep of the horizon from most any place reveals that the line of the land against the sky always has a slight angle, a subtle tilt.

The length of the view varies a good deal according to where I stand. Creek divides may block views over the next ridge half a mile away, yet from certain high ridges it is easy to sweep a quarter of a county with the eye. Contour planting, irregular field sizes and shapes, extensive pastures, soil-protecting field terraces, all unknown north of town, appear frequently in this part of the country, while field tiles are rare. The primary concerns about soil are reversed here from those on the flat land across the river valley; few farmers need consider problems in soil drainage, but all must worry instead about soil erosion.

There are rocks in places, and their location alone tells us something of how this land was shaped. The parent materials of the soil here are the same as north of town: glacial drift thickly frosted with windblown loess. On the ridges and the flatter uplands, where the loess lies deep, the soil is smooth and rock-free, but close to the edges of the uplands, where the land breaks into stream valleys, the water has cut downward through the loess and into the glacial drift, revealing cobbles and occasional boulders. Hauled in by the ice, they dot the valley sides and wash out to collect in creek bottoms.

There are irregular chunks of chert, hard and dense, resistant to the processes that smooth and round most glacial rocks, bits of shale, various colored igneous aliens from the Canadian shield, and other assorted well-traveled rocks, blotchy with lichen, mute as to their origins and past ports of call.

These are the rocks that crop out of the hillsides on my great-grandparents' farm south of Peterson; these are the rocks I dug out as a boy exploring the pastures and hillsides. I remember them peeping out of the long grass, encouraging me to look at them. I knew even then that they were a long way from home. Once in a while I dug out an ovoid and speckled one, a rock that had spent eons as bedrock in some unimaginable world. A part of me wondered if it could actually be a dinosaur egg. Not realizing that its glacial history was probably longer and as interesting as that of any dinosaur egg, I nonetheless hefted and shook any likely looking rock in hopes it might be light and that it might rattle. Had I known the real story of these rocks, that some of them had come five hundred miles inside a continental expanse of ice, I would have given up on dinosaurs and imagined glaciers instead.

Rod Burgeson's farm lies in this province of gentle slopes and hillside rocks. The forty-four-acre field just west of Rod's father's place rests astride a minor ridge; the land rolls gently off to the north and south, making a tractor working along the north fence invisible to anyone on the other side of the ridge. In the south portion of the field, where the land steepens as it falls toward a spring-fed creek, Rod and his dad, Glen Burgeson, have installed three field terraces. And along the south edge of the field, the land breaks into the short creek valley, and here, where the loess is thinnest, Rod sometimes picks up rocks.

Both the land north and south of Peterson are products of the Sheldon Creek glaciation and the subsequent action of water. While geologists know a good bit about how the ice and water worked in these places, there are still a lot of unanswered questions, questions that persist in great part because the ongoing erosion since glaciation has erased much of the story. Ever since the Sheldon Creek Formation, or the Sheldon Creek drift sheet as it is called, was outlined and identified as a deposit different from those that surround it, geologists have been digging at it, squinting at its stratifications, and poking fingers at topographic maps trying to figure out not only the details, but some of the major events that brought it into being. How did the ice behave in this area? Why has stream erosion had such an effect in some places, but less in others? Answers come slowly in muddled terrain. Where clues are thin and the trail cold, geologists put question marks on landform maps and present new theories with special care.

But not all landscapes around Peterson are the products of Sheldon Creek ice; some are newer and were formed by later ice or by other actions altogether. Because they are newer, they are easier to read.

Some miles to the east of Peterson is a boundary significant to geologists, and to farmers, but one easily missed by the casual motorist. It is easier to see on a map than on the ground, but, like most things on the landscape, it is a lot easier seeing it from either perspective once you know what you're looking for.

This boundary is the Bemis Moraine. It runs along the east banks of the Little Sioux River and Brooke Creek in eastern Clay County and northeastern Buena Vista County. This sometimes indistinct line marks the farthest westward extent of the Des Moines Lobe ice in the region, an advance called the Bemis advance. In melting back it left the Dows Formation, or Dows drift.

It is important to recall that the Wisconsinan glaciation was not a single advance followed by a long melt. Geologists know that the ice pushed forward irregularly, in different places and in different directions, sometimes covering new terrain, sometimes re-covering previously glaciated terrain, leaving specific deposits and landforms when the ice of each advance melted.

The Dows Formation to the east is much newer than the Sheldon Creek Formation surrounding Peterson; the Dows was left by the ice only 12,500 to 14,000 years ago; the Sheldon was deposited 20,000 to 30,000 years ago. Hence the Bemis Moraine separates a newer landscape from one much older.

The Bemis advance surged into eastern Clay County and across most of Buena Vista County and reached its maximum extent perhaps 14,000 years ago. In its melt-back, this glacial ice left some classic kettle-and-knob terrain and the Bemis end moraine. The ice pushed west as far as the Little Sioux River and Brooke Creek; both streams carried considerable outflow from the edges of the melting glacier.

The Bemis Moraine is a bit difficult to locate by observing the shape of the land. Compared with some, it is a faint end moraine, and since it so closely follows the valleys of the Little Sioux and Brooke Creek, its presence is masked by their effect on the terrain.

Nevertheless, the difference between the Dows and Sheldon Creek formations is easy to see if you look closely, especially along fence lines. Every farmer in the area knows the difference, even if most don't know the names. East of Brooke Creek on the Dows drift, generations of farmers have bent their backs hauling tons of rocks out of the fields, leaving them in great piles around gateposts and at field corners as cairns to the farmers' rock-devil. Where the Sheldon Creek to the west seldom has rocks at the surface, the Dows has rocks throughout; they infect fields, yards, and pastures alike. The explanation is simple: at the time Bob White's and Rod Burgeson's farms were being blanketed with a great cushion of wind-borne loess, burying their rocks, the Dows terrain was still covered by ice.

There is another evident difference between the Dows and the Sheldon Creek. On the Dows drift, most of the creeks and rills are missing. On this fresher glacial terrain, left as it was in lumps and hollows, there simply hasn't been enough time for an elaborate drainage pattern to develop.

In this way the Dows drift shows its youth. The few streams here show little valley development and few tributaries. Creeks flow sluggishly across the lumpy ground in swales that were dense tangles of prairie marsh before the water was drained and the prairie put to cultivation. So undrained was much of the area that streams had to be manufactured, dug by machine. Hence the hand of agrarian-minded humans is evident here. Creeks quite often run straight as a ruler for many rods—often in the cardinal directions, in accordance with the surveyed grid—and make their turns in engineered curves. In southeastern Buena Vista County, for example, some carry such romantic names as "Ditch No. 101." Picturesque, never; efficient at draining vast tracts of marsh to make productive farmland, yes.

Once I understood how recently the Dows Formation was deposited and looked at it closely, I could see its newness. From the air, with the sun at a low angle, this rumpled drift sheet does in places look like a dog's bed, especially when compared with the much older Sheldon Creek drift right next to it. On the Sheldon Creek, all direct evidence of the work of the glacier has disappeared; glacial lakes, moraines, and potholes have worn away. And on the fresher Dows, especially under the tools of farmers out to drain low spots to grow corn and soybeans, each day a little more of the glacial tread is erased from the surface.

Along toward the first of October these fields got dry and yellow under the combined action of the heat and sun. All through the slumbrous days of September the tall soldiers of the corn dreamed in the mist of noon, and while the sun rolled red as blood to its setting, they whispered like sentries awed by the passing of their chief. Each day the mournful rustle of the leaves grew louder, and flights of noisy passing blackbirds tore at the helpless ears with their beaks. The leaves at last were dry as vellum. The stalk still held its sap, but the drooping ear revealed the nearness of the end. At last the owner, plucking an ear, wrung it to listen to its voice; if it creaked, it was not yet fit for the barn. It was solid as oak, and the next day the teams began the harvest.

—Hamlin Garland, *Boy Life on the Prairie,* 1899

Chapter 8

Harvest

OCTOBER 2

The whole region is busy as soybean harvest hits full stride on a day before predicted rain. Local radio stations peg the chances of precipitation tonight at 90 percent, so farmers keep up the pressure to get as much grain into the bins as they can before the fields get muddy. On rural roads, and even on the streets of Peterson, there is a constant flow of harvest machinery and grain. Because of the heavy and slow farm traffic, it is not a day to be in a hurry to get somewhere.

Combines move slowly across fields and move from field to field as they finish each rectangle of grain. They are supported by a phalanx of trucks, wagons, and tractors hauling grain from the field to on-farm storage or to the elevator in town. Pickups run about retrieving repair parts or running other errands.

As it does every year, the town of Peterson has put up signs outlining a "harvest route" for farmers from the north bringing grain to the elevator. The posted signs keep heavily loaded wagons and trucks off the steep Main Street and direct them over more gentle grades to the scale at the elevator.

A variety of conveyances makes up the steady stream of grain haulers crossing the scale at the foot of Main Street. Tractors pulling multiple balloon-tired gravity-flow wagons alternate with trucks of all vintages and several sizes. A few of the trucks are genuine antiques with bulbous fenders and faded paint. Used only to haul grain at harvest time, they get all their miles during a month in the fall, then gather dust in the back of the machine shed for the rest of the year. At the other end of the spectrum are a few new trucks, big diesels, proudly bearing the names of sizable family farming corporations.

Janet Anderson, who runs the city scale, doesn't need any name on the side of a truck to tell her what to write on the weight ticket; she knows all the vehicles and drivers on sight and has no trouble determining to whose accounts incoming loads should be credited. Farmers often rent cropland in addition to their own, or a father and son may have a particular arrangement for splitting yields in which each party gets credit for alternate loads. As each vehicle settles on the scale, Janet slips a ticket into the printer and pulls the lever to print the weight, time, and date, then waves the driver on. A few moments later, but perhaps after several other loads have crossed the scale to weigh, the same vehicle returns empty, and Janet reinserts the same ticket to print the empty weight. The difference in weight represents the amount of grain dumped through the floor grates of the main silo building. Janet even keeps track of the driver; if he or she is in the cab for the inbound weighing when full and stands off the scale for the empty, the driver would get credit for, say, 170 pounds—or 2.8 bushels of soybeans that don't exist.

It has happened to farmers I know: they pull a load of grain into town with the pickup, weigh and dump, then forget to reweigh on their way out and stop for groceries, some roller chain, to have a tire fixed, and dinner at the café. Sheepishly, they return later after a phone call from Janet and after having tried to figure out what was and wasn't in the pickup when they crossed the scale the first time: "The groceries I remember, but was the dog with me?"

On each empty, or "tare," weigh, the driver hands Janet a rumpled lunch sack through the open office window. In it is a hatful of soybeans taken from the load just dumped. Janet hands each sample around the corner into the elevator office where the beans are tested for percentage of moisture and test weight, essential in figuring the price to be paid for the grain. Today the soybeans coming in average about 8 percent moisture.

I've watched elevator employee Boyd McGee take his sample as the grain flows out of a truck into the floor grates. As the grain flows fully, Boyd sweeps his hand smoothly through the stream from side to side, letting a sample of kernels—and any debris, which will see the owner docked on the price—fill his hand. He takes several sweeps and places each handful in the sack. Some elevators use various sorts of grain probes, but Boyd's method may well be more random and is certainly simpler. In any case, farmers watch as Boyd takes his sample; the specifications for an entire truckload of grain rest on these few kernels that pass through his hands.

The work today is steady, smooth. One vehicle pulls off the scale as another arrives. Janet carefully keeps track of her piles of tickets so that the tare and gross weights of each load get onto the same ticket. She is busy but never behind, never losing track of tickets or samples or names.

As Janet weighs one load, the driver, Kathy Brees, sticks her head out of the cab.

"You open 'til eight tonight?" she asks.

"We're open 'til it rains," Janet replies through the open bay window.

"That's great. I still have chores to do—I've got babies coming."

"I don't like pigs."

"Yeah, I can understand. This bunch is pretty grumpy—first-time moms—you remember how it was!"

They both laugh as Kathy drives off for another load.

In fact, many of the trucks and wagons that cross the scale today are driven by women. While gender roles are fairly distinct around here, as they are in most rural places, there has long been a tradition of women getting as dirty as men when it comes to field and livestock work, especially at harvest.

But whatever the activity, mothers are in charge of child care: in the cab of one truck crossing the scale inbound, I notice a two-year-old boy, sound asleep, curled against the side of the driver, his mother, who smiles and waves as she steers off the scale. In a few moments, she comes back across the scale empty, the child still asleep by her side, undisturbed by the noise and activity.

Soybeans are the name of the game these days. Corn harvest is only beginning, and only for those few who have their soybeans finished. Beans usually mature earlier and are more susceptible to harsh weather. Wind or hail can knock the bean pods from the plant, "shelling them out" onto the ground, out of reach of any machine. Today there is only one farmer hauling corn to town.

The land has undergone an astonishing change in the last weeks. All the cropland has turned from rich green to the pale colors that precede the white of snow. Pastures and lawns still show a little green, but anywhere there is corn or soybeans—which is nearly everywhere—the khaki of fall suffuses everything. The trees have begun to change in earnest as well. The hard ornamental maples in town have fired in just the last few days to brilliant reds and yellows.

Along the riverbank, a quarter mile or so from the elevator, the native trees have changed as well but haven't been as colorful about it. Here the soft maples, box elders, and cottonwoods put on much less in the way of a show, shrinking back instead from green to a sort of brown or gray. The change in density of the woodland is apparent; I can see white patches of the elevator through the foliage. There is the impression everywhere of worn-out leaves, of energy draining back into the earth where it will be safe from the coming freeze. The river is low: as low as it has been since I started coming here. Barring any holes beneath the murky water, I could wade across.

What's left of Rod Burgeson's cornfield has a funereal feeling to it today. Three weeks ago, while the corn was still green, he chopped the majority of it—ears, stalks, leaves—for silage, a rich livestock feed. The twenty-four remaining rows hold the gentle ridge, standing close, reminding me of Sioux burial scaffolds on a hilltop. The brittle leaves sound their death rattle to the fall wind in a voice very different from the soft rustle of summer-green leaves. There is still a hint of purple in the stalks, but the leaves and husks are the off-yellow color most anything assumes after having been bleached long enough by the sun. The ears are full and heavy and droop straight down. The tattered husks that cover them belie the rich life hidden within. Stripping one, I find full, hard kernels more bright, more colorful than anything else within sight.

Late in the morning, I stop at the café for coffee. Sue's is silent and nearly deserted. The electric fans that roared all summer have been put away, deepening the quiet. It's not yet cold enough for Sue to light the gas heating-stove at the back of the café. The only sound today is the scuttle of dry leaves blowing up Main Street. Sue and her waitress, Donna, sit at the front table, paging through catalogs. I pour my own coffee and read the signs on the bulletin board on the back wall. "For Sale—Home Grown Potatoes—Red, White or Russet. Donald Goettsch." No need for a phone number or address; anybody who would be interested in potatoes knows that Donald Goettsch is Sue's husband. Near the sign is a poster adorned with football players in dramatic poses. The banner across the top reads: "1990 Sioux Central Fall Schedules."

A few people come in for dinner; the special today is beef and noodles. Those who talk do so in low church voices, and even Sue has little to say today.

North of town, the closely cropped bean ground looks like worn corduroy. The plants have been clipped to within a few inches of the soil, and once they are processed in the combines, the stems and chaff get scattered back over the rows, returning the nutrients to the soil and softening the look of the ground, enhancing its suggestion of fabric. A south wind is rising, especially here in a place well away from the protecting influence of any trees or of the valley.

Bob White finishes a late dinner at home alone and prepares to return to the field. He picks up his dinner dishes, leaving a jar full of candy corn in the center of the table. It is a common centerpiece in the White household, a reminder of the corn still standing all around. Bob announces proudly that his son, Kevin, gave his girl a ring last night. Bob is just about finished with his beans and beginning to worry about his corn and the wind, and he is eager to get on to corn harvest.

"Oh boy," he says, "a good wind can sure cause a lot of ear drop—it's always a gamble. Letting 'er dry on the stalk too long can mean a 10 percent loss."

As we leave the house, the wind pulls the seed-corn cap from my head and sends it across the house yard.

"Hey," Bob exclaims, "that's a sign of rain, you know. Whenever your hat blows off, we'll get rain soon."

And indeed we do. During the night, we pick up a good three-quarters of an inch, and the harvest stops for a couple of days just where the machinery halted in the field. As I expected, the pattern of the day before is reversed: on October third, the elevator is deserted and Sue's is full and noisy.

Two weeks later, finished with soybeans, Rod Burgeson works to harvest his corn, including what he left in the forty-four-acre field to the west of his dad's place. Soybeans are done for the year in the region, and corn harvest is in full swing. Rod is a good way through his corn but hasn't been combining every day; there are cattle and hogs to feed, augers and harvest machinery to repair, and there have been several wet and snowy days keeping him from the field. The weather today is better, but the wind, despite being from the south, has a damp bite that makes all clothes somehow too thin.

Early this morning, with frost still on the ground, Rod sits high behind the plate-glass windshield of the International combine as it rumbles through another four rows of corn. His feet on the pedals are at corn-tassel level. We travel at precisely 3.2 miles per hour, according to the digital speedometer, fairly slow for someone who is eager to get the harvest finished.

"It'll be better when it dries out some later this morning," Rod explains.

Rod seldom says much as we grind our way through the field, not because of the noise and not because he needs to concentrate in some particular way, but because he seldom says much. In his early fifties, Rod has farmed all his life. Like many farmers, he farms half-and-half with someone else. In many cases the arrangement is with a landowner or a family member; in Rod's case, it is with his dad. As a result, Rod's fields, like many around the area today, are striped alternately with standing crop and stubble. Rod combines in alternates of eight rows; he is today combining his dad's half of the crop and will start on his own as soon as he finishes. By harvesting fields in such a fashion, each partner gets some of the thin corn near the creek and the good corn where the soil is deep and black.

We lumber back and forth across the field like some ungainly animal. Up high, the cab sways, and every movement is amplified. The combine maneuvers oddly through the turns at the end of each round; though they respond in a fashion to Rod's turns of the steering wheel, the snouts of the corn head don't seem attached to this machine.

On each pass, Rod watches closely to see that the combine head doesn't plug with too much wet corn. The combine has lots of dusty high-tech; electronic horns beep when the RPM is too low and at various other times when the machine is engaging and disengaging. Rod is very much at home and runs the thing like a pro, reaching for levers and knobs instinctively, without looking.

"On a good day with no breakdowns, I can do forty acres."

No more than a second after Rod says it, the head stops working altogether—no change in the din of the machine; the head just stops and corn quickly fills to cover it. Rod clambers off to investigate, pulls tools from his overalls, removes a shield to find that the main drive chain for the corn head—similar to a bicycle chain, except it is about an inch and a half wide—has jumped its gears. The chain is hot, dry, and stiff. With a couple of wrenches and a few minutes, we put it back on, smear it with grease, climb back aboard, and start off, only to have it jump off again in ten feet. Then again. Then it's off to town for a replacement.

Going to Peterson for the new roller chain, I'm struck by how mechanical the harvest is, how much of it is simply the push to get it done, to get the grain into safe storage. It makes sense: what farmer with any sanity would stand around admiring the corn in the field while a great storm bore down on the place? Yet something is missed somehow in not waiting an hour to begin and walking a half-mile row to experience the astonishing extent and energy of this waiting crop, at the moment just before it is taken from the earth. I remember how I walked through this field a couple of weeks ago, down a long row, lifting and feeling the weight of heavy ears hanging from dead stalks. I sense little ceremony in Rod, and I've seen little in any other farmer with whom I've worked at harvest.

At Ted's Shop in Peterson, we discover that the old roller chain is worn enough to have gained a half link in thirty. No wonder it won't stay on the drive cogs. With a replacement in hand, we are soon back on the farm installing it, and by 9:20 we're back in the field as the sun burns through the overcast to melt and evaporate the frost.

We advance steadily, the machine inhaling great draughts of standing corn. There is a hypnotic quality to the cornstalks disappearing against the advancing machine. As the snouts of the corn head slip past each stalk, snap rollers angle in to tear at it, seeking a bite; the slit between the rollers narrows as the machine moves forward until suddenly the stiff yellow stalk snaps downward, shucking off the ear as it goes, leaving it in the combine head. The shorn ear is carried back by the force of oncoming ears and is turned onto an open auger that pulls it to the center of the combine where it vanishes beneath Rod's feet and into the business of the machine.

Howling behind and beneath us, the guts of the combine spin, shake, and sort as they strip off husks, knock off kernels, spit out cobs and husks from the back end. The clean yellow grain augers into a high bin just behind the cab, piling deep and heavy. The bin fills with remarkable speed, almost a full load on each lap across the field.

After each trip across the field and back, we pull alongside a gravity wagon. They look like small railroad hopper cars with doughnut tires; each wagon holds about 250 bushels. Without dismounting from the combine, Rod manipulates a lever to swing a spout around and above the wagon, and he quickly empties the bin behind the cab. Two stops with the combine fill each wagon. Rod's dad, Glen, pulls empty wagons to the field with a pickup and sets them just about where Rod will need them as he comes out of the rows. At each round, Glen appears bearing an empty wagon just as we pull alongside another to fill. For several hours during the morning, there is always a full wagon waiting for Glen to take to the farm, one we are filling, and the fresh empty Glen brings.

We work our way back and forth through a sea of yellow-brown, eating up the crop at a great rate. I can't imagine that we won't be done by noon, but these are big fields. By ten the overcast is gone; the south wind dries the corn, and Rod boosts the speed to a steady four miles per hour.

As we go, we make sporadic conversation above the noise. We talk of the weather, of farming, of jazz, which is Rod's passion, and of his and Lorna's two grown children.

Of farming in his dad's day, Rod says, "They worked a lot harder in those days, but I suppose the mental strain of today makes up for it. Nobody then had to worry about being a half-million in debt like a lot of farmers these days."

Late in the morning, I notice the sun is perceptibly lower, more milky, diffuse, than it was a month ago. There is a sort of shimmer, a softness to the air and sky. And, despite the sun, it stays cold.

When Glen is called to other tasks, I take over the duties of hauling full wagons from the field to a big storage bin on Glen's place, which is just across the road from Rod's farmstead. The routine is simple, direct, and rewarding somehow as I watch the bin fill, even though I have had no role whatsoever in the success of this crop.

Each trip I make has the same rhythm. Each time I pull up to the bin, I stop the pickup in exactly the same spot in order to put the wagon's opening right above the auger that takes the corn into the bin; each time I start and rev up the tractor connected to the auger; each time I stand mesmerized watching the corn cascade from the wagon into the open auger; each time as I pull away, the tree branches hit the windshield in the same place as I swing wide to get the wagon turned around and back out to the field.

Each trip leaves a few minutes to kill while the wagon dumps and the auger boosts the grain into the bin. On one trip, I examine the storage bin through the hatch on the roof.

The thing is a marvel of grain storage. Not only does it store grain, the bin also dries it, aerates it, and even mixes it slowly and gently so that hot spots won't form to spoil the corn. Made of galvanized steel, the bin is a cylinder holding 10,000 bushels against all prairie weather save tornadoes. Empty, the bin has a floor big enough for a square dance. By means of a huge fan—today running hard—air is forced up through thousands of tiny holes in the floor and through the corn to dry it. Should mere air not be enough, Rod and Glen can ignite propane burners to heat the incoming air and dry even very wet corn.

But the most ingenious device is one that mixes the grain to prevent hot spots. Grain handlers know that spoilage begins when a small mass of corn, beneath a leak in the roof say, gets wet enough to mold. Molding corn generates heat and moisture; if left alone, it can ruin the contents of the entire bin and cause a fire as well. In addition to making sure the corn is appropriately dry, it makes sense to mix the grain often—or even constantly—to break up wet spots, hot spots.

Says Rod: "You've got to take care of corn. Sometimes people put it in the bins a little too wet, and it's fine while it's still cold, but then we get a few warm days, the stuff starts to sweat. If a farmer doesn't pay attention then, he'll open up the bin one day later to start hauling it to town and have nothing—the whole crop gone."

In the Burgeson bin, a small auger hangs down into the corn from an apparatus under the roof. The thing is called a "stir-aetor" and day by day works its way around the bin stirring and aerating the grain as it goes. It takes about half a day to make a complete cycle; in a few cycles, every kernel will have been moved.

While the wagons empty, there is also ample time to look at the corn itself. I scoop up a handful of corn from time to time as it pours from the gravity wagons and feel its texture and energy. The grain is silky, alive, full of power. Its pure color radiates the energy it contains. Since it is so fresh from the field and has been moved and augered but a couple of times, the corn has yet to generate dust; it is slick, slippery, but in no way oily. It tastes, well, like corn, crunchy, a little harder than a nut; a bowl of it would not seem altogether out of place at a cocktail party, or perhaps it could replace the candy corn in the jar on the Whites' table. While the wagon is yet fairly full, I climb the ladder and push my hand into the yellow grain, sensing each of the individual kernels touching my outspread fingers, my hand, my arm. Each kernel presses against me with equal pressure, with equal contact.

Later, while another load empties, I stand resting my arms on the side of the pickup and inventory the collection of stuff in the back. It is a typical collection for an around-the-farm pickup, an unsorted glacial drift of the variously discarded, lost, and soon-to-be-needed. I find: a spare tire (inflated), a coil of heavy fence wire (unbarbed), half a dozen fist- to head-sized field cobbles of two or three different types of rock, a long-disused water jug, two five-gallon plastic buckets, a two-and-a-half-gallon oil jug (empty), a sodden twenty-five-pound bag of medicated hog feed, a rusty coffee can, a small shovel, also rusty, a burned-up roller chain from some machine, and a corn knife. All of this is suspended in or supported by a one-inch layer of hay and old corn, mixed thoroughly with good Iowa dirt.

Surely, this too must be a palimpsest.

This is a time of grain in motion on the Burgeson place and all around the region. The day here began with corn moving gently in the wind on stalks in the field; seized by the combine, kernels are sorted from everything else and within hours are transported half a mile, augered twice, and spun into a bin where they are now stirred, aerated, and protected. Except for my running an occasional hand through it, the grain is never touched and hardly ever seen. Diesel engines, hydraulic cylinders, roller chains, augers, and electricity do the work, unlike fifty years ago, when farmers still picked corn by hand as they had for centuries.

In those days, every ear was handled individually. Art Johnson, who married my grandmother a few years ago (her father was also an Art Johnson; they're not uncommon around here), started farming in 1940, and, like most farmers in those days, he harvested, or "husked," corn by hand.

"We wore husking gloves and had a peg to tear off the husks. We did two rows at a time. If we'd had a lot of wind, we would have to bend down a lot to pick up corn from the ground. The corn we planted then didn't have the strong stalks that these newer hybrids have."

The farmer seized each ear from the stalk, husked it, and while reaching ahead to the next stalk, lobbed it into a wagon pulled alongside by steady horses. It was hard, repetitious, endless work.

Iowa author Herbert Quick wrote of the numbing work of corn husking in *The Hawkeye*: "Never look at the wagon, there is no time for that; never look at the horses—one can tell what they are doing by the movement of the wagon, and the sound made by their hoofs; never stop to pick off the silks or the little clinging husks; they can go in with the ears. And forget the sky, the clouds, the blood drawn by rosebrier or the sharp tips of the kernels of the 'hackberry' ears; forget everything but the economy of movement, the making of every second count."

Says Art: "It was hard, slow work, all right. We always hoped to get finished by Thanksgiving. It could get pretty miserable out there if we were late getting done or if we got an early snowstorm. It didn't go like harvest does now; a hand husker could only do about a hundred bushels in a day."

Late in the afternoon, Rod finishes his final round for the day and pulls out of the field for home. He has made good progress despite the breakdown and now has cattle and hogs to feed. He'll start again after chores in the morning and will be finished in just a few days. He'll rest well tonight because he's tired, and satisfied: since sunup he has harvested 6,000 bushels.

Well, it's like a friend of mine north of Linn Grove says. He lives out there on a century farm, and when I asked him how long his family has been there, he says, "We were here when they put in the river. It was a dry year so they had to bring in water from Storm Lake to prime it."

—Donovan Meyer, Peterson

Chapter 9

Diary of a River

Thomas H. Macbride, one of Iowa's early geologists and naturalists, came to Clay County in the last years of the nineteenth century and studied the region's geology, landforms, and natural vegetation. Macbride was the first scientist to make any sort of detailed study of the region. He traveled back and forth across the county, looking, thinking, measuring the slope of the land with his eye, examining field rocks and soil. No doubt he wrote his notes sitting on the seats of buggies rented from liveries in Spencer, Everly, and Peterson. But more than a scientist, he was an astute and analytic observer of both the great form and the small details of the landscape around him.

Macbride was puzzled by the odd characteristics of the Little Sioux River valley, particularly those of the valley where it passed Peterson: "That a prairie stream, draining a country destitute of rocky ledges or denser strata, should pick out a course so crooked is certainly a matter of curious interest. The contrasts shown when one compares different parts of the river valley are also very strange. The upper part of the valley from Summit township to Spencer and beyond is wide and shallow, flanked generally on both sides by beds of gravel. At Spencer the valley has widened to a broad sandy plain, some two miles wide and seven or eight miles long."

Writing of the valley downstream toward Sioux Rapids, Macbride noted a shift: "As we proceed southward all this changes. The gravel follows us of course, and is to be seen at intervals for the entire course of the stream, but the valley itself suddenly becomes narrower and deeper, the stream winds between high banks that are steep, precipitous, though of clay, cut on each side and gashed by sharp ravines, canyons of present or recent erosion. This feature becomes so marked that in Herdland township and in Lee township (Buena Vista county) immediately south of it, the river valley has long been designated as the 'straits'. . . .

"The same thing is seen at Peterson, ten or twelve miles by rail farther down the stream, and indeed throughout the whole course of the river from Gilletts Grove south and west. The bluffs of clay are in some places two hundred feet high, and the effect is picturesque in the extreme."

Of the valley and its steep topography two miles west of Peterson, Macbride wrote: "The proverbial section line road which elsewhere follows like a path of destiny the laws of the surveyor, here, for once, falls baffled, toils painfully up the channel of some lateral stream or ceases altogether, leaving the traveler by wide detours to find, if he may, some easier thoroughfare, some gentler gradient."

Macbride was among the first to observe that the middle section of the Little Sioux valley—the portion that enfolds the town of Peterson—was a great deal different from either the upper or lower portions. Along both the upper and lower Little Sioux, he saw manifestations of mature, older river valleys; they were wider, had gently sloping sides, and had had the time to develop a considerable number of tributaries. But what he found and identified in the middle section were characteristics of a much younger and quickly cut river valley: a narrow cross section, steep valley sides, a sharp break between the valley and preexisting terrain, and few tributaries. He also noticed that this odd middle stretch of river valley had an east-to-west orientation that ran in opposition not only to the usual patterns of rivers in the state, but even to the rest of Little Sioux itself.

A look at the state highway map makes clear that most of the rivers of Iowa follow two basic patterns, patterns set by the big rivers on the east and west borders of the state. Rivers that empty into the Mississippi flow generally southeastward, while those that drain into the Missouri flow generally southwest. And despite the number of rivers and the varied terrain they cross, the only real exception to the pattern is the Little Sioux.

The upper part of the Little Sioux—that is, the river north and east of Peterson—acts like a river that feeds the Mississippi; it flows steadily southeastward. It roughly lines up with the course of the Raccoon River, which is part of the Mississippi drainage system, making it look as though at one time the Little Sioux and the Raccoon were one river system leading to the Mississippi. On the other hand, the lower Little Sioux—that part of the river from a few miles west of Peterson to its debouchment into the Missouri River—makes its status as a Missouri River tributary quite clear by flowing unswervingly southwest for nearly ninety miles.

But the middle section of the Little Sioux, the thirty miles that connect the upper and lower parts, the river that flows past Peterson, runs west—even northwest for a bit—in defiance of both patterns. This is the only portion of any river in the state that flows so contrary to the normal drainage network. Something unusual happened here, and it didn't take Macbride and other geologists long to figure out what.

At a geological moment some 14,000 years ago, during the latter stages of Wisconsinan glaciation, the ice stood as a wall roughly fifteen miles to the east of Peterson; this was the Bemis advance nearing its southern and western maximums, edging its way from the northeast into the eastern parts of Clay and Buena Vista counties. It blocked and filled the Little Sioux valley at a point probably near Gillett Grove, damming the upper reaches of the river against the ice wall and forcing it to seek another outlet.

Where Peterson is today, and across some fifteen to twenty miles of open country between Gillett Grove and Waterman Creek, there was no river valley at all; probably there were low spots on the loess-mantled Sheldon Creek drift, but no valley.

The ice and glacial drift dam created what geologists call Glacial Lake Spencer; its shore line, flat floor, and lake deposits are still observable in northern Clay County. Lake Spencer, an expanding lake with no outlet, filled quickly with water pouring in from the glacier and from the river, itself a conduit for glacial meltwater. No one knows how long it took—a few years, months, or just weeks—but eventually the lake reached a surface elevation of 1,350 feet and found an outlet across the Sheldon Creek drift to the west, away from the face of the glacier.

It must have started as a halting trickle, hunting the low way across the landscape, but once positive outflow was established, the current must have surged dramatically as rushing water planed through the soft glacial drift. It must have quickly cut a narrow channel, a chute full of gray, cold water, choked with everything from silt to boulders, heading westbound pell-mell through the landscape.

The image of this spillover and rush thrills me. As a boy I spent rainy summer days building impoundments of various sorts for runoff water. Rocks, sticks, and a little mud would dam up a good few cubic feet of water, gathering a sort of potential energy almost as exciting as a box of fireworks. The goal was never to see how effective I could be at corralling and channeling water over the long term—irrigation, after all, was boring—but to race the incoming water in hopes that I could build a dam fast enough and high enough to make a really big blowout when the break came. The delight is there yet as I recall the first tentative breach, the trickle over the top, followed by the inevitable collapse of the dam, and a flood of Johnstown proportions washing all my toy soldiers downstream in one thrilling miniature disaster.

The creation of the middle part of the Little Sioux valley was a hydrological event of breathtaking proportions. Geologist Jean Prior, who is well acquainted with the facts of the case, shares my enthusiasm in imagining the event: "It may have taken months, it may have taken years, but there must have been some pretty interesting days." Surging water crossed fifteen or more miles of terrain, found the valley of Waterman Creek west of Peterson, and filled it with torrents of gray water. From then on, what was becoming the Little Sioux drained into the Missouri River via the lower course of Waterman Creek.

Macbride, who had no topographic maps, who would never see any of this terrain from the air, and whose only elevation figures came from the few railroad surveys in the county, figured it out. He wrote: " . . . the Little Sioux river has only recently, as things geologic go, made its way across the divide and found an outlet by way of Waterman valley down the Missouri drainage slope. The Little Sioux would thus seem to be a tributary to Waterman creek rather than the reverse."

Once the breach was made and the course of the valley established, Lake Spencer drained quickly. And the course of what is now the Little Sioux was changed for good.

Off and on over the next 2,000 to 4,000 years, the Little Sioux continued to work on its valley with meltwater from the shrinking Wisconsinan ice sheet. Year by year the water cut easily through the soft glacial drift, for the incline of the river was steep and the quantity of water considerable. As the river eroded downward, it carved a valley with steep sides and a very narrow floor. The valley sides expanded very little.

Then, some time about 10,000 years ago, the Little Sioux River shifted its hydrologic gears. The glacier had melted from the watersheds draining into the Little Sioux basin, reducing the water flow to a fraction of what it had been. In addition, the river had cut its valley downward to the extent that the gradient, the slope of the river, was diminished. And as anybody who has ever watched a steep mountain stream knows, the less the grade of a stream, the slower it flows; the slower the flow of the stream the less material it can carry. So, instead of expending most of its energy deepening the valley, the Little Sioux began to more actively deposit material across the valley floor. The sediment load available to the river now exceeded its ability to haul it away; the river began to aggrade more than erode; it began to fill its valley with alluvial material.

An aggrading river uses eroded material from upstream to build a floodplain, a broad, flat valley bottom deep with sediment. Some floodplains, like that of the Missouri River, are fifteen miles across; more commonly they cover the bottom of a narrower valley. Aside from the presence of water itself, alluvial floodplains are perhaps the most common feature of river environments, and except for rivers in V-shaped mountain canyons, most any river will get around to building one.

Thus the Little Sioux River has reached a point where it no longer works much to deepen its valley and instead concentrates erosional efforts on nibbling at the valley sides and on moving sediment by short hauls down the river. Now, in late youth, the valley no longer gets much deeper, only wider.

The Little Sioux valley running past Peterson demonstrates its comparative youth in another way: a paucity of tributary streams. This part of the valley is really more like a chute, a sluiceway connecting two better-developed parts of the river. The few creeks that do enter the Little Sioux along here are themselves new and have steep, V-shaped ravines. These are the creeks that daily work headward into the landscape around Bob White's farm.

The course of a river flowing through its own floodplain marks a line across the land that changes with the years, seasons, and sometimes hours. Rivers seldom run straight, and even when the banks have been straightened by misguided people who are fixed upon linearity, the course of the water will bounce from side to side like a cue ball in a rain gutter as it seeks escape. The curve of a free river is a tension between the driving forces of water against a resistant framework of soil, rock, and vegetation. Stone by stone, silt grain by silt grain, a river works at the landscape, and in so doing, bends its course. For a river, the state of being is always a state of becoming.

The Little Sioux not only seeks its own course, but seeks it again and again in seeming dissatisfaction with the one it has. The Little Sioux has meandered across the broad valley bottom, looping here, tightening a bend there, and finally cutting itself off to start new loops and whorls. The motion is that of a bull snake propelling itself across a road: loop advances on loop, sometimes angling off straight for a bit, then a swerve and a new cascade of curves pushes it off in another direction.

Once, washing dishes, I noticed the effect. As I held a cookie sheet at an angle under the faucet to rinse off the soap, I saw how a quarter-inch-wide stream directed across it mimicked most of the antics of a river meandering across a floodplain. The stream started straight and ran straight for just a second, and then it quickly turned out and bunched up into the loops and bends familiar to anyone who has seen a river from the air. Like in real rivers, the tiny flow made ever more erratic loops until it cut them off and resumed, however briefly, a straighter path.

The physics of water movement dictates that water flowing in the outside part of a river bend will be fastest, while that on the inside of the curve will be slowest. Along the Little Sioux, like most rivers, the banks on the outsides of curves are highest and steepest and the water below the deepest. Here the water is fastest and provides the greatest eroding power. Moving water, even at times of low current, cuts relentlessly at the point of contact between river and land. The banks here are concave; the roots of the grass at the very edge dangle in space, and the grass will soon fall.

On the opposite side of the stream, on the inside of a bend, broad, flat sandbars protrude into shallow water. Here silt, sand, and debris from upstream banks are dropped by the water as it slows down. The banks, if present at all, are usually low, and the water will be shallow for many feet out into the river.

By this unending process, river curves tend to become more pronounced, more extreme, to become horseshoe bends that reach nearly a full circle. In times of high water or storm, the narrow isthmus between loops is sometimes cut through, leaving the horseshoe bend as an oxbow lake and changing the course of the river overnight.

To wade the Little Sioux is to understand its elemental mechanism for change. As I stand in the current, my feet, even most of my calves, disappear in silty brown water. At low water or high, and in most any season, the Little Sioux

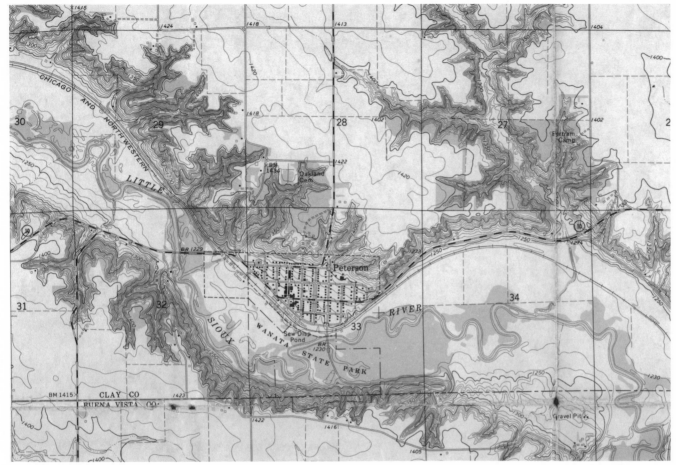

Detail from U.S.G.S. 7 1/2 minute map, Peterson, Iowa, 1971. While probably not drawn very accurately on the 1887 map (see chapter 14), the river has nonetheless changed its course in a place or two by 1971. Notice the steep walled valley and the short, barbed ravines that cut from it into the uplands.

will be coffee-dark with the suspended material of eroded topsoil. In time, after a long journey down the Little Sioux, the Missouri, and the Mississippi, that soil will displace a little more of the Gulf of Mexico, making Louisiana a bit bigger. Larger particles—sand grains—bombard my invisible feet as the grains work downstream. Sometimes these particles roll, sometimes they hang suspended just above the bottom, pulled always downstream. Depending on the whim of the current, particles of this bottom load, as hydrologists call it, may move many miles before settling, or may move only from one sandbar to the next.

It is easy to forget just how much extra distance meanders put in a river, especially if one is planning a day of canoeing. The Little Sioux demonstrates its sinuousity in the river course between Peterson and Linn Grove, the next town upstream. As the crow flies, it is just 5 miles between the towns. Via the "river road," which follows the bends of the valley, it is 6.9 miles, but in a canoe in the Little Sioux, it is 10.6 miles, over twice the air distance.

There are other details of this river and valley worthy of attention, clues that fill in other parts of this stream's particular history. Among the most common are alluvial terraces. Along segments of the river from Sioux Rapids downstream almost to its debouchment into the Missouri, the valley sides and floor are lined with broad shelves that mark former floodplain levels. They are vestiges of earlier valley floors and were left high and dry as the river meandered across its valley and continued downcutting.

Sometimes they are quite level, sometimes not; occasionally they are sharp and easily seen; more often they are rather broad and diffuse. Most often—on the Little Sioux and elsewhere—they are found on the insides of valley curves where the river meandered its way outward and away from them, but they do occur in many types of locations along the length of the valley. The key to finding river terraces is to look for a shelflike landform of most any size anywhere above the level of the present floodplain and below the level of the upland.

Valley terraces are made of alluvium, and since they are especially common in river systems that transported glacial outflow, most terraces in such valleys, including those of the Little Sioux, are made of silt, gravel, sand, and boulders that spilled out of the melting glacier. They not only represent former valley floors, but also represent cycles in the river's past where water slowed for a time and the river aggraded, or filled, its valley with water-borne earthen material. When glacial outflow increased again, the river resumed its downcutting, leaving parts of the old floodplain as high and dry alluvial terraces.

East and west from Peterson are numerous terraces representing at least three levels, or stages, of river downcutting. Geologists have traced these features along the valley sides and determined that the three levels represent downcutting during the draining of Lake Spencer some 13,000 to 14,000 years ago. But one needn't go outside the town limits to find an alluvial terrace; Peterson itself is built on one. This bit of geologic good luck and wise siting by those who platted the town explain why the Little Sioux, though it floods with regularity, has never flooded the town. The curve of the abandoned railroad follows the south edge of this terrace; the line of the now-abandoned Chicago and North Western was twenty-five feet above the level of the river.

But the most unusual, and the most haunting, reminder of the history of the Little Sioux River hides in a pasture five miles west of town. Few know of it, and its subtlety masks its importance to the degree that few would recognize it. This earthen relic, called a hanging valley, is one of the most unusual landscape features in the region.

Essentially it is an intact abandoned valley of the Little Sioux, a valley abandoned quite early in the development of the river. It stands high above the present floodplain at a point two miles downstream from where Waterman Creek joins the Little Sioux. Is it related to the breathtaking hydrological events triggered by the draining of Lake Spencer? Probably, but no one is certain just how. The best guess has it that the valley was formed during or shortly after the draining of Glacial Lake Spencer and was abandoned when the river changed course soon thereafter.

I walked overland to the hanging valley one March day after having located it from the air and was surprised at what I found. I walked east for some distance across muddy fields of the upland plains and quite suddenly came to stand at the lip of a miniature Little Sioux River valley. It is a perfect fossil from the glacial eons of northwest Iowa, a ghost from the era of wall-to-wall floods of meltwater. It is about fifty feet deep and a few hundred feet across, as compared with the present valley at a maximum of two hundred feet deep and half a mile to a mile across. The crisp details of this inactive valley have long ago succumbed to brome grass and erosion; the land features have softened, and the river course itself, filled with local sediment, has long ago disappeared.

I followed the old valley upstream, walking on the old valley floor so strangely bereft of a stream. It struck me as a surreal version of a river valley, as if a sculptor had carefully seen to its shape and larger elements, but, out of a desire for visual tension, had stopped short of providing an actual stream to run through it.

The best-preserved part of the valley is about half a mile long and at its upstream end stops abruptly at a startling view of the much larger and deeper present valley of the river. The old valley simply ends, is cut off, hangs high above the new. I stood on the floor of the old valley, with its valley walls to my left and right, and looked out and down another seventy or more feet to the river, its floodplain, and out to the horizon and the familiar hills of the newer valley.

If ever there was a place where the geomorphological past of this region emerges to be seen in today's light, this is that place. There is no more vivid way to know the history of this river than to stand at the north end of the hanging valley and contemplate, in one sweeping view, both the landscape of the last Ice Age and that of today.

Eddie Beck,
Eddie's Hardware

Main Street, Peterson, Sunday morning, July

    —The long distance telephone that is coming to Peterson has got as far as Sutherland and stopped.

    —Bill posters were here last week advertising a circus at Sutherland and Sioux Rapids July 26th and 27th. All bad things skip Peterson.

—Peterson Patriot, *July 21, 1898*

Dale Davis and Ken Syndergaard, Senior Center, November

Christian Kirchner home, May; built 1867

Gust Kirchner home, now owned by Peterson Heritage

Velma Walrath

College and Second streets, January

*Oma Rohrbaugh's
front door, April*

  The basic principle is this:
that all human landscape
has cultural meaning, *no
matter how ordinary that
landscape may be. It follows,
as Mae Thielgaard Watts has
remarked, that we can "read
the landscape" as we might
read a book. Our human
landscape is our unwitting
autobiography, reflecting
our tastes, our values, our
aspirations, and even our
fears, in tangible, visible
form.*
  —*Peirce F. Lewis,
    "Axioms for Reading
      the Landscape," 1979*

Pine Street, August

First United Methodist Church, August; built 1883, razed 1992

Restored
Peterson
blockhouse,
July

Kelli
Terrell,
Peterson

Eddie and Mona's wrenhouse, Peterson, August

America eludes categorizing. It is represented fully neither by the beautiful view nor by the profane. America can only be found in that vast space between the heights and the depths. Not a region but a place.

But if this place is not tangibly spectacular, it is eloquently representative of the people who made it. The product of successively inconsistent evolution, it is a place that has been molded by the ambitions, the failure and needs of each succeeding generation. Here on the face of America, on each street in each town and neighborhood, is the record. The adaptations each has made to his habitat are plainly evident, laid down one upon the other like the sediments in which the secrets of geological history lie, the record of the American evolution. And on the surface is today's topsoil, the organic medium where the everyday processes of life and death are depositing their own sediments.

—*David Plowden*, Commonplace, *1974*

West edge of Petterson, May

C. & N. W. R. R. TIMETABLE

GOING EAST   GOING WEST

Chicago Pass. 12:01 p.m.   *Iowa Pass. 4:29 p.m.*

Chicago Pass. 7:12 p.m.   *Dakota Ex. 9:03 a.m.*

Freight 1:00 p.m.   *Freight 1:15 p.m.*

Peterson—Spencer Stage Route

Leaves Peterson for Spencer, Mondays, Wednesdays

and Fridays at 9 a.m. and returns alternate days.

Carries passengers and traffic.

—Peterson Patriot, *January 20, 1898*

Little Sioux River floodplain, January

Elk Township, Buena Vista County, October

Clint Fraley,
Clay County Conservation Board

Oaks, Waterman Township, O'Brien County, August

Little Sioux River, July

Little Sioux River, December

Brooke Township, Buena Vista County, October

Big bluestem, Peterson Township, July

Up to that fateful moment, the prairie of the farm and of the township had been virgin sod; but now it bowed its neck to the yoke of wedlock. Nothing like it takes place any more; for the sod of the meadows and pastures is quite a different thing from the untouched skin of the original earth. Breaking prairie was the most beautiful, the most epochal, and most hopeful, and as I look back at it, in one way the most pathetic thing man ever did, for in it, one of the loveliest things ever created began to come to its predestined end.
—*Herbert Quick*, Vandemark's Folly, *1922*

Oh, that terrible day! Hour after hour they listened to that prodigious, appalling, ferocious uproar. All day Lincoln and Owen moved restlessly to and fro, asking each other, "won't it ever stop?" To them the storm now seemed too vast, too ungovernable, to ever again be spoken to a calm, even by God Himself. It seemed to Lincoln that no power whatever could control such fury; his imagination was unable to conceive of a force greater than this war of wind or snow.

—Hamlin Garland, *Boy Life on the Prairie,* 1899

Chapter **10**

1856–1857

DECEMBER 3

Before this morning, the dead grasses matted in pastures, roadside ditches, and along the river seemed the most colorless things in the world. They lay on the frozen ground, pale and dry, abandoned by all life. To look at them and consider their color was pointless; they had no color. But today the complexion of this landscape has changed altogether; Peterson got four inches of snow last night, burying all but an occasional spear and clump of grass. Now, by contrast, these beige sentinels seem rich and warm against the blanket neutrality of new snow.

People in Peterson awoke today to the unmistakable sound of the snowplow clearing the town streets. By eight-thirty, Max Wetherell has made at least two passes down every street and has scraped a good deal of the hundred-foot-wide Main Street, piling the results in a great conical heap at the center in front of the bank. The snow pile is tall enough that I wonder in passing if we shouldn't hang lights on it and call it a Christmas tree. It would nicely complement the real pine tree at the other end of the business block of Main Street, a tree that now shines every night with Christmas lights.

All over town, residents are hauling out their snow blowers, blade-equipped garden tractors, and even some old-fashioned shovels. As people get at it, the sound of personal snow equipment rises to overcome any that Max makes with the plow. Though most Iowans complain about winter, it seems a pro forma gripe; deep down, most get a perverse enjoyment from inclement weather, especially from this, the first measurable snowfall of the season, a storm that closed a few schools, made the roads good and icy, and transformed the landscape, as if by magic, overnight.

Light snow still falls, but the weather report makes clear the storm is over. And the lists of school closings make it clear that we missed the brunt of the storm. Few schools to the north and west of Peterson are called off, but to the south and east, everything is canceled because towns in that direction got as much as fourteen inches. Gray woolen clouds hang low, even in the valley; held above my head, my shovel end ought to disappear into them. The low clouds and thick snow muffle every sound.

Free of school, the kids scramble to earn money shoveling walks and driveways or head to the sledding hill behind the schoolhouse. Generations of kids have gathered there to test their sleds and cold endurance. The radio warns of icy roads and that "travel is not advised." But the roads aren't all that bad considering it's the Midwest and it's December. The bad roads detain neither the two long-haul semis that pass through town as I shovel our walk nor the morning coffee crowd at Sue's.

Most of the rural regulars are there, probably because nearly everyone, retired or not, gets around in four-wheel-drive pickups, and they don't want to be thought of as being stopped from their appointed rounds by a little snow. By this time of year, seed-corn caps have been replaced by wool hats and insulated caps; a few women wear scarves. As they enter, customers clump their boots on the rug at the door to shed loose snow, but the floor of the café is nonetheless thoroughly puddled.

Christmas is coming to the café as well. Sue has gotten the spirit and hung a paper Santa with a brace of reindeer above the booths, and there is a wreath on the front door.

"This is *real* weather," someone tells me with a grin. In a way I understand what he means, but wonder if it then means that a cool, partly cloudy April day, because of its ordinariness, isn't real weather. Given the fact that all weather, dull or extraordinary, is commented on at the café, I conclude in the end that all weather must be real weather. There are very few other topics in the café today. Claims of snow accumulations around the area are given close scrutiny; this storm, like most, came with wind, blowing some farm groves pretty full while scouring fields bare. In a back booth a young fellow loudly tells a story about how his pickup slid into the ditch this morning and how he dug himself out; the man sitting with him reads the paper and pays him no attention whatever.

The blacktop going north out of Peterson is surprisingly dry and clear. Since the wind is square out of the north, the cold air running down the middle of the road has little source of fresh snow. The east-west roads are a different story, as strong wind digs snow out of ditches along the north side of any road and trails it across to the south. Some gravel roads are nearly blocked.

On the prairie and plains, the amount of snow that winds up on any given piece of ground is affected comparatively little by how much actually fell. If the wind is right, half an inch of snowfall can collect five feet deep in a farm grove or on the lee side of a barn. Only on rare occasions here does snow come without wind; only rarely is there a deep, even cover on unprotected fields. I have a clear feeling of there being less snow out here than in town. The valley is the ultimate snow catcher; snow may blow for miles across open, level terrain to drop into the valley and give shovelers and snowmobilers therein much more to do than their neighbors on the hill. On the flats, winter means cold and wind; in the valley, it means cold and snow.

South of town, out where Rod harvested corn last fall, snow dusts the field. Frozen clods show black through patches of new snow, and the eight-inch-high corn stubble, looking like rows of miniature tombstones, is the only hint of color.

The river is slushed over today except for a narrow band of steaming water in the center of the channel. The stream has been trying to freeze over of late, with ice sheets extending further out, day by day, from the banks. But the river rises or drops a few inches, or we will have a couple of days of warm weather, and the ice shelves will disappear.

Today the accumulation of snow has thickened the water to the consistency of a milk shake. Nothing heavier than a chickadee—not even a bluejay—could walk on it without slipping in.

The character of the woodland along the river is the reverse of that of summer. When there are leaves on the trees, they mask everything but themselves; the dense foliage becomes the landscape, and the view is limited to a few dozen feet in any direction. Now, with trees stripped of leaves and the valley cloaked in snow, the surface and shape of the land are evident, the hollows and old river courses, the valley hillsides. The trees are distinct but are mere sticks before the land itself.

Late in the afternoon, I stop by the elevator and scale office to gauge the day from there. On the counter sits a small artificial Christmas tree, partly assembled, a string of lights nearby. In the process of setting it up, someone has been called to another, more important task. Beside it is a pile of give-away calendars and a big box of fresh, hot popcorn. As people go about their work, their paths are angled to pass the box for a handful.

Dale Roberts drives across the scale with a load of cattle feed bound for someplace, but otherwise people here are bent to paperwork. Farmers come in for feed and supplies and linger around the popcorn box for a time, then head home in the failing light.

Two snowmobiles headed for the river bottom whine past the scale office, the glare of their single headlamps dancing over the icy streets, while up in the middle of Main Street, somebody in a loader scoops at the snow pile, loading it into dump trucks. At four-thirty it is nearly dark, and the town snowplow, with Max Wetherell still at the wheel, makes a last pass down Front Street.

Peterson, like any town, city, or village, appeared where it did because somebody thought this site had advantages over others. The considerations are always livability, available resources, and transportation. The Plains tribes, when siting their lodges, considered protection from the elements, access to water and grass, and defense from their enemies. Most early American cities began adjacent to good harbors and in proximity to food-growing areas. Most midwestern towns established in the middle to late nineteenth century arose astride the railroad.

But not all of them.

On April 24, 1856, two brothers—John Augustin Kirchner, twenty-six, and Jacob Kirchner, seventeen—accompanied by one Ambrose Mead, arrived at the Little Sioux River just about where Highway 10 crosses the river today, west of town. The three of them were "land lookers": men in the act of finding new land for farms, for homes. According to a rather florid Clay County history published in 1889, they were men who took careful measure of things: "After a minute investigation, they discovered that this was a stream of clear water of sufficient force to furnish excellent water power. . . . After fording this stream and mounting the hill on the east side they beheld a vast field. As far as the eye could penetrate there lay before them acres upon acres of as fine a land as the sunlight of Heaven ever shone upon. The grass, then just emerging from the ground, gave striking evidences of the richness and fertility of the soil. The location was everything that could be desired and the land as productive as could be found in the section."

The men selected cabin sites, planted spring gardens, which they left to luck and the elements, and returned east for their families. Young Jacob stayed in Dubuque, Iowa, to purchase wagons and draft animals, and John Augustin—or Gust as he was always to be known—returned to the family home in Rensselaer, New York, for his parents and eight brothers and sisters. A married sister would remain behind in New York.

What Gust and his younger brother found at this bend of the Little Sioux River was not only good prairie land—for that was common, even ubiquitous, around here—but a solid stand of mature timber, a scarce resource in prairie country. They could use the wood as a universal building material and for heating and the standing timber for psychological protection. To people from the Hudson Valley, and so recently from Bavaria as were the Kirchners, the open prairie must have spoken of wind and desolation, the hope of great farmland, but never of home. To have trees at your back, the protection of shade on summer days, some interruption in the ache of sky and grass, must have been great comfort in so wild a place.

They also located a good site for a mill to saw lumber and to grind grain to flour. At the west end of the strip of timber was a spot where the river pinched in a bit between solid, high banks, a place where the stream riffled over a small rapid—a fine place for a minor dam, mill, and race.

Back in New York, the rest of the family awaited Gust's return. Among them was his young sister Charlotte. Some sixty years later she wrote a series of letters to her daughter describing the family's experiences coming west and making a home. Though the intervening years may have sweetened some recollections and soured others, the letters remain a useful narrative of the first Euro-American settlement in the region.

"In our family were eleven children, some little, some half grown and some grown up. I was a little, flaxen-

J. A. (Gust) Kirchner in later years, as a solid citizen of the solid town of Peterson. Photograph courtesy of Julia Booth.

haired, blue-eyed, ten-year-old and there were three younger. Your uncle, John Augustin, Gust for short, was the oldest. We thought him wonderful. He . . . had spent four years in California and could tell the most thrilling stories of his adventures there and of his trip across the Isthmus of Panama."

Gust had a touch of the adventurer in him. A broad and strong man, at the age of nineteen he had left home and joined the rush for gold. His mining rewards were modest, and he spent what must have been more profitable days as a carpenter in San Francisco and then went back east.

Now, in 1856, he returned from Iowa to his family waiting in New York, and together they departed on their journey west, leaving on the sixth of July. The trip from New York to the Mississippi River was by train; a ferry took them across the river at Dubuque.

Charlotte later wrote to her daughter of her first impressions of Iowa: "Your Uncle Jacob met us in Dubuque and we stayed there two or three days to complete the arrangements for our journey. There were but few buildings in the town and its whole aspect was very primitive. The hotel dining room was so full of flies that we hated to eat there. That was before the day of screens and fly swatting was not yet a popular pastime. Jacob had bought two teams of oxen and lumber wagons with bows over which blue and white striped ticking was stretched. We had also a large tent of the same material, which was to be our shelter on the long, slow journey from Dubuque to the end of the trail, the spot which is now the little town of Peterson.

"Your Uncles, Gust and Jacob, had been over the road twice, so that our camping places were carefully selected near water and with a wood supply, if possible. Sometimes it was late before our tent was up, our supper eaten, and all were ready for a much needed night's rest. In the middle of the day we halted for an hour or more to feed, water and rest the oxen and the cows. The weather was as good as we could expect, so that the camping was not unpleasant.

"We rested a few days at Cedar Falls, and when we moved on again we were accompanied by the Mead family, consisting of the father, mother and five children, and by two or three young men, altogether a large company. From this point westward the settlers were fewer and farther apart. The slow moving wagons gave us plenty of opportunity to look about; indeed, I believe that even the youngest of us walked most of the time.

"At Fort Dodge we left the last evidences of civilization behind us, and from there to the valley of the Little Sioux no plow had cut the virgin soil."

As if to welcome them to the West, the prairie that year put on a spectacular show of late summer flowers: "The prairies were one vast expanse of waving grass and blooming flowers. The prairie lilies, now practically extinct, were there in prodigal abundance. The prairie pinks, red, and white and purple, and the long purple spikes of the shooting star were among the most conspicuous blossoms; these last are still to be found along the byways and fence rows.

"Now and then we saw wild deer, and at least once a fawn was killed, which was a delicious change in our bill of fare. I remember, too, seeing a solitary buffalo. Our cooking was a most important event each day; your grandmother and the older girls did most of it, but no one but Gust could toss up the pancakes in the long handled skillet and have them come down neatly turned."

Finally, on August 24, 1856, the families arrived at what they called Long Grove; the place would later become Peterson.

"There was great gladness when, after weeks of travel, we came at length in sight of Long Grove. All alike, men, women and children, rejoiced in that welcome sight. I think that even the cows and oxen felt a thrill of contentment. The grove covered the steep hills on the south side of the valley of the Little Sioux river, forming a sort of amphitheater; this is still one of the beauty spots of Iowa. . . . Our tent was put up for the last time, and more securely, in the shelter of a large oak. The cattle were permitted to graze and rest, the wagons were unpacked and a permanent camp was made, while preparations were at once begun for the building of a house and of a shelter for the cattle."

So it came to be that the first dwelling that Peterson could call its own was a large blue-and-white-striped cotton tent.

The Kirchners were good candidates for success at the very edge of Euro-American settlement. Among family members were all the skills necessary for survival and prosperity on the frontier: agriculture, horticulture, animal husbandry, carpentry, and the mechanical and domestic arts in general. Apparently they were good planners as well; when Gust and Jacob first came west to select their claim, they brought with them seed stock for a large garden, the produce from which the family would come to rely on during the coming winter. The family arrived in northwest Iowa with a carefully planned selection of materials and supplies, and most of all, a bit of money, something always useful, even in the frontier economy 140 miles from the nearest store. In addition, they brought good business sense that allowed the family to make well on its investment. Gust certainly understood the economic advantages of being the first Euro-American settlers in the region, and of purchasing the best tract of timber for many miles. While the family was certainly interested in good farmland, there was going to be plenty of that for years to come; like settlers further west twenty-five years later who sought land with good access to water, Gust Kirchner knew that it was the limited resource—timber—that would repay them most fully for their efforts.

The spot they chose for their cabin was a natural and beautiful place for a homestead—it may even have reminded them of Bavaria. They sited their cabin a few rods west of the river on a terrace enough above the water to be safe from floods. The homestead was in a comfortable hollow, a widening of the river valley. To the south and west were tree-covered valley sides; to the north, a picture-window view of the prairie-cloaked valley wall opposite; to the east, the river. This place was, and is today, a safe harbor from the prairie winds, a pastoral setting fringed by trees.

In front of the cabin beside the river was the mill seat. Gust saw potential not only in the timber itself, but in his ability to saw logs into lumber for settlers soon to come. He knew that later there would be wheat to grind into flour.

Within short weeks the men in the family had cut trees and put up a modest timber home; it was a cabin tall enough for a sleeping loft above the main floor. They built it with a simple gable roof, four windows (complete with glass brought from Dubuque), a single door, and puncheon floors.

Today a glacial boulder marks the spot and bears a plaque identifying it as the site of the first cabin in Clay County. The place is half a mile west of Peterson, just south of Highway 10, on the west side of the river. The stone sits right next to the driveway of the old Gaston place, once a sturdy farmstead tucked into this little bowl but now fallen to ruin, barn and house slumping inward, the whole place overgrown. Its days are numbered; someone recently parked a bulldozer amid the buildings and coarse grass. This farmstead, itself as obsolete as the log cabin that stood here years earlier, has no relationship to the Kirchner homestead; the cabin was probably long gone before the first nail was driven in the Gaston house.

Meanwhile, as the Kirchners raised their cabin and livestock shelter, Ambrose Mead and his family did the same about two miles east, on their claim at the far end of the crescent of timber; no doubt the distant sound of Mead's ax at work in the woods gave comfort to the Kirchners, who felt themselves so deep in the wilderness and so far from "civilized" habitations.

Charlotte wrote of life at the new homestead: "The daily life of the family, from the youngest to the oldest, was indeed a busy one from morning until night. There was always something new to make—a rolling pin, pudding stick, a shelf for the water pails, or some other little help to make things more convenient, or perhaps something new was found which could be used for food. In the garden the uncles had planted in the spring, we had potatoes, roasting ears and a few other vegetables. We found plum trees loaded with red or yellow plums, trees festooned with wild grape vines which were covered with ripened grapes. Your grandmother found many uses for the fruit, while we children found the vines fine for swings and skipping ropes."

The Kirchner and Mead cabins were probably in the last stages of completion in September when Deputy Surveyor George Temple and his assistants sighted and chained their way across the township. He noted the timber, the valley, the river, and though he misplaced the Kirchner cabin, he mentioned the two new dwellings in the valley. Doubtless Temple and his crew camped near one or another of these cabins, and perhaps they shared a meal with the families.

The settlers knew the surveyors were coming and took great interest in their work. Until this land was subdivided into sections and quarter sections, until the families could provide a legal description of the land, and until they executed an actual purchase from the federal government, they had little recognized right to the land and their improvements. And where the survey lines themselves fell would make considerable difference. Once the surveyors had drawn their lines, it was technically possible to wind up with a newly plowed field sprawled in four sections—or even four counties. Since the survey took no account of topography or other land features, it was often impossible to claim, within a surveyed parcel of 160 acres, a particular stand of timber and a hillside spring; the line may simply and arbitrarily have fallen between them.

The Kirchner family, then, must have been dismayed to find themselves on the wrong side of two quarter-section lines, lines that separated them from both the timber along the river and the mill seat. By chance the lines that divided section 32 into quarters fell such that the cabin wound up in the northwest quarter of the section, the desired timber along the river in the southeast quarter, and the mill seat in the northeast quarter. Gust and his family could buy the entire section and still wind up with only a little of the timber, or they could move. The family considered their situation, and, empowered with the knowledge of the exact survey lines, selected a new site for a new claim half a mile east across the river, a claim that would encompass much of the best woodland along the Little Sioux.

Peterson became a town in part because the Kirchners' first cabin wound up in the wrong quarter section. Wanting the timber and mill seat in their claim, and being forced to move across the river to get them, the family built their second cabin at a place not only on the same claim as the timber, but also at a place excellent for a town site. Here the family claimed, and soon bought, all of section 33 plus the east half of section 32, which included the mill seat. The center of section 33 would later be the site of Peterson.

George Temple could hardly have packed his survey compass and moved on to the next township when Gust headed back to Cedar Falls for supplies and also, apparently, to encourage others to join him and his family along the Little Sioux. In early October, Gust returned west laden with foodstuffs—and no doubt nails, hinges, and windows for the new cabin—and with the James Bicknell family, to whom he had sold—sight unseen—the 160-acre claim where the cabin stood.

Jane Bicknell was eighteen when she traveled west with her parents that year. Her cryptic diary survives: "Oct 1, 56. Father, mother and I are on our way to the Little Sioux. Started Sept 30. Last night we camped at Parot's grove. There are three teams of us. Mr. Kirchner that lives on the Little Sioux has agreed to take us out there and let us have his claim for $260.00."

It is a puzzling entry. Inasmuch as the Kirchners had not yet had to pay a cent for either claim, it strikes me as odd that Gust would expect payment and that the Bicknells would essentially agree to pay twice for the land, once to Gust and later to the U.S. government, which itself had only officially come into possession of it, by virtue of the survey, just days earlier. The price itself seems fair; at the time U.S. government lands were bringing $1.25 an acre, making an ordinary claim of 160 acres worth $200; adding $60 for the cabin was probably reasonable considering the labor and materials involved in building it and their rarity this far west on the frontier. Perhaps Jane is accurate as to the price but not to whom it would be paid; $200 would go to the government for the land and $60 to the Kirchners for the cabin. In any event, the deal was amicable; Jane and Gust would be married the next year.

The Kirchners quickly set to work on the new cabin as the Bicknells prepared to move into the old. The new dwelling went up in what is today the northwest corner of Peterson. Writes Charlotte: "All hands were now doubly busy, as they wanted to build the new house and move before cold weather, there was no time to lose. The new house was built about a half a mile from the first one, on the opposite side of the river, near the foot of a hill with a deep ravine at the west. A little east of the house site a spring of purest water bubbled up, partly from the bluff and partly [from] the flat ground below. This furnished an abundance of water and never froze. The second house was like the first in size and style, a fair shelter from the now fast approaching winter."

That year the Kirchners, the Meads, and the Bicknells were not the only people to build cabins in the region.

Eighteen-fifty-six marks the beginning of the so-called pioneer era on the lands of northwest Iowa. In towns along the Mississippi and in places back east, new words, new place names, entered the vernacular: Sioux City, Spirit Lake, the Raccoon River—or "Coon" as most call it, even today—and the Little Sioux. As the Ohio Country had earlier and like Dakota would a few years later, northwest Iowa began to draw the attention of a land-hungry nation and of Euro-American settlers with visions of neat farms, towns, and cities.

Considered very little in this movement toward the north and west were prior claims to the region; forgotten in this early dash to the Little Sioux was the fact that a handful of other people were still here and that they had another name for the river: Ea-ne-ah Wau-de-pon. The legal claims of all the Sioux peoples had been officially extinguished by treaty in 1851, but not all tribal groups concurred. Even as the Kirchners were at work on their cabin, hunting parties of Yankton and Wahpekute Sioux ranged across northwest Iowa seeking dwindling deer, bison, and other game. These were to be the last days of hunting by Native Americans on the northwest Iowa prairies.

In 1856, up and down the Little Sioux, along the Missouri River to the west and the Raccoon to the south, small groups of settlers pulled their wagons to rest in the shade of native trees along prairie rivers. Within minutes of unhitching oxen from heavy wagons, they set to work in classic frontier fashion, building shelter. And like the Euro-American settlers before them, who built towns along the Ohio, the Mohawk, the Shennendoah, these people built cabins of logs.

The Kirchners and other settlers along the timbered stretches of these prairie rivers were among the last to live out the story of the Euro-American log-cabin frontier. The means of settlement, and the entire structure of the endeavor, would soon change as fast-building new railroads overshot any notion of a "frontier" or a "line" of settlement.

Peterson, or Long Grove as the Kirchners first knew it, stood at a point of both spatial and temporal change on the classic frontier. The cabins built here were among the last of the log-cabin frontier, a frontier that, in many minds at least, extended back to the very first European settlement on the eastern seaboard of the continent. Almost everywhere east of here, settlers had begun their new lives in thick-walled, hand-hewn log cabins; by 1856, people everywhere were turning away from this heavy and slow construction method as canals and railroads began to bring milled lumber and manufactured building materials to growing towns and rural areas. Within a few short years, the railroad would bring a new sort of Euro-American frontier to the lands of Dakota; if the log cabin symbolizes the earlier frontier, surely the tar paper shack and the balloon frame cottage must symbolize the dwellings of the frontier further west and a few years later.

Sometime in November, seventeen-year-old Jacob was dispatched to Cedar Falls, the nearest place of any size, for supplies. He traveled with two older men who lived up the valley. The fall had lingered that year, and the prairie was open and free of snow, so the men assumed they would have an easy journey with wagons and oxen. They had covered the 140 miles to Cedar Falls and over half the way back to the cabins on the Little Sioux with their supplies when the first blizzard of the season overtook them. The wind-driven snow accumulated quickly on the matted prairie, and very soon the men were forced to abandon wagons and provisions in hopes of saving their lives.

They arranged to leave their livestock with a settler on Lizard Creek, but before they could resume their trip on foot, a second storm engulfed them. According to Charlotte's letters, the men huddled in the unprotected wagons on the prairie for three nights until the storm abated. Finally, when the weather cleared and the wind died, and after preparing food for the fifty-mile trip, they left the wagons and started for home on foot over hard miles of deep prairie snow.

Charlotte later wrote her daughter of the ordeal: "For three days they struggled on through the snowdrifts before they reached the Little Sioux river. They rested in holes dug in the snowbanks, and became so exhausted and discouraged that they were repeatedly at the point of giving up. Finally Mr. Bell declared that he could not take another step and that the snowbank should be his grave. After vainly trying to persuade him to follow them, your uncle drew his pistol and said that he'd shoot him if he did not get up and march on. He started then and when they really saw the trees on the bank of the river he was ahead of them all."

The waiting family had almost given up on Jacob by the time he returned.

"Only that morning father had said, 'I thought and dreamed about the boy all night; I am afraid that we must give him up. I know they must have started back before the storm and no one could live on the prairie in such a blizzard.'"

But Jacob did return, late on the 23rd of December, with feet badly frostbitten; it was months before he could walk without pain.

Storm followed storm across the prairies that year: heavy snow, great winds, arctic temperatures. Perhaps no winter since has equalled the winter of 1856 and 1857 in northwest Iowa. On January 18, 1857, Fort Ripley, Minnesota, registered a low of minus fifty degrees Fahrenheit. The blizzards that year are credited with wiping out the last of the elk in Iowa.

Though the families on the Little Sioux were in little danger of actual starvation, winter, without the supplies left back on the trail to Cedar Falls, was a lean time. They had earlier provided well for themselves, and now most families cautiously shared their larder with others who had less so that no lives were threatened.

Charlotte remembered that winter: "In all the annals of Iowa there has never been recorded a severer winter—such quantities of snow, such fierce winds and such intense cold. It was a winter that would have been a trial in a furnace heated house with all modern conveniences, near a well stocked store and without any fear of famine, wild beasts or savage Indians."

And there were Indians to contend with, people a good deal more hungry and cold than the new settlers. While the Kirchners, Bicknells, and Meads were trying to stay warm as they awaited word of Jacob's fate, a band of beleaguered Wahpekute Sioux, probably hungry through much of the fall because of a lack of game and now probably desperate because of the ferocity of the winter, was camped along the river not far from the Bicknell cabin.

Jane Bicknell wrote in her diary on December 16, 1856: "The Indians were in here again this morning to get something more to eat. After they had gone an old squaw came in and I helped her take off her blanket and she stayed here a spell and we gave her something to eat. . . . Father went over to Mr. Kirchner's to have Gust come over here. . . . Found the old squaw here, gave her something to take with her and then Gust told her to 'puche-kee' which is Indian for 'go.' Then he put on her bonet and pinned her blanket around her. Father took her budget and carried it a little ways for her and then put it on her back and came back. We could hear her cry a great ways. She was so lame she could scarcely go. There was thirty Indians been here in all. In the evening Gust brought his singing book over and we had a sing."

They had arrived late in the fall, just before the storms of that violent winter came on. These Wahpekute Sioux, a branch of the Santee Sioux, were led by Inkpaduta, a minor leader among the tribes, and as the blizzards came, were camped close to the Bicknells. Probably the Wahpekute had camped in this hollow along the river before; no doubt they recognized it as a place safe from the winter blast. What did they think this year when they found a new cabin here?

Wrote Charlotte: "We had been very eager to see Indians. Late in November they came to the house, one or two at a time, to beg food. There were several tepees in the shelter of the woods near the river, and near the Bicknell house. . . . They were very friendly and did not molest the cattle nor anything else that belonged to the settlers. One day an Indian offered a bright ten-dollar gold piece for our nice dog, but the dog was not for sale. They smoked the peace pipe, and once one of them offered me a paper of pins. . . . We were not at all afraid of them after a few days, although I think we were never quite sure that it was safe to trust them."

Neither group had much trust in the other, and what little there had been was soon betrayed.

The Wahpekutes moved south as soon as the weather eased enough to travel, probably sometime in January, probably in search of game, but weren't long in returning upriver.

After some disturbance with new settlers near Smithland, sixty miles downstream on the Little Sioux, the group of about seventy Wahpekutes—some sixty women and children and ten men—returned up the Little Sioux in February. Among the men, at least, the mood had changed. All along the river, from its mouth at the Missouri clear to Spirit Lake, there were new cabins, new in the last year, a peppering of settlers that the Wahpekutes knew was the start of a great flood. There was little game, in part because of hunting on the part of the settlers, but also because of the severe winter. Now the snow lay deep, and the Wahpekutes were no less hungry than the whites, and perhaps a good deal more so. They must have grown ever more angry at the presence of these invaders.

Years later, Charlotte remembered the time: "On the morning of February fifteenth we knew that the savages were camped a half mile away, but what they might do we did not know.

"Everyone was watching the path to the woods from which the Indians would come. Soon nine warriors appeared, walking single file, hideous in their war paint. Gust opened the door as if to welcome a friend and the dog rushed out, barking. They shot the dog and pointed their guns at Gust. John stepped back and said, 'Father, they have shot Gust,' but a moment later Gust came in smiling and the fierce band with him. First of all, they took the only two guns in sight and two of the Indians stood guard while the others plundered the house.

"One of our oxen had died a short while before and the carcass had been brought to the house to be fed to the pigs and chickens. They saw this meat and by signs ordered some to be cooked. Someone understood and soon a kettle was filled and boiling. The meat was hardly thawed before they were ready to eat it. They had found a jug of molasses, which they poured onto their plates and in which they sopped the meat, which was still dripping blood.

They ate and ate, using their fingers, and presented a sight so disgusting that I can never forget it. After this ravenous eating they acted less savage. They took, or were given, the pillow slips from the beds, in which each one place a few pounds of flour or meal.

"The next day, after shooting two oxen, which they left, they broke camp and went to the Mead home at the east end of Long Grove. We watched them as they passed the house on snow shoes. The squaws had great bundles strapped on their backs and often a papoose on top. The dogs were harnessed to pole drags and were so heavily loaded that they had to be helped along. We counted about sixty squaws and papooses and ten warriors, and felt much relieved to see them move on, altho' we little knew what unspeakable horrors we were escaping."

The group moved upstream late in February of 1857, the men growing more bellicose as they went. At the Meads', they ransacked the cabin and kept two women briefly as captives, then released them unharmed. They traveled upstream, terrorizing settlers at Linn Grove and Gillett Grove, and then moved on to Spirit Lake.

No one knows just what triggered the massacre at Spirit Lake. Inkpaduta left no memoirs, and the Euro-American versions, especially as they relate to Native American motivations, are unreliable. Whether it began because of built-up anger over white settlement, hunger, the loss of game, an altercation with a settler there, or simply the shock of seeing several new cabins on the shores of the Okoboji and Spirit lakes—a holy spot for the Sioux—we can never know. Whatever the cause, early in March 1857, Inkpaduta and his men killed thirty-four settlers and took four captives, two of whom were later killed and two released.

The interactions leading up to the Spirit Lake Massacre, like so many others between whites and Native Americans on the frontier, were characterized by mistrust and ignorance on both sides as to the other's tenets regarding possession of land, general social conduct, and trade.

The Santee Sioux—Inkpaduta's people—had signed the treaty of 1851 relinquishing all claim to lands in parts of Minnesota and western and northwestern Iowa. For the land they were to be paid ten cents per acre and were promised annual issues of blankets, firearms, and provisions. But much of the money and most of the material was waylaid by private traders. Inkpaduta's demands for food from the settlers may have had as much to do with retribution against the whites for unfulfilled promises as it had to do with hunger.

Euro-American writers have said that Inkpaduta took no stock in the treaties that bound this land over to the

U.S. government. Perhaps he wanted no part of them, even though most of the rest of his people had moved west and north to find game and escape the coming settlement. Perhaps he felt his people's claims to this place, in spite of the treaty, still far exceeded those of these new cabin-builders. His people had hunted and traveled here for several generations. He knew the lands to the east were filling up, and now he saw the same happening here. The game was gone; his people were hungry.

Certainly the new settlers felt they had every right to settle on this land—it was owned by the U.S. government, was it not? Clearly, too, they felt their Christian ways superior to and more civilized than those of the Santee Sioux, and they were afraid of these people, who, to them, seemed entirely brutal and unpredictable.

The Spirit Lake Massacre ended the brief history of Native American and Euro-American interactions on the line of the frontier in northwest Iowa. Inkpaduta and his people are said to have moved west after the killings; some accounts have him, as a very old man, fighting Custer at the Little Big Horn.

In years to come, even as late as the turn of the century, the Euro-Americans who settled around Peterson saw some Native Americans, usually as they passed through following the pathway of the Little Sioux River valley. Sometimes they camped along the river below the town, as Ida Sitz Martin recalled from her childhood in the 1890s: "They would camp sometimes in the spring, and sometimes in the fall. While here the medicine men would go to the timber and gather roots, leaves, and different things to make their medicine with. Some I remember they used for dyes for their painted faces: blood root, ginseng, foxglove, slippery elm bark and many more. I remember one of the Indians giving mother a gray shawl."

And if there are people of Native American blood living in the area today, they have blended into the culture of the late twentieth century on the former prairie.

Long ago, a child, when very young, observed a certain star in the heavens, which he regarded more than all others. As he grew up, his attachments for the star increased, and his mind became more and more set upon it. When able, he went out to hunt, and while traveling, weary and alone, not having very good success, this favorite star came down to him, and conversed with him, and conducted him to a place where he found bear, and plenty of game. After this he was always a great hunter.

—Ioway Indian story

A very near approximation to a true meridian, and consequently to the variation, may be had, by remembering that the pole star very nearly reaches the true meridian, when it is in the same vertical plane with the star Alioth in the tail of the Great Bear, which lies nearest the four stars forming the quadrilateral.

—Instructions to the Surveyors General of Public Lands, 1855

Chapter 11

Gods in the Soil

Though Inkpaduta must have felt strong bonds with this land, his people, the Wahpekute, a small tribe of the Santee Sioux, had had only a short and passing history in what became northwest Iowa. While many native groups have lived in their ancestral homes for hundreds—even thousands—of years, the Sioux were comparative newcomers to the area. In the early eighteenth century, the Santee, Yankton, and Teton Sioux tribes were pushed out of their villages near Mille Lacs in east-central Minnesota by better-armed tribes to the east. The Sioux had been a woodland tribe of hunters, gatherers, and farmers; in fact, "Wahpekute" is said to mean "Shooters among the Leaves."

The Teton peoples went west to Nebraska, the Dakotas, Wyoming, and Montana, displacing several other tribes. With the advent of the horse, the Teton Sioux emerged as the classic buffalo culture when they rose to become the dominant cultural force in the northern Great Plains prior to white invasion.

The Yankton and Santee moved south and west, the Yankton settling in eastern South Dakota and the Santee spreading out along the Minnesota River in southwest Minnesota. By about 1750, both groups must have ranged well into northwest Iowa on hunting journeys, and the Sioux peoples claimed the territory as their own. In 1804, Lewis and Clark reported contact with the Yankton and described them as a nomadic tribe that hunted "between the Missourie & River Desmoin, on the Little River Sioux." In 1850, a Major William Willams, later of Fort Dodge, estimated that there were 150 lodges of Sioux living, hunting, and traveling across northwest Iowa, none of them apparently in permanent villages.

The Santee tribal groups did not migrate into a vacuum as they expanded their hunting range across northwest Iowa; they were enemies of the Ioway Indians and certainly must have clashed with them. But, like the Santee, the Ioways—and the Otoes and Omaha—had little real control over or interest in the land of northwest Iowa. Then, as now, this region was off the beaten path; not exactly unclaimed, the prairie here was central to no tribe of historical times.

The Sioux tenure here was fairly short, perhaps a hundred and fifty years, and they established nothing more permanent than migratory hunting camps. In fact, among hundreds of archaeological sites in the region, archaeologists ascribe none to the Sioux; evidence of their time here is found only in the historical record and in the odd discovery of isolated Sioux artifacts.

The Little Sioux valley was a natural home for people who didn't travel by pickup truck and get their food from California like we do today. There has always been water here and at least some wood to furnish fuel and shelter. And while it took a steel plow finally to cleave the prairie sod, there have always been open, alluvial soils along the river, seedbeds suitable for cropping with wood and bone tools. To several prehistoric cultures, the prairie, woodlands, and bottomlands of the region provided bison and other game, ample fish, clay for pottery, plant materials for baskets and mats, plus stones, feathers, flowers, leaves, and shells enough for a vivid ceremonial life.

It is also a natural pathway. It makes a sheltered, though less than direct, route from the Missouri River on the southwest to the lakes and rivers of Minnesota to the northeast, and the deep valley would provide cover from enemies, protection lacking on the open prairie.

Northwest Iowa has been home to numerous cultures since the time of first human occupancy here, thought to be some 12,000 years ago. There is little doubt that humans hunted mammoth in the shadow of the glacial ice. Small bands of nomadic Clovis people ranged widely across North America toward the end of the Wisconsinan age; they grew no crops and had no way of storing food against shortage and so were impelled by aching bellies to follow the herds wherever they went. Archaeologists have never found a Clovis campsite in Iowa; Clovis people apparently never stayed in one place around here long enough to leave sufficient trace for scientists to discover a hundred and twenty centuries later. What we know of the Clovis and other ancient peoples here comes from discoveries of spear points and other scattered artifacts.

Unimaginably ancient Clovis spear points and only slightly newer Archaic ax heads turn up once in a great while among field rocks and soil. They seem to appear during planting season after a field has been disked and when farmers move most slowly over bare ground. The event of such a find turns a field stone into a mystic tool used inconceivably long ago by a people we can hardly picture. My mind balks at the gulf between the eight-row corn planter and tractor halted in the middle of a field and a hunting party of skin-clad people hacking a freshly killed mammoth into portable pieces. Could it actually have happened here, on this spot?

Much later, other peoples came, and they left a more certain imprint on the region. At about the time of Christ, a culture now called Woodland developed on sites scattered across the Midwest. They established villages in northwest Iowa and lived here successfully, and apparently comfortably, for nearly a thousand years. The landmarks these people left are well known. They built the Effigy Mounds in eastern Iowa and thousands of more ordinary ones scattered across the Midwest. Woodland people brought with them the ability to make pottery, a skill that today makes understanding their culture a great deal easier. Few artifacts survive as well as ceramics, and no other artifacts so vividly recall the individual work of their creators.

Other groups arose, probably out of Woodland peoples, including the Great Oasis and the Oneota, who are considered ancestors to the Ioway Indians of historic times, and the Mill Creek, who for about four hundred years called the Little Sioux valley their home.

These groups left hundreds if not thousands of archaeological sites sprinkled across northwest Iowa. There are bison-butchering sites, old villages, encampments, cemeteries, and probably ceremonial sites. Only a few sites have been methodically excavated and studied; others are at least known and mapped; some are as yet only hinted at by subtle surface marks or variations in soil coloration. Others must lie buried beneath alluvium, or more modern deposits, and may never be found. It should not surprise us that everywhere we turn there is a place of ancient occupancy; people have lived here for a hundred and twenty centuries. I sometimes imagine that under my every footstep, whether on town sidewalk, plowed field, or nature trail, must be secrets left by those who lived here long before section lines, high school basketball, and rural free delivery.

These people left broken pottery, abandoned or lost stone tools, and the bones of butchered animals in their middens; haunting, maddening, tiny facts that lead only to a universe of new questions. Did the children play rough one day and knock over this vessel? Were these stone tools abandoned, or were their owners killed or run off by invaders? Was someone angry at herself for misplacing this hide scraper, not seen since the buffalo hunt last fall? In museum drawers there are potsherds, collected and numbered, that bear the fingerprints of their unknown maker, pressed into the wet glaze a thousand years ago. When she finished this vessel, did she hold it up to the sun to look closely at it? Was she proud of her work?

The Mill Creek people intrigue me most. They lived here recently, as prehistoric events are measured, and more than any other culture before or since knew the Little Sioux valley and its tributaries—particularly the steep regions between Sioux Rapids and Cherokee—as home.

Archaeologists think the Mill Creek people emerged as a separate culture about A.D. 900, establishing their own village patterns and styles of pottery and tools. They lived in small villages scattered along the Big and Little Sioux river valleys and immediate tributaries and flourished here for about four hundred years, almost three times longer than Euro-Americans have been here.

According to archaeologists, the Mill Creek culture was a "distinct local development"; manifestations are not known outside of northwest Iowa. And these were not prairie peoples, since all of the known village sites are found in valleys. For reasons no one will ever know with certainty, Mill Creek peoples were particularly drawn to the deep, gorgelike valley of the Little Sioux River and its tributaries between Sioux Rapids and Cherokee. There are twenty-one known sites here, all within the valley complex and within twenty miles of Peterson. Like many prehistoric cultures, Mill Creek people left their faint imprints on the landscape and middens full of questions.

For a time archaeologists debated the origins of the Mill Creek people, for their appearance was somewhat sudden for such a distinct culture. The riddle is not altogether solved—and perhaps never will be—but most now agree that the Mill Creek people developed out of local Woodland and Great Oasis cultures and were not, as some had thought, the product of a long-distance migration from Cahokia, Illinois, and the large prehistoric culture flourishing there at the time.

Mill Creek villages were generally situated on the alluvial terraces of the Little Sioux or its tributaries. Most were at stream's edge, but a few were sited some distance above the river or creek, yet still within the valley complex. None were on the upland prairie outside the protection of the valley. The close proximity of the villages suggests that, while the Mill Creek people lived in separate communities, their larger cultural life may have relied on gatherings of people from all villages. Certainly they traveled among the villages easily, and the Little Sioux valley must have been crisscrossed with trails.

Much of what we know about Mill Creek people and culture comes from one village site carefully excavated in 1974. Archaeologists call this place Chan-ya-ta, which is said to be Siouan for "at the woods." Unlike many of the Mill Creek sites that are on the heavily farmed floodplain, and have therefore been disrupted, Chan-ya-ta is on a small ridge within the valley and has never been disturbed by more than grazing cattle.

Chan-ya-ta holds the top of a small pasture knob above Brooke Creek, some six miles southeast of Peterson. The site is small, surrounded by trees, with sharp ravines on three sides. The spot is easy to miss; it is one of dozens of likely sites for a prehistoric village in the area, and is only distinguishable by some fifteen faint surface depressions marking what were once probably dwellings. It has been 500 years since the Mill Creek people left this place; that there is yet some surface evidence of their lives is quite surprising.

Archaeologist Joseph Tiffany, who has done the greatest amount of study here, describes Chan-ya-ta as a "small hamlet." He thinks about fifty people lived here at a time, but no one knows what the Mill Creek people did with their dead. There is only one human burial associated with the site: that of a child found in a flexed position, buried in a simple grave without ceremonial objects, pigments, or adornment.

While archaeologists claim to excavate in search of answers, their work in fact always generates ever longer lists of questions. They stand on the island of what can be known and shovel soil into the sea of what cannot. Trowels seek answers, but in every potsherd or cell of carbonized seeds brought to light—in fact, in every shovelful of earth archaeologists carry and screen—only more questions arise about more unknown pasts. Who was this child? What was done with others who died here? What else is here that we cannot see or imagine?

Some years ago, a construction crew working beneath the streets of Anthon, Iowa, fifty miles downstream from Peterson in the Little Sioux valley, uncovered a skeleton. Murder was at first suspected, but examination proved the remains to be that of an adult Oneota woman, dead several hundred years. But there was an unusual aspect to the skeleton: archaeologists were startled to discover an arrowhead wedged between two of her vertebrae. The wound could not have killed her, for there was clear evidence of bone growth around the arrow point.

The arrowhead was Oneota. Was she wounded by her own people? Did someone's target practice go awry? What did the village healers do to relieve her pain?

I am always drawn by freshly turned soil. Whenever I plant a tree, walk across a freshly disked field, or stop at a place where a foundation is being dug, my eye scans the dirt, looking for things I cannot name. I have never found anything significant nor even particularly interesting, but I always look closely for what the soil might hide. Digging in the yard of a house we once owned, I frequently found artifacts of historic times: broken bricks, fragments of colored bottles, bits of broken teacups—even an enameled doorknob, once. These were unimportant artifacts, suggesting nothing more than the fact that our yard was fill, and not very clean fill, but I always reveled in my finds; somehow even a shard of ordinary window glass, no older than windows in our own house, for having been lost, buried, disconnected from its past, took on some quality of mystery.

The people of Chan-ya-ta and at other Mill Creek sites in the Little Sioux region were farmers, gatherers, fishers, and hunters, similar to many Native American tribes of historic times. They lived in semi-subterranean, rectangular, earthen lodges supported by tree branches, similar in many ways to those of later sedentary Plains tribes like the Mandan. Inside many of them, and scattered throughout the village, were storage pits for food. From these food caches comes much of the fragmentary evidence we have about Mill Creek subsistence.

Certainly the prairie sod was too tough to break with simple wood and bone tools, so their corn, squash, beans, and sunflower patches would have been staked out in the alluvial soil of the valley bottom. No doubt their gardens were sometimes washed away in summer floods, bringing lean times next winter. While their cultivated crops were the mainstay of their diet, bison played a great part as well. Even though there seem to have been deer and elk in the region at the time, the Mill Creek people had a preference for bison, as evidenced by the great numbers of bison bones found at the site and the comparative paucity of others. Nevertheless, the Mill Creek people did not hunt or rely on the bison in a fashion similar to the later Plains tribes. According to archaeologist Tiffany: "The fact that Mill Creek groups hunted bison is undeniable. It is highly improbable, though, given their deep river trench/farming orientation, that they would have spent a lot of time on the high plains or the rolling, tall-grass prairie hunting bison. Summer hunts of the magnitude of those recorded for historical Plains Village groups are not really feasible without the horse."

The prairies above and all around the Mill Creek people were probably of small import to them; certainly they gathered some materials and food here, but their lives were structured by the valley and its resources, its protection.

But why did they settle along just this part of the Little Sioux? Except for a number of sites along the Big Sioux River to the west, all of the known Mill Creek sites are along some thirty miles of the Little Sioux River or its immediate tributaries. One of the resources that may have attracted these people here could well have been the same that many years later sent Gust Kirchner back to New York to bring his family west: timber.

According to Tiffany: "It appears that the most important natural resources to Mill Creek groups were easily tillable soil, potable water, wood, and availability of large game (bison, elk, and deer). These factors are fundamentally related to the landforms of the region—the Mill Creek sites in the Little Sioux are confined to a section of the river valley where the trench is deepest. The landscape near the river in the section of the Little Sioux valley from Cherokee to Linn Grove is more rugged and consequently has more timber and game potential. Since the channel is narrow and meandering, flooding does occur periodically, supplying an easily tillable, fertile soil. Negative evidence is also supportive; that is, no Mill Creek sites are found on rivers with broad treeless valleys like the Floyd River, nor are any known from the headwaters area of the Little Sioux in the Iowa Lakes region, nor south from where the Little Sioux valley begins to broaden substantially at Correctionville."

When the first white families arrived here in 1856, they carefully sized up the resources before building cabins. To them, as to the Mill Creek people several hundred years before them, timber for homes and fuel was important, as was good agricultural land. The Kirchners knew they could break the prairie sod; Mill Creek people knew they didn't need to, given the abundance of alluvial soil. By 1856, game was but a small part of the diet of settlers in northwest Iowa; hunting pressure from the Indians to the west and the whites moving in from the east had all but killed off the large animals. The Kirchners, after all, were thinking of cattle, not deer and bison.

Today the bison are gone, of course, but in recent years, the deer have come back, especially since they no longer have natural predators. My great-grandmother Edna Johnson never saw a deer as a child and never got over the delight of seeing them flourish again in the late 1970s.

Archaeologists are of the mind that Chan-ya-ta and perhaps other Mill Creek sites were not occupied for the full 400 years the culture existed. In fact, Tiffany believes that Chan-ya-ta may have been occupied for a total of only twenty-five to thirty years spread out over that time. There is clear evidence at Chan-ya-ta that newer houses were built on the sites of the old, suggesting that people returned periodically to rebuild the old village and live there again.

Environmental degradation is the most likely cause of the Mill Creek people's periodic departures. The inhabitants may well have exhausted the timber, game, and available cropland and may have been forced to abandon sites to allow nature to replenish them. Though there was timber here and at the other village sites, even fairly small populations so dependent on wood for shelter and fuel could deplete a limited woodland in short order. Historic times provide a comparable example. The only thing that saved the Kirchner woods from destruction was the advent of the railroad: a bit of the forest of Wisconsin was cut and hauled to Peterson to build pine homes, and coal from Kentucky came to heat the homes, saving enough woodland that a forest preserve could later be established where the Kirchners and Meads once cut logs for cabins.

Subtle evidence from another Mill Creek site in the region reinforces the possibility that Mill Creek people degraded the area enough from time to time to force them to move out. Here, near the bottom level of the site, archaeologists found the bones of a particular species of squirrel that prefers hardwood forests; higher and newer layers yielded bone evidence of another species of squirrel, one that finds its home in brushy thickets. It suggests that woodland was heavily cut in the area, and then grew up to brush and second growth, much less useful for building lodges and heating them.

Even though archaeologists have unearthed, studied, cataloged, and filed thousands of artifacts from Mill Creek sites, we know very little of Mill Creek material culture; only things made of stone, pottery, and bone have survived several hundred or even a thousand years in the Iowa soil. No doubt they employed grasses to weave baskets and mats and used wood for myriad practical and ceremonial purposes. Grasses, feathers, leaves, animal skins, soft stones and hard, sand, seeds, bark, shells, flowers—it was an environment rich in raw materials, rich in possibilities for decorative and practical applications. I wonder about individual tastes in the decoration of clothing, lodges adorned with personal items, and children playing with dolls made of corn husks. There must have been family heirlooms, even for a people who lived without furniture, snapshots, or mass-produced figurines.

Nevertheless, there are some strong clues about Mill Creek aesthetic life. Their pottery takes many forms—probably as many forms as there once were Mill Creek potters. Many of the clay bowls and jars unearthed at various sites have handles that are effigy heads and tails. A bowl might be a raccoon, the handle on one end being the head, the other the striped tail. Many sites reveal clay and bone objects that must have had decorative, ceremonial, or entertainment purposes. Bone ear spools, circular objects of painted clay, drilled and carved deer toe bones all must have been worn by certain tribal members or may have been game pieces for some long-forgotten game used to pass the time on a cold winter afternoon in a warm lodge.

Sometime about A.D. 1300, the Mill Creek people left their villages on the Little Sioux for good. Archaeologists suggest some possible reasons. Beginning about A.D. 1250, the climate became hotter and drier, perhaps causing food shortages. Combined with human-caused environmental degradation, a few years of poor conditions may have been enough to cause the Mill Creek people's hegira.

Another theory involves trouble between Mill Creek people and another group in the region—the Oneota. It is clear from pottery found at many sites in the area that Mill Creek people did not trade ceramics with the neighboring Oneota. Mill Creek sites contain no Oneota pottery, and vice versa, suggesting enmity between them. In addition, about a third of the Mill Creek village sites show evidence of fortification; Chan-ya-ta is protected on three sides by ravines, and on the fourth it appears that the residents dug a ditch. Clearly the Mill Creek people were worried about someone. Archaeologists think it likely that pressure from the Oneota was responsible, at least in part, for the out-migration of the Mill Creek.

Radiocarbon dating of artifacts from village sites and other evidence provide reinforcement for this theory.

Carbon-14 decay tests indicate that Mill Creek people had altogether left northwest Iowa by about A.D. 1400; shortly after, the Oneota established a village north of Cherokee near the center of former Mill Creek territory.

No one can be exactly sure about just where they went, but several scholars, Tiffany among them, think the Mill Creek people might have gone west, up the Missouri River, and blended in with the Mandan and Hidatsa tribes. There are considerable material and cultural similarities, suggesting a strong connection.

The Oneota were by no means newcomers to northwest Iowa. Archaeologists think they emerged as a distinct culture around A.D. 1000, probably rising from the great prehistoric culture at Cahokia, Illinois. Oneota villages were larger than those of Mill Creek and much more widely distributed; Mill Creek people preferred to live in small villages in close proximity to one another, while Oneota villages were larger and broadly dispersed all across Iowa and in parts of Wisconsin, Illinois, Missouri, Nebraska, and Minnesota. The Oneota and their descendants lived in what became Iowa for nearly nine hundred years, some thirty-six generations.

And unlike the Mill Creek, the Oneota seem to have adapted better to the change in climate that occurred around A.D. 1250. Evidence from their village sites suggests that when croplands began to dry up, they farmed less and hunted more; later Oneota sites reveal less in the way of grown crops and more in the way of large mammal bones, indicating a shift in food habits as they adapted to new circumstances.

A few Oneota sites reveal something new: first contact with European goods. Mixed with potsherds and flint chips in later village sites are glass trade beads, copper and brass, and metal utensils, suggesting that as early as the late sixteenth century, such goods had made their way here from European sources, hinting of great changes to come.

Scholars in several fields have puzzled over the connections between prehistoric native cultures—those we know only from archaeological evidence—and the historic Indian tribes. Of course, to any culture where written history is merely a stepchild of oral tradition, the connections are obvious, and the concerns of archaeologists, anthropologists, and historians are thought of as oddly pointless. The Hopi are certain they are descendants of the Anasazi; why look further? But European rationalism makes certain proof necessary.

Such proof is hard to come by. Connections among groups of people are best traced through similarities of language patterns, something that can be done only with living groups like the Cherokee or Sioux. Nobody has any idea what language the long-extinct Mill Creek people spoke. Scholars must instead compare the material cultures—arrow points, pottery, dwelling construction—left by both the prehistoric and the historic peoples in hope of forming some link.

Other clues come from geography. At times archaeologists and historians can plot concordances of archaeological sites of a particular group with the village sites of certain tribes at the time of first white contact. Using old maps—often wildly inaccurate—and the diary entries of people who were themselves using those maps—and therefore lost much of the time—scholars have, nonetheless, been able to pinpoint the locations of certain Indian villages. The crucial questions are, where were the villages, and who was living in them when the first French traders stepped into the firelight to share the pipe?

Using such evidence, scholars have formed a strong link between the prehistoric Oneota and the historic Ioway Indians; the Oneota clearly seem to be the ancestors of the Ioway and several other tribes. Mildred Mott made the first foray in 1938 when she linked them by means of comparing known Oneota sites with Ioway village sites mentioned in the earliest historical records of Iowa. She found strong correlations, and, in the years since, the connection has been strengthened by various means to become accepted fact.

In a sense, certain groups of Oneota became Ioway by virtue of the sudden appearance of visiting whites; they moved instantly from the sphere of the prehistoric to the historic. The Oneota didn't notice their transition to Ioway; certainly their name for themselves didn't change with the advent of these strangers seeking buffalo hides and beaver pelts.

In 1700 the lives of the Ioway were little different from those of their ancestral Oneota. They lived in semipermanent villages scattered widely and thinly across the state, farmed and hunted, often ranging far from home, and by then enjoyed some of the benefits of the Euro-Americans' metal and glass.

But change was coming. By about 1750, they had acquired the horse, and although this greatly extended their hunting range, they never turned their backs on agriculture. Soon smallpox reduced their numbers, and by 1830 they had ceded their lands in Iowa and moved south, squeezed out by the Sioux to the north and west, and by whites and the Sac and Mesquakie (Fox) tribes to the east. The Ioway, who had lived in Iowa for as long as nine hundred years and who would give the state its name, were displaced to Missouri, Kansas, and Nebraska, and finally to Oklahoma.

Then, for a short time, about twenty years, it seems northwest Iowa had no permanent residents. The widely scattered Ioway village sites disappeared into the prairie, while hunting parties of Sioux roamed freely over open country in pursuit of bison, deer, and elk. How many people wandered back and forth across the region, no one can know, but in all those grassy miles a few bands of traveling hunters would dissolve into the prairie. Free from all their enemies, the Yankton and Santee doubtless thought little about the smoke from their cooking fires giving away their presence; their next and last enemy was the white race, who were still in the act of crossing the Mississippi River to the east.

This is the time I think of most. It was a sort of interlude, a time between, a moment when few lived here and few traveled through. Certainly back through the eons of prehistory there were many times, longer times, when humans were so few in this area, but this time seems so real for being so recent. What few trails there had been grew back to grass; in fact, white surveyors and settlers reported only a handful of faint paths when they began arriving after 1850. There were as yet no green lumber towns and no longer any sprawling Indian villages, no barking dogs, no squash patches, no cornfields of any kind.

Very many good quarter sections were spoiled by being driven full of stakes and gorgeously displayed on paper, while the only perceptible improvements were the aforementioned stakes, and the only citizens gophers, who held the lots by right of possession, and who seriously objected to having their range intercepted with cottonwood stakes.

—N. Levering, "Recollections of the Early Settlement of Northwestern Iowa," 1871

Chapter 12

Townbuilding

JANUARY 31

This morning the thermometer stands at seven above; the ground is hard as iron, and the gray snow and ice are only a little softer. The sky is a great clear dome, filling every shadow with blue. Throughout the day, thin, high cirrus clouds will move smartly out of the west, aloft on great winds. They will pass hour by hour, quickly, and will leave nothing but more hard blue sky in their wake. The eastbound jets that pass over will arrive early in Chicago, Cleveland, and Pittsburgh, pushed by intense jet-stream winds. Those going west will be diverted to routes north and south to avoid fuel-consuming headwinds.

We've had snowfalls, some substantial, some mere skiffs, a couple icy and wet. It is deeper on the lee sides of everything, but thanks to a wet, heavy snowfall a couple of weeks back, the fields are covered with about eight inches, making it a painfully bright landscape, even under the low sun of January.

Rod's cornfield offers a chance for a study of the variety in snow. Different kinds of snow abound in the area, varieties that Arctic dwellers could probably differentiate and name. We had a sleet storm recently that sealed the older snow like a thin sugar glaze seals a cake. This stuff will never again drift before the wind. But since the sleet fell, we've had a skiff of fresh snow—maybe it would measure half an inch—that now blows across the icy layer looking for a crack or low place to lodge. This loose snow is pretty worn; the flake points are broken off, and a handful of it looks more like sand grains than snow. Looking toward the sun in the south, differences in the sheen are apparent. The fresher snow collects in little drifts, making dull patches on the shinier ice layer.

The roadside ditch beside the cornfield is filled with a couple of months' accumulation of fine-grained, siltlike snow that has settled itself into a consolidated mass. The snowplow has passed recently, widening the track, and has shoved and broken it into large irregular chunks. The blocks are strong and light for snow; this must be igloo snow. As I walk among them, the chunks rub together with a sound like that of one cinder block being pulled across another. Leaning against a fence wire is a piece of it pushed up by the plow; the wire's heat and vibration have sawn through three-quarters of the block.

Rows of chopped-off broom handles stick up through the snow. I remember that these were once huge, green corn plants, but it is impossible to believe that anything ever grew here. It seems a century ago that the climate changed and all living things disappeared, leaving only ice.

The snow is a sort of parchment, similar to the land itself in the way marks made by humans and others upon it can be read by those who come later. On the frozen river and adjacent banks today is a welter of marks. Snowmobile tracks run down the center of the channel, curving back and forth to follow the bends; amid them are cross-country ski tracks. Deer paths creep out of the brush on either side and warily cross the river, and my own footprints from my last visit are still faintly visible. Dog tracks, rabbit tracks, and those of a mouse, probably awakened by a growling stomach, make their purposeful ways through the bottomland.

The mouse first stuck its nose up out of a big clump of reed canary grass, made a few tentative steps into the open, gained in confidence, and crossed open terrain in a series of short hops. I can see where its cold paws hit the loose snow, even its tiny tail print, as it scurried across a path made by a snowmobile and worked its way around some other clumps of grass to disappear some twenty-five feet from where it started, vanishing into an old deer footprint melted out by the sun. I look into the hole to find matted grass, but nothing looks back at me. This mouse is spending a comfortable winter beneath the snow. The loose mat of grass, buried in snow, is an open network of food and shelter; a mouse, or more likely thousands of mice, move, stay warm, and eat grass seeds, protected and never needing to show themselves to hungry owls or hawks. Indeed, this mouse left a one-way trail, and there are no other trails popping up anywhere nearby.

It is possible to read some of the activity in town by snow prints as well. The stuff is pretty well stomped down in many places or piled up out of the way, but the age of a path and its frequency of use are still pretty easy to see where kids cross a backyard on the way home from school or where Swede Rohrbaugh parks the elevator fuel truck in the same place in front of his house every noon. At one place in town I find a surprising rectangle of snow-free ground, a glimpse back to late fall and dead grasses. Fresh wheel tracks leading away from the rectangle reveal the source as a recently moved automobile, one that had sat still since before the first snows fell.

A long drive north of town makes clear that little is happening in agriculture. A few farmers are out doing livestock chores, but most places are free of outdoor human activity. Nobody goes outside who doesn't have to. I wonder if farmers watch afternoon game shows in the winter. Traffic is very light, on gravel and blacktop roads alike.

Late in the afternoon, the sun streams in the small front windows at the café. I am late enough that Jean Saunders has already drained the last of the coffee, so I sip decaffeinated instant. My boots, like those of a couple of other customers, leave puddles on the floor.

The place is warm, too warm really, and patrons sit in relation to the heating stove according to their thermal needs, some close and others distant. Sue is making closing-up noises around the café, so I tip my cup and head for the door just as the sun dips behind the Masonic lodge across the street. As I close the door behind me, I notice that the Christmas wreath is still on the front door.

At a quarter to five at the elevator, the low sun still slants in the west windows of the office. Though no one comments on it as they put trucks away and begin to close up, everyone seems relieved that the sun is beginning to make its slow way north again.

On a summer day in 1941, some of Peterson's sagacious businessmen pass the time on the sidewalk of Main Street. At left, with his back to the camera, is the author's great-grandfather, Art Johnson. Photograph courtesy of Peterson Heritage.

Starting with the construction of their cabin in the fall of 1856, the Kirchner family made a primitive, make-do farm life for themselves on the alluvial terrace that was later to become Peterson. Since for the early years the nearest resupply point was Cedar Falls, 140 miles east, what they didn't have, they simply did without. Like pioneers before them to the east, they built furniture for their cabins, made baskets of willows, used dull files for ice skate runners, and, after oat harvest, collected the fresh straw and wove it into men's and women's hats.

That first spring, 1857, Gust and his brothers turned the prairie sod for the garden and for crops. It wasn't the first sod broken here; the first came the year before, when Gust, Jacob, and Ambrose Mead chopped holes in the prairie to plant seeds and then went back east to retrieve their families. Of the new, more formal plot near their home, Charlotte later wrote: "The first breaking was a large garden near the house, which Grandmother and Grandfather took as their own special care, and the little seed bags that had been so carefully selected in the East, and stored in a strong bag, were brought out, and the busy parents planned their first garden for their new home. . . . In all that catalogue of seed, if they had been catalogued, there were even apple seeds."

Breaking ground for garden or crops, the men drove six oxen each on two big breaking plows in order to cut the prairie sod; sisters Charlotte and Lena followed, dropping handfuls of corn at three-foot intervals for "sod corn."

And so new lives took shape in a new place.

Gust had been wooing Jane Bicknell since he brought her family west in the fall of 1856, and Jane's diary reports his eventual success: "We was married Oct 17, 1857, went to Ft. Dodge with one ox team. Was gone from home 7 days."

A month later, Gust had finished building a new log house a few yards east of his parents', and he and his bride moved in. Wrote Jane: "Cabin 24 by 16. A span of horses, a yoke of oxen, a colt, 5 cows, 2 calves, 2 pigs, 3 chickens, one breaking plow, one common plough, table, chairs, stove, 60 yds coton cloth. . . . I think we are very well situated." Elsewhere she reports, "When we commenced had 30 acres of breaking, 2 big wagons, one shed and provisions to last a year easy, and about $375 in money lent."

Of the 320 acres Gust and Jane owned, 80 were timber, encompassing the best of the woodland along the Little Sioux. In addition, their land encompassed nearly all of what would later become Peterson.

A year later, in 1858, Jane again took stock of their worldly goods and marked an increase of one horse, three cows, four pigs, ten chickens, 500 bushels of corn, 150 bushels of potatoes, 15 bushels of carrots, 10 bushels of rutabagas, a bushel of beans, and a half-bushel of onions. The prairie soil was beginning to share its prosperity.

Clay County was organized at Peterson in an election held October 12, 1858; the polling place was Ambrose Mead's cabin south of the river at the east end of the woodland. Party loyalties were evenly split with nine registered Republicans and nine Democrats. Of the eighteen men who voted in the election, fourteen were elected to some office.

Year by year, settlers from the East came to the Little Sioux to scout for good farmland or business opportunities, and some stayed to stake claims. Several families acquired land from the Kirchners, in what is now the northwest part of Peterson, and built their own homes of logs, or even sod, near the Kirchner homestead. Peterson became a small village.

On their scouting trips, many "land lookers" camped at the Kirchner settlement and watered their thirsty horses in the spring that bubbled out of the hillside behind the two cabins. Certainly whenever land lookers came through, there must have been spirited conversations and the sharing of news around the tables at the two Kirchner places. Can there be any doubt that Gust and his parents, brothers, and sisters, once they took a liking to potential newcomers, did everything they could to encourage them to stay and make a claim? Like so many Euro-Americans who came west, the Kirchners wished to encourage others to settle with them in order to reconstruct familiar institutions they had left behind to the east.

But people came slowly, and a good few went back. The Panic of 1857 stopped many, and fear of more trouble with Indians caused many who might have come this far west to settle in places less remote. The census of 1860, the first for Clay County, registered eighteen dwellings in the county (all were along the Little Sioux); seven were listed as "unoccupied."

In 1858 the village came to be called Peterson. The origin of the name is lost with those who might have told the story. The Kirchners called this place Long Grove after the trees along the river; that this name wasn't attached to the post office is probably because there already was a Long Grove in Iowa. But why did it become Peterson? Most frequently written and told is an implausible story about a fellow named Howard Peterson who came west looking for a mill seat. According to the story, he stayed here long enough to help the few citizens apply to the government for a post office. Some versions say he was illiterate but nonetheless wrote a letter to the postal department requesting an office and suggesting his own first name as the official name. Why Howard, why not Kirchner? At any rate, the reply came back that there was already a Howard in Iowa—which was true at the time—and that the post office would be named Peterson instead. Shortly after, so the story goes, not being sufficiently captivated by the idea of living in a town named after him, and probably not being eligible for the postmaster's job because of his lack of reading and writing ability, Howard Peterson headed on west, never to be heard from again. That last part could be true; there is no Howard Peterson, nor any other Peterson, listed in the manuscript census of 1860, the first for this area, nor in the census of 1870. Meanwhile, Gust Kirchner, who could read, was appointed postmaster in 1858.

It's an entertaining, loose-jointed story with plenty of openings for a good breeze, and yet somewhere in it are probably kernels of truth, but now, more than a hundred and thirty years later, they are impossible to sort from the chaff.

It strikes me as odd how some facts persist unchanged—Peterson has been Peterson since 1858—but other facts, especially those that might shed some light on some of the unchanging ones, disappear altogether while no one is looking. Certainly everyone who lived here in 1860 knew the true story of the name, but because it was so commonly known, no one thought it necessary to record it. The great appeal of history always centers around the ellipses, those facts that drop out of the matrix of the past, facts that might explain the simple, enduring, and nagging mysteries.

Perhaps the descendants of a Mr. Peterson gather from time to time someplace for a family reunion. And perhaps they collect around the map of Iowa at each gathering to look at the name of a little town in the northwest part, and someone tells the story of how the place came to be named for their long-dead ancestor. If they do, I'd like to hear their version.

In August 1862, the Sioux uprising exploded in Minnesota, only a hundred-odd miles north of Peterson, reigniting settlers' fears of Indians. The Santee Sioux, their lands given over to settlers and the U.S. government and driven to starvation by corrupt Indian agents, attacked forts, settlements, and isolated pioneer families in what was one of the bloodiest conflicts in the guerilla war between Indians and white settlers. As many as a thousand people on both sides were killed.

Panic engulfed the frontier. Stories of approaching war parties, a few true, but most false, washed back and forth across the region as Euro-Americans fled south and east to safe haven. Most of the white settlements at the frontier from Minnesota south through Iowa were abandoned for weeks or months. For a time the residents of Peterson and other scattered settlements along the Little Sioux retreated to the small strongholds of Sioux City and Fort Dodge.

The United States was in the midst of the darkest hours of the Civil War and could not afford to send any detachments of regular soldiers to protect the settlers on the frontier. As a result, in September 1862, Iowa governor Samuel Kirkwood created the Iowa Border Brigade, a 250-man volunteer force, hastily trained and dispatched to build and occupy a line of small forts along the frontier.

The men built a series of seven simple stockades that stretched from Sioux City to Iowa Lake, including one at Peterson; this structure was completed in April 1863. It was a small, triangular affair with two sides of 100 feet and the third of 150 feet. Like a compass needle, it pointed north. Along the south wall, the brigade built stables, a kitchen, and officers' quarters. A ten-foot gate opened to the northwest, toward the scattered houses of the settlement nearby. At the north point, the garrison built an eighteen-foot-square blockhouse with the second story turned forty-five degrees to the first in order to provide a clear field of fire in all directions. Both levels sported rows of small gunports.

Both the stockade and the blockhouse were built from timber cut in the Kirchner woods south across the river; the blockhouse itself was of jointed oak and ash timbers ten inches square.

In order to save time, wood, and labor, the stockade, instead of being the typical enclosure made of standing logs with sharpened top points, was built as a massive plank fence. At least two of the walls were built with six-inch-thick boards set upright in the ground.

For the next two years or so, a detachment of one or two dozen Border Brigade volunteers, and later Union troops, were stationed at the Peterson fort, providing protection for local settlers as scouts rode up and down the chain of forts, maintaining communication and providing something suggesting a line of protection.

Although the fort must have seemed impregnable and must have been a great relief to settlers who had thickened along the Little Sioux, it could not have withstood a dedicated assault. From a strategic standpoint, it was too small and rather poorly designed. The gunports of the blockhouse were small, which precluded aiming at nearby targets. Overlooked in its construction was the fact that marksmen along the south wall of the stockade would have to shoot through gunports from inside the cramped stables—right over the horses' heads. It was a fort that might protect people in the event of attack by incidental bands of hunters or warriors but would never withstand any massed, larger-scale assault.

The Sioux uprising came to its end even before the Peterson fort was completed. At the battle of Wood Lake, General Henry H. Sibley and his force defeated the Santee on September 23, 1862—only five weeks after the uprising began. On December 26, thirty-eight Santee were hanged in Mankato, Minnesota, for their part in the affair. Nevertheless, for the next couple of years, tensions remained high on the frontier, even though it is likely that no Indians, hostile or otherwise, came within miles of Peterson during the time of the fort's active duty.

Sometime in 1865 or 1866 the fort was abandoned; the scare had ended, and quickly the wood was scavenged for other uses. In timber-poor country such as this, the lumber from the stockade was shortly reapplied to build homes, barns, fences. The blockhouse, however, remained intact and was moved to a farm two miles west of town. The upper story was rotated into line with the lower, making a more conventional structure, and it was used for years as a dwelling, later a farm building, then abandoned.

No one knows today precisely where the Peterson fort was originally built, and there is nothing visible in town to suggest its site. There is a plan for the structure, but on no map or document is there any indication of a landmark or witness tree from which a bearing could be drawn to locate subsurface remains of the structure, if any exist. The best guess is that Highway 10 passes through the center of the old stockade, right about at Park Street. Workers digging sewer and water lines turn up odd unrecognizable things from time to time, but it's anybody's guess whether this stuff is from the fort or merely fill from later construction projects.

In 1977 Peterson Heritage, the local historic preservation group, acquired and moved the long-abandoned block-house two miles back to Peterson, and in 1985 they began restoration. Volunteers disassembled the eighteen-foot-square building, replaced many logs, rebuilt it according to the original plans, and placed it on a concrete foundation as close to its original location as could be guessed and the highway allowed. In September 1986, Peterson Heritage completed the work and dedicated the structure. Today the blockhouse, minus stockade, stands on the center boulevard of Park Street at the intersection of Highway 10, glimpsed by passing motorists and occasionally toured by school kids on field trips.

In the early 1860s, during the time the fort stood to protect settlers, the tiny gunports of the blockhouse looked out on trampled prairie and the fields of the Kirchner homestead. A few hundred yards to the northwest was the insecure settlement of Peterson, and between the village and fort there must have been a well-worn path as settlers and guardsmen alike made trips back and forth. Except to the south along the river, the hills were bare of trees. The landscape near the fort would have been trail-worn and barren; the detachment's forty horses would have made short work of nearby grass, leaving the prairie to mud and dust.

The view through the gunports today bears no resemblance to that 125 years ago. For one thing, the view is now through squares of plexiglass, which keep the sparrows out. Where border brigaders once sat on the prairie and cleaned Austrian rifles in preparation for Indians who never came, homeowners now rake leaves and weed flower beds. There are houses, yard ornaments, mature trees, gardens, power lines, birdbaths, garages, sidewalks, lawn furniture, traffic signs, streetlights. Looking out through the gunports of the blockhouse, I find little connection between a quiet small town in the late twentieth century and a nineteenth-century prairie fortress. They seem to stand apart by more than time alone; they exist in separate worlds.

In 1863 a soldier looking out through a gunport on the northwest side of the blockhouse would have looked upon the newborn village of Peterson, but it is hard to know exactly what it looked like. Charlotte Kirchner's letters to her daughter are silent about the layout, character, or extent of the settlement, and photography wouldn't get to the ordinary places on the frontier until much later. The earliest map of Peterson is the 1881 plat filed when the streets were laid out in preparation for the arrival of the railroad; it doesn't depict structures that existed when the plat was drawn.

From the census and from Charlotte's letters we know that by 1870 there were both a store and hotel in the village. In one of her letters, Charlotte writes about the gala opening of the first retail establishment for many miles around: "When the first store was built in town, they decided to have a calico dance—everybody was invited, and the young people came from far. Aunts Lena and Julia and I had new dresses. . . . The uncles had blue overalls with white shirts with red or blue socks. They came from Old O'Brien, Linn Grove and other places. We had a fiddler for music, someone called the changes, and had a plate lunch—we had a wonderful jollification."

The census of 1860 had registered 52 people as residents of Clay County; all of them resided along the Little Sioux, most of them in the southern part of the county. By 1870, Clay County boasted 1,523 people, 44 of whom lived in or near Peterson. Gust and his brothers had built a sawmill on the river near the Bicknell cabin by this time, making building construction a much more practical matter. Near the store was the hotel; it was probably more of a boardinghouse. The census lists 9 people living or staying at the hotel in late July 1870: Albert Wheeler (the hotelkeeper), his wife and son, an attorney, two farmers, the owner of the store and his clerk, and a real-estate agent.

While the census of 1860 had listed the occupations of most men in the county as farmers (no occupations had been listed for women), that of 1870 began to report specialization in the growing population. In the Peterson area, the census taker listed a miller and a blacksmith, and Charlotte Kirchner was identified as the schoolteacher.

By 1867, the Kirchner family had convinced father Christian Kirchner that it was time for a modern house to replace the eleven-year-old log cabin. The women were tired of trying to keep house in such a crude structure. Charlotte wrote: "I think I have said very little of the pests that claimed an abode in the cracks of the logs. We had mosquitoes, flies, and the most hated, vulgar bedbug, and no amount of care on the part of the patient, faithful housewife could keep a log cabin free from their constant company. Humorous readings, and the jokes on the gullible housewife by the wily agent with his sure exterminator of the night-prowlers would have been humorous if it had not been such a serious question to the housekeeper.

"The building of a modern frame house in 1867 or 8 was no small task. There were no lumber yards. Your Uncle Gust had his saw mill, and the trees had to be cut, taken to the saw mill, sawed, sorted for the different kinds to be used for siding, studding, flooring, shingles, etc., and left to dry. The limestones were picked up on the bluffs, and the hair from animals saved to mix in the sand and lime. . . . I asked Will about it—he said all native timber was used—the siding and shingles were cottonwood, and the finishing wood was black walnut. The nails, paint, windows, blinds and doors were mostly brought from Fort Dodge, which was a major task, as there were no bridges or graded roads, and the Iowa sloughs were a terror to the stoutest heart."

It was the first frame dwelling in the county. Built on a simple hall-and-parlor plan with a central stairway, the story-and-a-half home must have drawn attention and Sunday callers from counties all around. The large-windowed and wallpapered rooms must have seemed palatial to people so long cooped up in dark, damp cabins.

Many things change in a century and a quarter, yet much stays the same. Visitors to Peterson today can sit in the parlor of this same house, a parlor nearly unchanged from the time the house was built. By luck, and out of a concern for history, this house was spared extensive remodeling, additions, and outright demolition. It exists today, restored and carefully maintained by Peterson Heritage, in a condition very close to that of the time of construction.

While the house is there and even the spring that provided reliable water, the homestead itself has undergone considerable change. Charlotte described the homestead at about the time the new house was built: "Grandfather planted black walnut trees—one he called Lena's, one Julia's, one Lottie's—that was for me. There was a path from the house to the road with beds of flowers on each side. On the west was the orchard and on the east side, the well-kept, large vegetable garden."

Today the homestead is a park and the historical complex for Peterson Heritage. The few hundred feet to Fourth Street are now smooth mown lawn; there are no walnut trees or orchard, nor have any of the outbuildings survived. Walnut trees live a long time, but there has been none here in my memory. Where the orchard once was, kids now play on modern playground equipment; where the garden was now stands the Rock Forest School, a one-room school-house moved in from the country, currently used as a museum. Until very recently there were huge elms; the last of them, a fine giant, succumbed to Dutch elm disease in 1990. But thanks to energetic citizens and in the spirit of tree-minded settlers, Peterson has planted dozens of new trees in the park, trees that would make old Christian and Magdalena Kirchner glad.

What did this village look like in 1870? Probably pretty barren and uninviting. There must have been a few new homes made of lumber sawn at the mill, mixed in with a number of log cabins, and a few families may yet have been living in sod houses. The Kirchners had been planting trees from seed since the spring of 1857; by 1870, the orchard near their homestead might have cast a few square feet of shade during the hot days of July. Except for the trees the Kirchners planted, there were probably few others in the village. The only mature trees were along the river to the south and west, some distance away.

In terms of the arrangement of buildings, Peterson was certainly an informal village, but probably not altogether unplanned. The infant town was all on land first claimed by the Kirchner family, and they no doubt sold or leased lots according to some loose plan. Judging from the few remaining buildings of the preplat era, it seems likely that structures were put up in relation to an informal road that tended generally east-west, and later became Fourth Street, though there is evidence that some buildings might have been shifted to conform to Fourth Street some time after the town was formally platted.

Livestock roved loose, like it did on most of the Iowa frontier. Jane Bicknell Kirchner reports in her diary the progress of Gust in building fence—of raw sawn lumber or split rails—to exclude horses, cattle, and hogs from their fields. With the arrival of the first blacksmith sometime prior to 1870, the village became more lively as the ring of hammer and anvil carried through the valley above the low of cattle.

Soon after the sawmill was built along the river, the county officers voted to erect a courthouse. C. H. Brock-schink of Peterson, perhaps the only bidder, won the job with an astounding $6,000 bid, and, according to at least one source, later sought an additional $1,500 for unforeseen work. The two-story wood-frame building he put up was the size of a modest house and stood in the village of Peterson. That he was paid at least $6,000 for the job suggests that Clay County politics, like those of several frontier counties at the time, were not altogether honest.

Home seekers must have passed through the area often, now that the threat of Indian attack had diminished. While Peterson was not near any main traveled road, the people of Iowa continued to look west, sending farmers, land speculators, and tradespeople to the region. The area would not boom until the railroad arrived, but by 1870, a few new fields amid the prairie grass were beginning to grow oats and corn.

In 1870 hardship touched the Kirchner family when Jane Bicknell Kirchner died, leaving Gust with four children. In 1871 Gust remarried, and he and his new bride, Rachel Williams Kirchner, soon built and moved into a fine new house along what is now Fourth Street. This house, like that of his parents a few hundred yards west, still stands and has been carefully restored and maintained by Peterson Heritage.

Peterson lost the county seat to the newly platted town of Spencer in 1871, and the courthouse building in Peterson became the most expensive barn anywhere around. Peterson was located in the far southwestern corner of Clay County; Spencer was centrally located, allowing people easier access to the county seat. In addition, there was talk of a railroad for Spencer and a boom there.

Even before the Civil War, everyone in Iowa was talking railroads. To take advantage of Iowa's deep black soil, farmers needed markets; access to markets meant transportation, and, in the latter half of the nineteenth century, transportation meant railroads. While separated from much of the world by miles of yet unbroken prairie, the people of Peterson kept close watch on any developments that might mean a column of locomotive smoke on the horizon. When the Iowa Falls and Sioux City Railroad, later the Illinois Central, was completed through Storm Lake and Cherokee in 1870, the residents of Peterson and the surrounding countryside suddenly had a much closer connection with the outside world, a connection that was only twenty miles away. Ten years later, the Chicago, Milwaukee and St. Paul Railway built its line through Spencer. At about the same time, the Toledo and Northwestern Railway, a construction company of the Chicago and North Western Railway, made plans to build a branch line from the east through Peterson; no doubt the residents of the village could talk of little else. This would be the opportunity to make the place into a real town.

The arrangement was simple. The Western Town and Lot Company, itself a subsidiary of the Chicago and North Western Railway, entered into a contract with Gust and Rachel Kirchner to develop their farm into a townsite. The land company was to survey the site, subdivide lots, and act as sales agents, and the Kirchners were to provide the land. The company was to receive half of the proceeds from the sale of residential and commercial lots, Gust and Rachel the other half. Gust no doubt would be a good salesman on-site, and the land company and the railroad would combine efforts to promote Peterson as a fine place to settle. It was a contract that worked to benefit all parties.

Rachel's imprint on the town persists to this day. A staunch fighter for temperance, her vision of the new town included no alcohol. On every abstract for every piece of property in town even today appears this admonition: " . . . no spiritous liquors, except for medicinal purposes, shall ever be sold on said premises; and upon breach, grantor, their successors, heirs or assigns, may re-enter said premises and hold same as their former estate."

Townsite speculation was a very profitable practice for railroads, and, with the good luck of being where a railroad wanted to build a town, and with the right contract, it was very profitable for the owner of the land. Most often towns were platted on land granted directly to the railroads, allowing the company to reap all of the profits from land sales. While such quick sales were an excellent short-term benefit, railroads understood the long-term value of populating the town with merchants who would get yard goods and implements by rail and the countryside with farmers who would ship great quantities of grain and livestock to market.

By the latter decades of the nineteenth century, railroads in the Midwest had learned a great deal about the business of planning, establishing, and promoting towns along their growing lines. Each company had developed basic plans for townsites that ultimately created the majority of towns in western Iowa. That so many of the towns along a particular line are so similar in their grid pattern, street width, block and lot size, is easily traced to standard practices of each railroad. While Peterson became a fairly typical town for the North Western, it is one of the few that had any history prior to the arrival of the townsite surveyors.

Most railroad towns were laid out as rectangles (except when terrain interfered) with straight, wide streets, a concentrated commercial area, and uniform sized lots, and, perhaps most important, were carefully oriented toward the railroad. Some early towns were platted with Main Street facing the tracks, but later plans had the central commercial district jutting off from the railroad at right angles in what has come to be called the T-town. Railroads were smart to arrange their towns' Main Streets so they pointed to the railroad; it allowed them to build their station at the end of the most important street in town. Many towns wound up with their star institutions at either end of Main Street: the railroad station at one end and the public school at the other.

For Peterson, October 1881 marks the turn from being a frontier village to being a real town. That month the survey crew arrived with a wagonload of stakes to grid out streets and lots on the alluvial terrace above the river, on the Kirchners' cropland, and over the old site of the long-ago-dismantled Peterson fort.

From the old village, the new formal plat expanded east and south, initially developing about a dozen new blocks. The standard block was four hundred feet long by three hundred feet deep, although several were truncated by the curve of the rail line along the south edge of town. Main Street, the axis of activity in any midwestern town, was laid out two blocks east of the existing village. It ran north and south and was placed to give merchants to come ample room for building. Lots on Main Street were staked out twenty-five feet wide. Such narrow lots were pretty much standard for commercial areas in any railroad town and allowed numerous merchants to push up to the sidewalk, lending a prosperous image to a town. In the residential areas, lots were fifty feet wide to better accommodate spacious houses, gardens, chicken coops, and stables.

The layout of streets, too, signaled the important center of town. While most streets were planned with a width of eighty feet, and Fourth Street, which passed through the existing village, was laid out at only sixty-six feet, the perpendicular Main and Elm streets were both surveyed at one hundred feet in width.

There were thirteen full blocks and seven partial or truncated blocks, for a total of twenty. While the plat must have seemed immense to anyone who explored the town-to-be, the plat would prove smaller than the demand; Gust and Rachel Kirchner would eventually make three additions to the town.

When the surveyors had finished, residents of the village could stroll along avenues staked across corn stubble and grazed-over prairie to see the new town. It is easy to imagine Gust and Rachel driving a buggy slowly back and forth between the rows of stakes, down imaginary streets in the future town, talking of homes, trees, fences, gardens, children, schools, and churches all rising amid these rows of fresh stakes. Driving down Main Street, Gust might have imagined banks and stores abutting the wide sidewalk, and Rachel would have found comfort in knowing she'd prevented any saloons from finding a home here.

At the foot of Main Street, down the hill toward the river, near where the scale office is today, lay the path for the railroad. Perhaps work on the embankment had already begun. The depot would be built here where Main Street ended at the tracks. A great change was about to occur.

The railroad arrived in 1882, and from that date Peterson has been a busy and bustling little town, with fair prospects of considerable commercial development. The Chicago & Northwestern railroad has performed a good act for the little town of Peterson, and has been instrumental in transforming it from a town in name to one of business activity. Its citizens are moral and upright; its business men sagacious and enterprising, and the town a pleasant and delightful place to dwell. Besides many social organizations, there are two churches, and several secret societies, all in a healthful state of prosperity and well attended.

—*History of Clay County,* S. J. Clarke Co., 1909

Chapter 13

Main Street and the Railroad

The scale office, where Janet Anderson spends her working days, is homey, and even on busy days is quiet. On any day the radio will be playing softly in the background, usually tuned to KICD in Spencer for country western music, local news, and weather. Janet has photographs of her family on and around her desk and pictures on the wall. In one corner sits an oak rocker where she is sometimes able to do a row of cross-stitching between weighs.

The office has a bright bay window that looks north out over the scale; it also provides Janet with an end-on picture of Main Street and a good view of much of the center of town. Most of the town's activity is visible through the window, and the scale, right at her feet, is one of the busiest places. Along with Main Street, she can see the library, Highway 10, seven of the town's intersections, most of the town's businesses, and the fire station. If Janet hasn't seen it, it probably hasn't happened yet. In fact, until the fire department and ambulance crew began to rely on radio pagers, the town emergency number rang here and the scale operator threw the switch for the siren to alert everyone of the emergency. And even today, as more tradition than necessity, Janet listens for the time signal on the radio and blows the town siren every weekday at noon.

Janet's phone rings from time to time, but not to bring news of a fire or car accident; occasionally she gets a call from someone who is looking for a spouse, a neighbor, or a friend. With her comprehensive knowledge of vehicle ownership in the area, Janet can scan the horizon out the window and cover about 75 percent of the likely stopping-places in town.

"Yes, his pickup was up in front of the post office about an hour ago," she'll say, or, "She must be on her way home; I just saw her go east on 10."

The bay window looks directly up the sidewalk along the west side of Main Street. The walk goes north past the old concrete watering-trough in front of the library, crosses the highway, and runs past the bank and up along the row of business buildings. Looking from the window, I am struck by just how precisely the buildings line up against it. They obediently toe a line traced by survey stakes set out over a hundred years ago.

To satisfy my own curiosity, I recently measured the distance between the storefronts facing each other across Main Street. The 1881 town plat says the distance was to be a hundred feet, the golden mean of main streets in railroad-planned towns. I borrowed a tape, and at a moment when traffic was quiet, a sort of moment increasingly common in Peterson, I stretched it from the front of the hardware store on the west to the front of Sue's Diner on the east. Within an inch it read a hundred feet.

I had hoped Sue wouldn't see me doing it, but she misses little. As I held the end of the tape to the front of the café, I heard the booming voice at the window just above me, "Just what the hell are you doing?" I had my response ready. "Figuring out where to put the freeway."

"Ha! That'll be the day!"

The entire street is two and a half blocks long: a block of residences, a block of businesses, and a short block of neither.

The north block of Main is all residences except for the Baumgarten Funeral Home on the west side and Hass Insurance on the east. A parkway runs down the center of this block, with an American flag at midblock and a large pine at the south end, right at the upper end of the business district. At Christmastime the tree is bright with strings of multicolored lights.

At the opposite end of Main Street, the south end, stands the elevator and scale office. Close by was the Chicago and North Western depot years ago. Nearby, on a triangle of land, sits the Kirchner-French Memorial Library. It is named for Lena Kirchner French, sister to Charlotte and Gust, and for Walter French, her husband, who willed their 200-acre farm to build and maintain a library in town. Nearby, a lighted sign says, "Welcome to Peterson." Across the street is a large former livery barn now used for machinery storage.

In between is the single block of businesses; years ago a few merchants spilled north into the next block, but even by 1910 people could see that Peterson had reached the limit of its growth, and soon all commerce had shrunk back south toward the railroad.

The condition of Main Street today can be read in the utilization of the lots. Including the easement for an alley that was never built and several lots that were originally platted to face Second Street, there are in effect sixteen lots on each side of the business block of Main. Each is twenty-five feet wide as platted by the Western Town and Lot Company. Seven lots are altogether vacant; another five are held by abandoned and slumping buildings; four belong to recently closed businesses, the buildings now used for storage. That makes sixteen lots, or half the total number, that are derelict or vacant. The town has worked to see that the gaps don't become eyesores; it has planted grass in the openings and has provided picnic tables, flower boxes, and playground equipment.

There are nine businesses here: T.K.'s Bar, the hardware store and laundromat, Peterson State Bank, the *Peterson Patriot* office, veterinarian Q. Sundberg, Quality Equipment (steel fabrication), Tom's Clover Farm (groceries), Sue's Diner, and Brown Plumbing and Heating. Mixed in are the Senior Citizen Center, the Masonic Hall, and the post office.

Most of the buildings are single-story. A few are two-story, but space is at no premium here; second-story windows are either blank glass or boarded up. Until recently, a sign hung on the door of the barbershop: "Will Close April 30th. I am retiring. Thanks for your patronizing all the years. I will miss you all. Thanks, Wendell." The barbershop closed in 1988.

Peterson's Main Street businesses, and the few businesses elsewhere in town, are trying hard to hold out against both the shrinking population and its increasing tendency to commute to county seats for work and shopping. The job gets tougher every year.

Businesses in Peterson do offer a considerable range of goods and services. If you need drill bits, steak, roller chain for a combine, a grilled cheese sandwich, work gloves, a tire fixed, gasoline, light bulbs, your income taxes figured, postage stamps, instant coffee, traveler's checks, an ice cream cone, automotive fuses, bananas, or even over-night film processing, you can get them here. But if you need a washing machine, new eyeglasses, a bottle of scotch, a prescription for Lasix, the latest Robert Ludlum thriller, a new pickup, a Madonna compact disc, a taco salad, blades for a John Deere silage chopper, a pile of two-by-fours, or even a daily paper, you'll have to go to Spencer, Storm Lake, or Cherokee.

Members of my family have had a stake in Main Street's livelihood over the years; the John Deere shop stayed in the family until it was sold in 1970. Twenty years passed, and then, on October 20, 1990, my folks invested in the future of Main Street and bought the Peterson Mercantile and adjacent laundromat. For Mother and her husband, Eddie, it was almost an impulse buy; we had talked about it over coffee a couple of nights before, just after the sale bill appeared in the paper.

Business had been poor at the Mercantile, and rumors abounded that the place would close and that Peterson would have another empty building on Main Street.

"Peterson has to have a hardware store; we can't just let it close up and die," said Eddie as we sat at the table.

"You could run a hardware store," suggested Carol to Eddie. "You know what farmers need, what they come into town for."

Mother and I agreed. Eddie was silent for a few moments. He had for years run a large family cattle and farming operation; when the stress overcame the rewards, he handed it over to another family member and had been working for other farmers much of the time since.

"I've been wondering about it," he said, looking into his coffee cup.

Mother offered, "Well, the place can't go for too much in Peterson." We talked of what the store might bring, and Mother and Eddie eventually settled on the top price they might pay.

"Let's think about it more and then see how it goes at the sale," said Eddie.

We spent much of the evening discussing what a good, small-town hardware store should be like and what we could do to start a new business successfully in such a small town. What would draw people to town? We made lists of merchandise, talked about how important it was that Peterson not lose another business. And we wondered what would happen.

Sale day two days later was cold and rainy, making the cloaked crowd on Main Street seem like a cemetery full of mourners attending the funeral for another town business, or a restless flock of vultures waiting for a stricken animal to become a carcass with the blow of the auctioneer's gavel.

Mother sat with coffee across the street at Sue's; she was damp and nervous. Carol, long a lover of hardware stores and their secret bins, perused the soon-to-be-sold stock. I stood in the gray rain, but not with Eddie. He moved at the edge of the crowd, pacing, as the building, minus stock, went on the block first, at eleven sharp.

The auctioneer called and the assistants pointed and yelled, and it was impossible to tell who was bidding and who finally bought. It was over within minutes, and I wasn't even sure Eddie had bid on the place until I located him in the crowd afterward and asked him.

"We bought her, we bought her," he said. He looked pleased, and relieved. They had bought two buildings making fifty feet Main Street frontage, one with an operating laundromat, the other now in the process of emptying as the auctioneers sold off the contents. My folks had bought both buildings for the price of a good used car.

"At that price, what have we got to lose?" wondered Eddie aloud.

The November 1 issue of the *Peterson Patriot* carried this small ad: "Eddie's Wash and Dry, Peterson. Open 7:30 A.M.–7:30 P.M. We appreciate your business."

Five weeks later, the front page of the paper announced:

"NEW BUSINESS TO OPEN IN PETERSON

"Eddie and Mona Beck are gearing up to open a new business on Main Street in Peterson. The doors of EDDIE'S HARDWARE will be opening in a week to ten days in the location of the former Peterson Mercantile. The store will be a small hometown hardware store geared to serving the community and farmers in the area. 'I've been in the farming business all of my life and I am very aware of the farmer's needs,' Eddie said.

"The store will start out with a small general hardware inventory. But, 'Any suggestions as to additional inventory or services needed will be greatly appreciated,' Eddie said. He added, 'Our inventory will grow with the needs of the community.'

"Hours for the new store will be from 7:30 A.M. to 5:30 P.M. Monday thru Saturday."

It turns out that Eddie had begun to develop a vision for the place from the time we first talked about it. In the weeks after the sale, as he and Mother prepared for their opening, he said little, but moved through the processes of getting the store ready with the steadiness of someone who had set up a hundred hardware stores in the past. He perused catalogs, ordered stock, arranged shelving, set up his workshop in the back, hung lights, painted, arranged his newly arrived merchandise, and in half the time it would take someone to write a business plan for the banker, hung a sign in the front door. OPEN, it said.

He also put up a big sign above the door identifying the business. It is a good example of his vision for a small-town hardware store. He described it to me one day just before he built it. On plywood he planned to arrange simple stick letters made of painted wood; with a mixture of uppercase and lowercase, they would spell out "Eddie's Hardware." Clearing my throat, I affirmed his ideas, and then proceeded to adjust them based on college-educated ideas about typography, design, and readability. He politely paid attention to what I said but, to his credit, ignored my suggestions altogether.

Within two days the sign was up and facing Main Street for the world to see. It is simple, readable, informal. More than any manufactured or professionally designed sign could, it conveys the character of the place, the character of the owners, and a feeling for what will greet customers when they enter the store.

Inside, the place looks like any other hardware store at first glance, but quickly details begin to accumulate. Bird sounds fill the background as parakeets and canaries flit about in two big cages. A pair of giant steer horns, with a Sentry Hardware hat hung on one of them, hovers above the drill bits and saw blades. In the spring, the big windows cast light across long trays of pepper plants, tomatoes, petunias, marigolds. The shelves are well stocked, but it is easy to see that Eddie cannot carry the breadth of selection that a big store in Spencer can. His strategy is to carry what people need most of the time and to order the rest. Month by month, the stock and selection grow as Eddie seeks to fill out his merchandise lines. The store has a feel that suggests there ought to be a big potbellied stove in the center, with half a dozen town idlers warming their feet around it. The place is not perfectly tidy; Eddie's habits and the birds see to that, but things are easy to find, and Eddie knows his stock well.

Business doesn't boom, most days, but Eddie has found other ways to increase trade and income. At times he is busy in the back room, repairing windows or fixing something else someone brought in. In addition, he makes hydraulic hoses, mixes paint, replaces hammer handles, builds and sells bird feeders. Eddie stays busy, and, with the laundromat, brings home enough to keep the place going.

The big windows in the front look out across the quiet Main Street toward Sue's Diner and the post office. As people pass, Eddie looks up and waves, just as merchants have on Main Streets for a couple of hundred years. Now, on days when the wind blows snow as fine as ground glass and just as sharp, he looks out the window with an impish grin and says, "Gee, I sure as hell wish I could be feeding cattle on a morning like this."

I had never been upstairs in the hardware store until Eddie and Mother bought it, even though I had frequented the store since I was very small. The place has been a hardware store for many years; I remember visiting Fastenow's Hardware before we moved to California in 1957, and it was an old store even then. The upstairs is divided into offices with a hall running along the north side. In hopes of attracting a dentist, a lawyer, maybe even a palm reader, these offices were partitioned off, probably at the time the building was built in 1916. At the front of the second floor is a large, bright meeting room. To the best I can figure, these offices were never occupied, never rented, and the meeting room was never the home of the Odd Fellows or the Masons.

On any given weekday, there are anywhere from zero to twenty vehicles parked on the broad street. People's weekday activities downtown are observable in the pattern of cars parked on Main Street at different times. The first vehicles of the day usually appear in front of Sue's by six-fifteen. By midmorning, vehicles cluster in front of the post office and the Senior Center across the street. The mail is distributed to boxes by nine, and most days see a good card game or two around the tables at the Center. Meanwhile, all day long, occasional cars come and go from in front of Eddie's Hardware and the bank at the end of the block.

By two o'clock, the street is down to one or two vehicles. Late afternoon brings a small flurry of activity at the grocery store, and by half past five, Main Street is empty.

My memory easily reaches back to times when the heart of town was busy six days a week, or at least it seems to me that it was, now that I look at Main Street today. Old people used to tell of times when it was really busy, back at the turn of the century when on weekdays the sidewalks were full of people and the street was jammed with horses, buggies, and wagons—gridlock in 1900.

But my own best recollection is of summer Saturday nights, long evenings when the stores were lit up and busy, and the street was parked full of round-fendered cars, chrome glinting under dim street lights, and people walking the sidewalk from store to store. The town was lively, especially if there was to be a band concert or a baseball game down at the field across the tracks. Downtown teemed with voices and familiar faces, and the café stayed open until ten, where I often sat with my hands around a cheeseburger, sipping a short bottle of Coke through a paper straw.

Sounds and smells come back to me easily. Both were enhanced by warm, moist air and the lingering twilight of summer. In the John Deere shop, a pedestal fan churned the scents of fresh green-and-yellow paint on a new tractor, oil, peanuts, and sweeping compound. Laughter and conversation were more common on Saturday night; both the farmers and my grandparents were less busy and more willing to talk of local events.

While supermarkets today smell of plastic and disinfectant, Peterson's two grocery stores—Hansen's and Brees'—smelled of cut meat, wet sawdust, fresh bread, and bananas that were getting a little too ripe to sell. I can still hear the screen door slam at Hansen's.

The drugstore next door to Hansen's smelled of cigars and strange potions, shampoo and a hint of perfume. A giant pendulum clock near the door slowly ticked off the minutes as I scanned the comic books from the rack nearby. As long as I bought one once in a while, which I did, Ernie Tigges was always glad to see me. With my nose in a new comic book, I would sit on one of the wire-backed chairs and drink a Green River from the marble soda fountain.

Up the street, the White Front building held the variety store, complete with long, low counters partitioned by thick glass dividers. Sometimes I thought I needed a new eraser or a protractor, or would be sent after some sewing notion or a roll of tape. On Saturday nights, Fastenow's Hardware store was open, and it smelled of machine oil and paint, and had that electric-train smell of ozone to it somehow. I am happy to report that Eddie's Hardware, in the same building, has the same smell today. Next door was the Sioux Dairy, filled mostly with kids eating ice cream. Then came the Peterson Hatchery, with a big Purina checkerboard on the front; no need to guess about the smell—chicken feed and chicken droppings. From the bar next door emanated the sounds of happy tipplers, the scent of cigarette smoke, chewing tobacco, and spilt beer, especially on any warm night. Across Main Street, Wendell Brown stayed open late to cut hair.

On the street, great concentrations of insects formed clouds around the streetlights, and traffic was heavy; one actually had to look both ways before crossing. In those days there was a band shell in a vacant lot on the east side of Main Street, and farm people and townspeople alike sat in and on their cars listening to the community band saw its way through one popular tune after another. Applause was hard to hear from such a scattered crowd, so the audience signaled its approval at the end of each number with a flourish of car horns. The sounds of engines, slamming car doors, and conversation gave the downtown a vibrancy, a glow of energy that I wouldn't fully appreciate until it was gone. These days, Main Street is altogether deserted on Saturday nights, and the only sound is the hum of the beer sign at the one remaining bar.

Peterson grew with vigor once the railroad came in 1882, as the censuses of 1880 and 1885 make clear. The manuscript census of 1880 listed only six dwellings for the village of Peterson, and a total of 31 residents, 228 for the whole township. There were but four people engaged in any sort of nonagricultural or nondomestic work: a blacksmith, the Methodist minister, a storekeeper, and his clerk. The miller lived across the river, outside the village. There was no longer anyone listed as a hotel keeper, no land speculators, no real-estate agents, no lawyers. While farmers were trickling into the surrounding countryside, the village of Peterson had clearly lost ground from its population of 44 ten years earlier.

Five years later, in 1885, the trains had arrived and the picture had changed dramatically. The census listed a full thirty-four dwellings in the platted part of Peterson and 151 residents. There were painters, storekeepers, draymen, lumbermen, several carpenters, a bridge builder, a good many laborers, three blacksmiths, and a telegrapher and depot agent. The hotel was back in operation and housed, in addition to its owners, a laborer, a blacksmith, a stock dealer, a butcher, a carpenter, and two masons.

Soon after the Chicago and North Western arrived, Gust must have ceased to cut timber in the woods south of town and must have ceased running the sawmill. There was simply no way that a local mill, dealing in walnut and oak, could ever compete with the freight cars full of pine that began to arrive as soon as the rails were spiked in place to the loading dock.

Though the Kirchners were in on the deal, the railroad actually built Peterson and set the patterns that still organize the place. The railroad, with the Kirchners' help, not only planned, promoted, and sold the town to settlers and merchants, but it also brought them from far points to make homes here. It transported the stuff from which they built a town and a society: sawn lumber from Wisconsin, bolts of cloth, plans for churches, red bricks, the latest sheet music, garden seeds, uniforms for the baseball team, desks for a school. While residents provided all the labor to build Peterson, about all they could provide in the way of raw materials were glacial cobbles to lay up for building foundations.

The railroad was essential to Peterson's success as a nineteenth-century small town in another way. Once the settlement expanded much beyond the size of the 1860 village, residents would have soon exhausted the timber along the river, and, without the railroad to bring coal, Peterson could not have warmed itself.

One by one Main Street lots sold and sprouted business buildings. Like frontier towns everywhere, Peterson soon had its selection of green-lumber storefronts, complete with slab board signs. Several were quite small. The first barbershop on Main Street, two millinery shops, and a windmill and pump dealership were single-story structures, each measuring less than twenty by twenty-five feet.

The old hotel and general store in the original part of town probably persisted for a time, but by 1890, most businesses had concentrated on Main Street, with a couple of places on Elm Street a block west.

The earliest known photograph of Main Street was taken about 1890. The gray image was published in the 1956 centennial edition of the *Peterson Patriot* under the catchy headline, "Main Street as she looked way back then." The original print seems to have since disappeared. The photograph was taken from the center of the street near the top end of Main looking south toward the railroad, providing an opposite-end view of the street to that from the scale office today. Evidently the unknown photographer intended to make a comprehensive view of the growing business street.

In the photograph, two rows of wooden false-front buildings face off and trail down the street into indistinctness. A few have two stories, but most have only one. The buildings are new but have a drab, raw appearance that matches the gray landscape and sky. The sidewalk is limited to a few squares of planking in front of the better buildings; otherwise, the center of this town is a sea of raw soil or mud, a rude place where the structures seem afloat without foundations. A dark figure in a brimmed hat stands near one building. The quality of the photograph is as muddy as the street, making it difficult to tell if there are wagons or other people about. It is impossible to determine the season since there are neither shadows nor a single tree or shrub; this Main Street had been cornfield only a few years earlier. The prospect is one of drafty buildings set amidst drabness, themselves adding to the drabness of what seems to be a March day on the Iowa frontier.

A resident of Peterson today, taken back in time to that spot and moment, would recognize little of the scene. As many as five buildings from that time still grace Main Street, but they have undergone considerable change and would be hard to recognize. The insightful modern viewer might notice the particular slope of the street down toward the river and the fact that the building fronts were then, and still are, exactly a hundred feet apart.

The town grew briskly for a decade or so, but it could not be considered much of a boom except by those who had lived here through the decades of stagnation prior to the coming of the railroad. All over the nation, towns were being platted and promoted, and many of them clearly offered more in the way of business and agricultural opportunities. Footloose farmers, merchants, and artisans could choose among options in a dozen states as land was opened for settlement and towns were platted everywhere. Land prices in northwest Iowa had risen far above the $1.25 an acre the Kirchner families and other original settlers had paid in the 1850s; by 1892, an acre was going for $15 to $20. Many farmers were looking to places farther west, where land was still cheap.

While Peterson had only a few years when it resembled the tar-paper boomtowns farther west, where hotels, restaurants, and blacksmith shops were unloaded from flatcars en masse and arranged to form an instant town, Peterson is no less a manufactured entity, no less a town made possible by the Industrial Revolution. Everything beginning with the very plan of the place was a mass-produced good, a standard, interchangeable part. Except perhaps for old times' sake, by 1899 no one collected any oat straw to hand-make hats; there were six stores in town that sold hats, better hats made in factories in the East.

By the last decade of the nineteenth century, Peterson was well enmeshed in the regional and national economy. A certain amount of the region's grain and livestock stayed here for local consumption, but most of it went east or west by rail to the markets at Chicago and Sioux City. From the beginning, farmers in all the new places on the prairie had seen themselves not as subsistence growers, but as members of a larger market economy.

Petersonites knew themselves to be part of the national culture as well. The railroad and its parallel telegraph line brought the news of the Spanish-American war, the circus and chautauqua, the Sears and Roebuck catalog. The railway station, situated at the foot of Main Street, was a focus of town life. Residents knew by heart the times of the six trains through town every day; town idlers met every one of them and sized up everyone who arrived and departed. And in those years before radio, residents crowded around the telegraph key in the depot anytime there was an election or a disaster.

A hundred years later, the chronology of Main Street is easily read in the materials used to build its structures. A glance at either side of the street today reveals a variety of media: wood, brick, a small bit of high-quality dimensional stone, and an occasional foundation laid up with round glacial rocks, stone-boated in from the hills and fields. There are walls of sheet and block glass, cinder block, concrete, aluminum, and even plastic. There is a clear time line here, one expressed in a sequence of structural building materials starting with wood, moving to brick, then to what must be called assorted materials, and, finally, to metal.

From 1881 until about 1894, all Main Street businesses in Peterson—indeed all buildings in town—were constructed of sawn lumber shipped in by rail. Single- and two-story balloon-frame shop fronts rose at the edge of the board sidewalk, standing cheek by jowl and selling general merchandise, groceries, harnesses, meals, haircuts, women's hats, pumps, and windmills. Second floors held fraternal lodges, doctors' offices, and, later, the telephone office. Because of fire danger and the primitive quality of fire equipment, most structures were separated by a fire break just wide enough to provide easy passage for town kids.

By 1899, Peterson was looking to brick. Most considered it more beautiful than any other material, except perhaps stone, and it certainly had advantages over wood-frame construction when it came to fire, but most of all it lent an air of permanence to a frontier town coming into the twentieth century. The two banks in town, like banks everywhere, wanted to promote the image of safety and security and became the first structures built of brick. In 1894 the Peterson Bank was laid up in red brick at the center of the block on the west side of the street; today the building is the Senior Center. The other, a much larger two-story structure on the corner to the south, became home to the First National

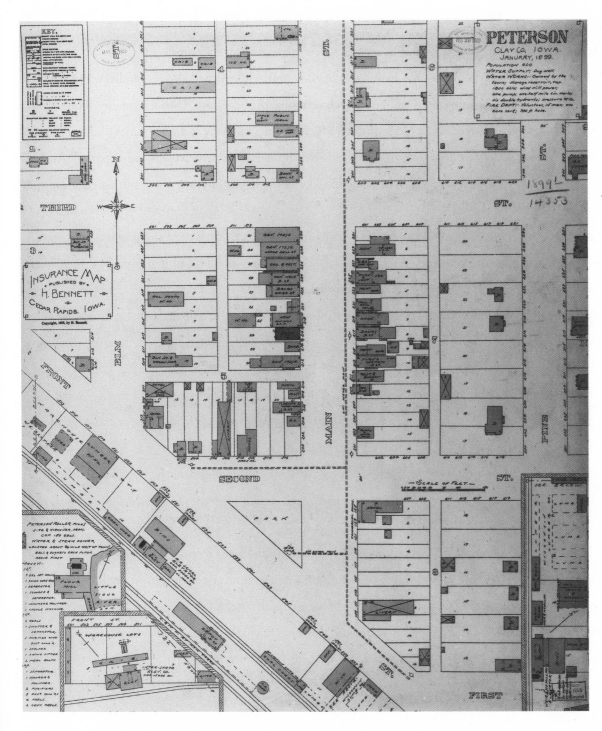

H. Bennett insurance
map of downtown Peterson,
1899. The Main Street
buildings seem to clump
toward Third Street, to the
north and away from the
depot, suggesting a town
plan that hoped to make
the intersection of Main
and Third the key
commercial corner in town.
The brick Peterson Bank
hedged its bets and was
built in the center of the
block on the west side of the
street. Today the building
houses the Senior Center.
The twenty-five-foot-wide
lots make clear just how
small some of these early
structures were.

By 1914, when this
Sanborn Company map
appeared, most of the recent
construction on Main
Street had taken place to
the south, toward Second
Street and the railroad
depot. The big new bank
on the corner had gone up,
and Batcheler's Ford
garage, across the street to
the west, was quite new.
Apparently, by 1914,
Peterson realized that the
commercial part of its
Main Street would not
grow beyond the single
block it now occupied and
that being near the depot
counted for more than
being near the intersection
of Main and Third.

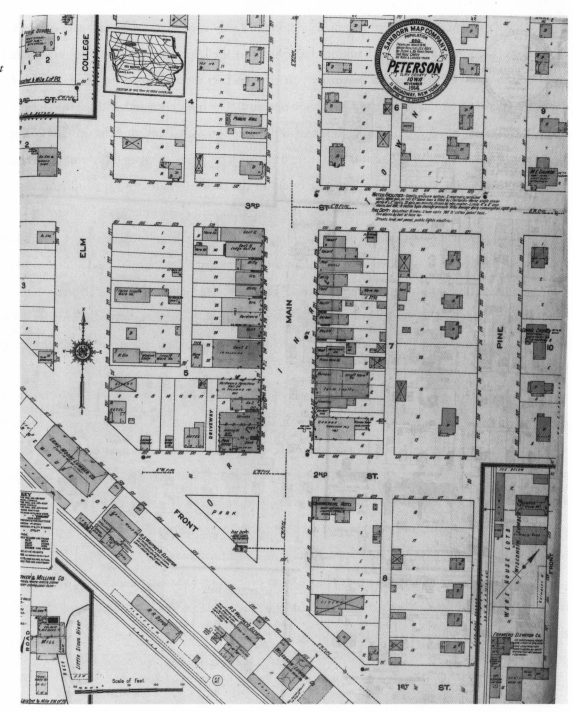

Bank a few years later. Both were trimmed in stone, a rarely used material in this part of the state because of the distance from stone quarries. The bank on the corner was the largest building in town, save perhaps the bins of the grain elevators down at the tracks. For many years the upstairs rooms housed the offices of the *Peterson Patriot*, the dentist, a doctor or two, and the town telephone operator. The building stands today, remodeled several times, at the corner of Highway 10 and Main Street. It serves as the Peterson State Bank, and the upstairs is empty.

Soon after the turn of the century, another brick structure took its place on Main: the White Front, a striking general store building spanning two lots. The bricks of the facade were fired with a brilliant, vitreous, white glazing. The roof and floor have long ago fallen in, but the brick front still gleams like a new Auburn.

Prior to World War I, builders began working with a new material—cement block. It looked a bit like stone, and it was as strong, but block was cheaper than brick. Sometime before 1914 the Tumler and Fedderson store was built of cement block and, about the same time, the Batcheler Garage, which later became the John Deere shop. Cement block was seldom ornate and had none of the warmth of brick—especially white-faced brick—but it was functional and comparatively inexpensive and therefore quickly earned its place on Main Street, not only in Peterson, but all across the country.

At the beginning of World War I, Peterson boasted but one vacant lot on the business block of Main Street and twenty-eight buildings, ten of which were either of brick or cement block. From then until about 1960, Main Street structural materials changed little. During those decades some builders experimented with tile brick, asbestos shingle siding, and asphalt paper pressed to resemble brick, but not until just after midcentury did several new materials gain favor. These came coincident with the urge to remake Main Street. During my teen years and later, I watched wood paneling, glass brick, plywood, and structural aluminum make their appearance on Main Street as buildings were redone, either to reflect more up-to-date designs or to make them look old-fashioned.

Out of a desire to remake the cinder-block front of the John Deere shop, the new owners had carpenters clad the front in dark, weathered siding and add on a Dodge City–style saloon overhang, complete with wood shingles. All that is missing are hitching posts to complete the effect of a faux western town. What started out as a legitimate postfrontier Main Street building has been redone in a modern style that could be called "Old West tourist trap revival."

The latest trend in building materials is evident in Brown Plumbing and Heating, next door north from Sue's. This structure is the newest on Main Street and perhaps the first since about 1940; some have opined that it will be the last. The structure marks the ongoing trend of construction not only on Main Streets, but anywhere in the farm belt. Built of dimensional lumber on a poured concrete floor, the building is clad in corrugated aluminum, altogether cheap and quick to put up. Plain as a T-shirt and entirely undistinguished, it has no pretensions of being anything but a utilitarian shelter for a business. The only signal to its purpose is found in the sign on the front of the building: "Amana Cooling & Heating—Brown Plbg. & Htg."

And in fact, except for the sign, the place could be most anything: a restaurant, a meeting hall, corporate offices for a trucking company. Never beautiful but endlessly flexible, these materials make airplane hangers, cattle sheds, and bus stations, with equal ease and equal lack of character.

Although it is very hard to trace their exact lineage, there are five buildings on Main Street today that seem to date from the first generation of construction. To the best I can determine, they are the first and only structures to have occupied these lots and were built sometime between 1882 and 1905. On the west side of Main at the corner of Third Street is T.K.'s Bar; south seven lots is the Senior Center, once the Peterson Bank; on the east side of Main is the abandoned and slumping Huntress Cafe; and two doors north, Sue's Diner.

Sue's may in fact be the oldest building on Main Street, though it is impossible to determine with certainty through abstracts of deeds, old fire-insurance maps, the Peterson histories, and what few photographs exist of the north end of the east side of Main Street. For many years photographers preferred to make their images of Main Street from the south end; for many years there were several trees standing between that vantage point and the building that today is Sue's, effectively obscuring it from eyes prying into the past.

For the fifth building, the record is a little more complete, though there are still gaps. In 1901 William H. Like opened a pool room in a single-story, false-front building that measured about eighteen by sixty feet. It was probably a new structure, but there is evidence suggesting that it could have been an older building moved from across the street. Built of wood, it could have easily fit on any small-town Main Street in the country and could have housed anything from a hat shop to a poultry hatchery. Given its simple design and construction, those who built it must have imagined it to be temporary, a structure that would fill the bill until larger, more permanent business houses—probably of brick—were built.

An exterior photograph from the time shows the pool hall well patronized along a muddy Main Street clogged with farm wagons and buggies. In the window, with his back to the street, is a man; he might be chalking a pool cue or pouring a drink. Like many such places of the time, the joint bore no signs to suggest the nature of the business therein.

What Rachel Kirchner thought of this pool hall is not recorded. Even if the place served alcohol, there is no reason to believe that it was the first in town to do so. And even by 1901, residents must have known that her edict on every deed in town prohibiting the sale of spiritous liquors was probably not legally enforceable.

In any event, 1914 saw Halver Berg buy the building and William Like move to a new location. The chewing tobacco was scraped off the floor and the building became the H. H. Berg jewelry store. The store stands in the background of a photograph of the Armistice Day parade; a Model T truck chugs slowly up Main Street, decorated by the Red Cross, with three starched nurses standing in the back. All the buildings in the photograph, including Berg's, and the parked cars along the street are festooned with bunting and flags. On the back of the print is written: "Nov 11–1918, peace parade." The storefront has been remodeled since Mr. Like ran the pool hall; the front windows are now bigger, of plate glass, and the doorway has been recessed.

For some years a Mr. Clausin ran a part-time photo studio in the back room of Berg's store, but, for reasons now forgotten, and at a time no one seems to remember, the back room of the building was taken off. In any event, Berg operated his jewelry store here until his retirement in 1957; then, for many years, the place was home to an insurance agency run by Loren Reed, and today it is a satellite office for veterinarian Q. Sundberg.

Meanwhile, through the decades, the buildings on either side came and went. The millinery shop to the south closed and was torn down; it was soon replaced by the cinder block Batcheler's Garage. To the north, an implement shop and harness shop came down around 1934, leaving three vacant lots. Today the back part of those lots is home to the aluminum-clad building of Quality Equipment.

The Berg Jewelry building, as my grandmother refers to it yet, is easily identifiable today as the same structure from the turn of the century. Though now sheathed in asbestos shingles, the plain high facade is unchanged and altogether original; the simple foundation is original. To this day, the building has no running water, no plumbing whatsoever.

It puzzles me to think that this small frontier building would persist and remain useful when so many larger and more substantial brick-and-cinder-block storefronts around it have been abandoned long ago. During our time in Peterson, the larger, two-story, cinder-block Tumler and Fedderson store right across the street was torn down. It was newer and was once sturdier, but it didn't last as long as this little wooden building. The survival of the smaller buildings, like the Senior Center, Sue's, and Sundberg's office, while bigger, more grandiose buildings have fallen into themselves, attests to the fact that Peterson was to remain small. The small structures have persisted because of their smallness, their low overhead, their suitability to the small market.

These days in William Like's old pool hall, Halver Berg's old jewelry store, Loren Reed's old insurance office, Janette Sanders sits close to an oil heater, beneath a pressed tin ceiling, answering the phone and listening to the business band radio, just where farmers once shot pool and gazed out at a muddy street nearly a hundred years ago.

In an odd way, this building is the prototype for two other, very different buildings on Main Street: the saloon-fronted and abandoned John Deere shop next door and the new aluminum-clad Brown Plumbing and Heating building up the street. While Sundberg's office is a true frontier storefront, one that would be as much at home in early Cheyenne as in Peterson, our western mythology, driven primarily by the motion picture industry, has taken these buildings and returned them to us with theatrical makeup. Where a simple false front was good enough for the real Dodge City, the Hollywood version, and the tourist-trap version that followed, had to have more texture, to show more contrast to the drab actuality of the frontier. Hence, where reality gave us a simple clapboard storefront, cinema imagination gives us weathered barn boards of plywood; where architectural fact gave us awnings of canvas and bull nose tin, Hollywood revival gives us an overdone caricature in wood and shingles.

In a different way, the Sundberg building is a prototype for the aluminum-sheathed sheds appearing everywhere in the Midwest. At the turn of the century, the easiest and cheapest way to build a building was to erect a balloon frame and sheath it with wood; today that bill is filled by poured concrete floors and wooden uprights sheathed in corrugated metal. And like the Sundberg building, which has been home to several different businesses, the metal-clad Brown building is universally flexible. Small-town thinking has always embraced utilitarianism, and the best example of it from 1900 has been updated by another from the late twentieth century.

The railroad through Peterson is gone; it built Main Street and then abandoned it. The branch line lasted just short of a hundred years. The tracks reached town from the east in July of 1882 to the jubilation of the whole town; they were pulled up during the summer of 1981 to only mild dismay. Never more than a tertiary line, passenger service here ended about 1950, and freight traffic ebbed to the point that each time a train went through town, people commented on it. "I wonder if that was the last one," they'd say. Finally the last one came, with a crane on it, and pulled up the rails behind as it went slowly through town. The line had been weedy and unkempt long before I began to hike it as a kid. Most of the rail, and probably the rotten ties as well, had been there since before the turn of the century.

. . . Up to that fateful moment, the prairie of the farm and of the township had been virgin sod; but now it bowed its neck to the yoke of wedlock. Nothing like it takes place any more; for the sod of the meadows and pastures is quite a different thing from the untouched skin of the original earth. Breaking prairie was the most beautiful, the most epochal, and most hopeful, and as I look back at it, in one way the most pathetic thing man ever did, for in it, one of the loveliest things ever created began to come to its predestined end.

—Herbert Quick, *Vandemark's Folly,* 1922

Chapter 14

Earth Upside Down

MARCH 6

The wind gets up early today, as it often does when winter begins to soften. It shakes steady and hard through the bare trees, even down here in town. But this is no spring breeze; the wind is raw out of the northwest and the temperature about twenty-five degrees. March on the northern prairies is neither winter nor spring; there are rare springlike days, and there are commonly those that pretend to be winter, but most are simply crummy days whose best function is to mark time until spring actually arrives. March is the month of frozen mud.

Outside the kitchen window, beyond the rattling trees, a cold moon hangs over the grain elevator, fading in a predawn sky. The growing gray light begins to illuminate a landscape that would be gray in the warmest sunlight. It is still a long time until good weather.

At six-thirty streetlights burn bright, and lights are on in kitchens and upstairs bathrooms all over town. There is even a light in the office at the school. A few cars leave town going north, west, or south with commuters to jobs in Spencer, Cherokee, and Storm Lake. An empty school bus rolls by on the highway.

At the cafe, Sue sleepily makes the rounds with the coffeepot as Mavis Stoner comes through the front door. She slams it behind her, leans on it, and proclaims to all: "Just heard on the radio of a farm in Clay County that sold for twenty-four-hundred dollars an acre—what do you think they'd give me for mine?" No one answers, but she quickly falls into conversation with those at the front table. The farm economy is doing better after the hard years of the 1980s, years that saw a clear decline in the fortunes of rural areas and towns like Peterson. Though land prices have rebounded, the fortunes of many smaller farm operators and their small towns remain endangered.

On the back wall at Sue's today are three sale bills, two from Sioux Rapids, one from Pocahontas. All three are farm sales. Each bill lists two or three hundred acres of land and associated farm buildings, plus older, smaller farm machinery, some of it antique, assorted household goods, appliances. The same economy of scale that makes it impossible for the dime store or the local drugstore to compete with Wal-Mart increasingly gathers farm ground into ever bigger and bigger parcels. The land described on these sale bills will be sold; what fences that are left will be pulled down, and unless the house and buildings are something special, they and the grove will be razed and burned. It takes a lot of room to turn a sixteen-row corn planter.

The farm couple or widow selling out will move to an air-conditioned apartment in a county-seat town, Storm Lake or Pocahontas, and will no longer watch each June for the peonies to open and won't know it when the winter birds come looking for the bird feeder in a sheltered yard that is no longer there.

These days the snow has sunk into the fields north of town, but it will come back this month once or twice if only for a few days. The soil looks to be warming and looks to invite the plow, but it is still frozen solid, every clod a rock.

Dirty snow, March snow, plugs the ditches still, and over the past weeks has melted back into grubby piles that contain as much dirt blown from the fields and gravel plowed from the roads as snow and ice. Matted dead grass is beginning to reassert itself as the predominant texture of the land. All over the area things are re-emerging from the snow; everything from Styrofoam cups to lost tools and a newspaper from December that one never found.

As I walk the river bottom, the air roars through the trees, keeping the few birds that spend the winter here close to shelter. Only the crows seem not to mind, and they flap their way downriver, crabbing sideways in the stiff wind. There are only three colors to the world on such a March day: the yellow-tan of dead grasses, the powdery blue of the sky filtered through gauzy clouds, and the gray of everything else—trees, earth, old snow, water, automobiles, streets, buildings, and people. Such March days exist to provide contrast to the warm days to come; wind and gray make the warming and greening of spring the feast after the hunger.

Late in the morning at the elevator, the scale office business is quiet. Says Janet: "Yesterday there were a lot of people bringing grain to town, but today the wind and cold is keeping the farmers home. Grain will blow off of a full wagon if it's too windy, and very few like to haul grain when it's so cold. But let it warm up or the price jump a few cents, and we'll be busy. A couple days ago the price went up ten cents a bushel and all kind of beans came to town."

The weather forecaster comes on the radio in the background and reports a wind chill of four below zero.

Rod's cornfield is an alien place on such a day; cold as Mars and bleak as the moon, there is little here save disked-over corn stubble and frozen clods. Except for the melting of the snow, the field hasn't changed materially since October when Rod made a pass over it with the disk to loosen some of the corn roots and stubble. In fact, I am the only person who has been here since then, in a third of a year. The land waits now for warmth and rain, waits for the sun to move north and strike the soil squarely to grow grain another season.

A full decade before the first store building went up on Main Street in Peterson, white settlers had begun to take up prairie lands to the north and south of town. By the time of the 1870 census, there were sixty-one men listing their occupation as farmer in double-sized Clay Township, Clay County, which included the thirty-six square miles that hadn't yet been split off to become Peterson Township. That amounts to sixty-one farmers for seventy-two square miles, and since the average purchase at the time was probably about 160 acres, it suggests that less than a quarter of the land was owned by people who were actively making farms.

Certainly far less than a quarter of the land had been broken and planted to crops; an 1868 estimate claims that 1,682 acres in all of Clay County had been put to the plow. That amounts to less than half of 1 percent, an average of three acres per square mile across the county.

White settlement here was still very new, and breaking tall-grass prairie for farmland was mean, hard work. It took power and time to invert an ecosystem that had taken several thousand years to develop. Roots of prairie plants were deep, strong, and woven into a dense mat of great strength. A typical breaking plow had a stout wooden beam seven to twelve feet long, with the front resting on a pair of steel wheels. The share was of steel in the best of them and could turn a thirty-inch wide furrow. The machine, depending on its size, required anywhere from six to twelve oxen to pull it, or somewhat fewer animals if a breaking crew used stout horses. A good operator with a good team could break one and a half to three acres of prairie per day.

Contrary to what most people believe today, breaking plows didn't plow deep. According to L. S. Coffin, who wrote about breaking prairie in 1902, not long after the last of it had been turned: "The main object aimed at was to secure as complete a rotting of the sod as possible. To this end the plow was gauged to cut only one and one-half to two inches deep."

This practice cut the plants at their most vulnerable point just below the surface and, when the sod was turned, buried the roots just deep enough that resprouting was unlikely. In order to cleave the roots, the share, or "shear" as many Iowans of the day called it, had to be kept sharp, necessitating frequent stops so the cutting edge could be refiled. Plowing around the outside of an eighty-acre plot, the plowmen were required to stop at each round to sharpen the cutting edge.

According to Coffin, plowing marshy ground was especially difficult: "In many places the sod in these 'sloughs' was so tough that it was with the greatest difficulty that the plow could be kept in the ground. If it ran out of the ground, this tough, leathery sod would flop back into the furrow as swiftly as the falling of a row of bricks set up on end, and the man and driver had to turn the long ribbon of tough sod over by hand. . . ."

By 1870, there were a few black rectangles of cropland amid the miles of prairie and a confusion of wagon tracks leading from Peterson in each direction to a slowly growing number of pioneer farms.

In those early days, farmsteads on the prairie were primitive. Treeless and fenceless, they provided little more than marginal shelter for humans and livestock alike. A few families started out in sod houses; others bought local timber from the Kirchners or the few others along the river who had trees big enough for marketable logs and built small log houses. By 1867, Gust Kirchner had his sawmill running, ending the short era of the log cabin in the area. Settlers could now haul rough-sawn lumber to their land to build better houses, better farm buildings. And soon the railroad would bring lumber by the trainload.

The sharpest impressions of this time of transition on the Iowa prairie come from those who were there, and none are more vivid and true than those of Hamlin Garland and Herbert Quick. These two regional authors lived during the days of sod breaking and farm building on the Iowa prairies and wrote about the changes with a nineteenth-century sense of the dramatic and with the detailed keenness possible only for writers who had observed the change firsthand. Garland, who left us such autobiographical volumes of Midwest literature as *Main Travelled Roads, A Son of the Middle Border, A Daughter of the Middle Border*, and *Boy Life on the Prairie*, was among the first to draw a realistic, if somewhat romantic, portrait of life on the prairies of early settlement, the newborn society, and the personalities of the region.

Herbert Quick is best known for a trilogy of novels detailing Euro-American settlement in Iowa. *Vandemark's Folly, The Hawkeye*, and *The Invisible Woman* together form a chronology tracing the lives of those who sought to change the grasslands to farms and towns. Similarly, Quick's autobiography, *One Man's Life*, brings to focus the specifics of his own experience as a child growing up in early Grundy County, Iowa.

In *One Man's Life*, he describes his family's move to a freshly broken farm in north central Iowa, probably about 1875: "Half a mile beyond stood our new house. It was a building which many farmers nowadays would not think good enough for a henhouse; but it was ours. There was a magic in this word. A block of this black, turned-up sod half a mile long and a quarter wide was ours. That house with sides of boards running up and down and with no lath or plaster was home. The stable was made of crotches cut in timber and set in the ground, with poles over the roof, which was covered with prairie hay spread on with a pitchfork. We had no knowledge of any such thing as thatching. The teams turned in before the door, and goods were unloaded, the stove was set up for the house warming and the cookery, and we were installed in the Hagen Place, as we afterward came to call it.

"We were farther out on the prairie than ever before; but the settlement was now spreading over the whole country like a rash, of which we were only one of the numerous pimples. The doom of the prairie was coming upon it."

While Quick's family began on a farm where a great deal of the "ground breaking" work had already been done, most began with only a rectangle of prairie marked out by survey stakes. There were a million things that must be done at once, not only to make this piece of grass a home, but also to begin a producing business that would feed a family. There was new breaking to be done, crops to put in, a vegetable garden to plant and tend so that the family would not starve come winter, a well to be dug, and a house and some sort of shelter for livestock to be built, out of materials that were not necessarily close at hand. And as soon as time allowed, farm families planted trees to break the prairie wind. They planted seeds for fruit trees and dug saplings along the river—fast-growing species like silver maple, willow, and cottonwood—to surround their simple homes.

The need for groves was as much psychological as it was environmental. A human being is the tallest thing on open prairie, and from the start people sought to build structures and plant things that would dwarf themselves and bring some relief from too much horizon and too much sky. There is something unnerving about being so exposed, so vulnerable, and people rebelled against it by planting trees and eagerly tending their growth. As soon as there were trees to put your back against, the place would become home.

Cow Vandemark, the protagonist in *Vandemark's Folly*, relates to the reader certain difficulties of prairie settlement: "We early Iowa settlers, the men and women who opened up the country to its great career of development, shivered through that winter and many like it, in hovels that only broke the force of the tempest but could not keep it back. The storms swept across without a break in their fury as we cowered there, with no such shelters as now make our winters seemingly so much milder. Now it is hard to convince a man from the East that our state was once bare prairie.

" 'It's funny,' said the young doctor that married a granddaughter of mine last summer, 'that all your groves of trees seem to be in rows. Left them that way, I suppose, when you cut down the forest.' "

From the very beginning, midwestern farmers saw themselves as commercial operators; though farm families would grow a certain part of their own food, they saw their livelihood in terms of selling grain and livestock to railroad-provided markets.

Until the railroad came, they made do. Herbert Quick writes of Cow Vandemark's first days of work as he begins to turn prairie into a farm: "As I looked back at the results of my day's work, my spirits rose; for in the East, a man might have worked all summer long to clear as much land as I had prepared for a crop on that first day. This morning it had been wilderness; now it was a field—a field in which Magnus Thorkelson had planted corn, by the simple process of cutting through the sod with an ax, and dropping in each opening thus made three kernels of corn. Surely this was a new world!"

The first crop the first year was actually planted not in soil, but in the overturned sod. It took a couple of years for the turned sod to decay, or "mellow," into topsoil. Once the soil softened, farmers extended their range of crops and planted them in more efficient ways. "Sod corn" soon gave way to smooth fields of wheat, barley, and rye, and in a world where horses provided the only power greater than a man's back, farmers raised oats to feed them. Wheat varieties engendered considerable experimentation, some scientific, some not. Whether the breeds were tested or not, they carried engaging names: Red Chaff Bald, Black Sea, Wild Goose, Scotch Fyfe.

In the early days, before all the land was taken up and turned to crops, farmers used the shrinking prairie as a great livestock range. Much of the unplowed land was owned by speculators who were waiting for the price to rise, and some quarter sections had not yet been bought from the government; nobody was making any attempt to farm great tracts of land, especially the wet, undrained prairie. As a result, the remaining grasslands became open range for cattle, sheep, horses, and even hogs. It fell to the young boys to spend their summer days as herders, early cowboys in a sense, who were put in charge of small herds of livestock and were to keep them together and out of any crops. The practice persisted until the 1890s, when the prairie had shrunk to the point that open range grazing was no longer practical. Not until then did farmers begin to plant domestic hay for their animals; not until then did they consider the need for fenced pasture; not until then did they turn their young boys to other, less adventuresome tasks.

The 1870s were hard times for most people in the United States, and no less so for new farmers in northwest Iowa. The Panic of 1873 and the depression that followed all but stopped land sales in the region and thus the inflow of settlers. What did flow in were great plagues of grasshoppers. They had made their first appearance in 1867 but were at their worst from 1873 to 1878. Wrote Arthur Allen in his *History of Northwestern Iowa*: "Their first appearance resembled the approach of a storm cloud, so dense and numerous were the swarms. An ominous buzz, like a battery of distant sawmills, and the darkening of the sun's rays, were the next evidences of the approach of the weird, mysterious danger. Then, like a dense, dun blanket, the insects settled upon the fields and gardens of growing wheat and vegetables, stripping everything green down to the ground in an appallingly short period."

Making this all the worse was the grasshoppers' preference for small grains like wheat and oats, garden produce, and fruit trees over the less succulent, and more durable, native prairie species.

Continued Allen, "Billions upon billions of eggs were then deposited in the ground about half an inch below the surface, where they lay until the warm winds and sun of spring hatched them out."

What agony it must have been during that long winter of 1873–74, a winter of economic depression to begin with. In addition, you knew that if financial times didn't kill you, the seeds of complete agricultural destruction had been laid by the billion all around you during the summer, awaiting only the turn to spring to rise and finish you off.

Allen quoted a settler in Fort Dodge: "No amount of cultivating the soil and disturbing the eggs seemed to injure or destroy them. I had two hundred acres of new breaking, and as soon as the frost was out [in the spring], commenced dragging the ground, which exposed the eggs. The ground looked as if rice had been sown very thickly. I thought the dragging . . . would destroy them, but I believe that every egg hatched."

Year after year they came back. Some years they destroyed everything; other years they hit some counties hard and barely touched others. Sodbusters in Nebraska, Kansas, and Dakota, plus thousands of Iowa settlers, were devastated and went back east. Then, in 1879, mysteriously, the plagues ended. A few grasshoppers hatched out that year, making farmers anxious, but then disappeared, never to return.

Because of the depression, because of the grasshoppers, the population of northwest Iowa grew sluggishly, if at all, during the 1870s. The western tier of four townships in Clay County—including Peterson Township and village—grew from a population of 310 in 1870 to only 570 a decade later; many of the new residents may well have been backwash from the frontier, retreating east from Dakota and taking up land in Iowa, where, despite the plagues, the grasshoppers weren't as bad as farther west. During the same period, the village of Peterson actually lost residents: some 30 percent of its small population left during the decade of the 1870s. These were not flush times.

But with the departure of the grasshoppers, the return of better economic times, and the arrival of the railroad in Peterson in 1882, growth came to the region. As the steam whistle changed the village into a town, it wrought a manifold change on the rural landscape, as boxcars of manufactured goods and affordable materials streamed toward the new settlements. From Peterson and every other town along the rail lines in the newly broken prairie, farm wagons full of lumber, farm machinery, tools, and even some store-bought dry goods, radiated into the countryside. Better farm implements improved the lot of farmers, and shacks were replaced by houses—most of them modest, a few quite large—and rude stables were one by one replaced with commodious barns, quickly becoming the symbol of farm prosperity.

Other buildings went up during this first boom in farm construction. By 1890, the well-equipped farm had, in addition to a snug house and barn, a granary, a hog house, some chicken houses, a smokehouse, a wood house, a washhouse. Many farms boasted a dozen or more specialized buildings clustered around the house and barn. Above it all hovered a windmill, and all around grew young trees striving to overtop it.

A common commodity in thousands of boxcars coming west in those days was barbed wire; while this innovation is given credit for dividing the open range farther west, it also was the final link in the domestication of the Iowa prairie. Prior to its advent, there was simply no way to enclose fields and pastures in this treeless land. Quickly now, unfenced prairie gave way to corn and oats, and the valley-side hills were fenced in all directions to become pasture.

Choices in crops had shifted as well. Because of the trouble with wheat rust, grasshoppers, and other insects, wheat had fallen into some disfavor, and corn had moved in to take its place. Corn's popularity as a reliable crop in the north was enhanced by the development of early-maturing varieties that helped ensure a good harvest before fall freeze. In 1889 Clay County averaged a 35–40 bushel-per-acre harvest of corn, very good for those days, but tiny compared with the 150–200 bushel-per-acre harvests of today.

The land was filling up, but, in Clay County at least, not evenly. A sample of three townships from 1887 provides a clear example. Clay Township, just north of Peterson Township, led the county in the number of farmsteads with ninety-four in its six-by-six mile square. The township also boasted eight new single-room schools for a growing population of students. Several square miles in the township had five or six farmsteads each, making things downright neighborly. Clay Township, being crossed diagonally by the shallow Willow Creek watershed, was well drained; all a settler had to do was plow under the prairie and plant crops. This was preferred land.

On the other hand, much of Peterson Township was either river bottom, steep valley side, or, north of town,

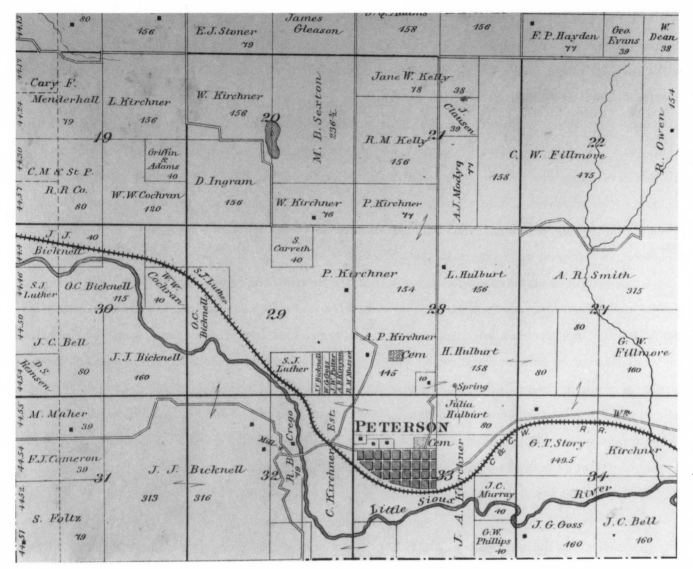

Excerpt from Peterson Township map, Inter State Publishing Co., 1887. The prairie of Peterson Township was fast disappearing under the plow when this map was drawn. That the Kirchners had been interested in the timber along the Little Sioux River is indicated by their claims along the river in the south half of section 33. The mill seat is in the northeast quarter of section 32. Note how the river loops three times across the section line between sections 33 and 34. Almost all these family names, including Kirchner, are gone from the Peterson phone book today.

largely flat, unsloped prairie. In any wet year, great pools of water would persist in the many low spots on the flat prairie. As of 1887, there were only fifteen farmsteads here, and five schools, including the one at Peterson itself. Dense settlement of Peterson Township would wait until land that was easier to farm was all taken up and until field tile could be dug into the soil to drain the many low spots.

And in the southeast corner of Clay County was yet-unorganized Garfield Township. Here, on the Bemis Moraine, the land humped and rolled, with little in the way of organized drainage, leaving ponds, sloughs, and cattail marshes thick across the landscape. Here, as of 1887, there were only eight farms on the whole thirty-six square miles, and not a single school.

As is true for much of the rest of the United States, people of particular ethnic backgrounds tended to settle close together. In 1887 a good many Germans had bought land south of town. The Welsh took up farms to the east of Peterson: the township cemetery along Highway 10 is still known as the Welsh Cemetery. North of town, in Clay Township, the Danes made a strong showing, with Canadians, Swedes, and Germans lagging behind. Around the area was a peppering of Norwegians, English and Scottish, Dutch, and a few Irish. The same year in Peterson Township, including the town of Peterson, most people were U.S. born, with thirteen Germans (the Kirchner family alone accounted for a good many of them) and nine Swedes.

It would not, however, be fair to describe this part of northwest Iowa as any sort of ethnic stronghold. In all townships and in Peterson itself, native-born men and women far outnumbered immigrants; according to the census of 1885, 80 percent of the residents of Clay County had been born in the United States.

While these ethnic and cultural differences were for a time borne out in different language, food, and dress (and persist today as ethnic awareness and "heritage" activities), they actually made little difference here in how people farmed, whether it was in styles of farmstead structures, spatial organization of a farm, or crop and livestock selection. While it is true that farmers of different ethnic traditions brought with them various skills and inclinations, they quickly learned the efficiency of new methods and new crops and understood the advantage of labor-saving machinery. Very quickly both the farmer from upstate New York and the farmer from Denmark adapted to the new conditions of soil, climate, markets, and technology.

As the land began to fill up, the routes of travel began to change to conform to the section lines. When the land had been mostly open prairie, settlers followed wagon tracks that avoided low spots but generally ran fairly straight from town to the home place. As prairie on either side of a section line became farmland, the roadways were increasingly squeezed into the sixty-six-foot-wide corridor astride the section line, irrespective of terrain. In places this forced travel into low spots, making horse-drawn vehicles negotiate sloughs and cross streams at less than opportune spots.

By 1900, there were trees. In farm groves the biggest trees would have reached up only about twenty-five feet, but by then they made enough shade that a threshing crew could get some relief from the midday summer sun. And they had already begun to slow the great winds.

A great change had taken a mere thirty years. In 1869, at the beginning of settlement on the open prairie around here, some ancestors of mine, Anson and Helen Allbee, bought 160 acres of prairie in Clay Township. Recently discharged from the Union army, Anson used his war scrip to buy the land. Everything around them was prairie, so they used it to build themselves a sod house. There were a few other settlers in the township and only a little bit of fresh plowing; it was "new country."

In the three decades to the turn of the century, they saw the reversal—the literal overturning—of mile upon mile of prairie. They watched it change year by year from a land of wild plants to a land of fields dotted with sturdy new groves, barns, and two-story houses.

Neither Anse, as he was known, nor Helen, nor any of their three children left diaries, so I have no clear sense of their lives on that land during those years of revolution, and I have no sense of how deeply they understood the magnitude of the change. Many, if not most, pioneer stories pivot on the romantic notion of being on the cusp of some great advance in civilization, but, living amidst the revolution as they did, could they ever fully grasp its meaning? I wonder what Anse thought when he climbed the new windmill for its periodic oilings and took a moment to sweep his eye along the horizon. Perhaps he was filled with acrophobia and thought only of being back at soil level, but looking out above the grove across miles of new plowings and plantings must have made him wonder at the change he was part of.

And when it was all gone, did he and Helen miss the prairie? For a people so concentrated on fields and barns and trees and fences, it was easy for the last of the prairie to slip away unbidden. Perhaps Hamlin Garland summed it up best in *Boy Life on the Prairie*:

"It was a changed world, a land of lanes and fields and houses hid in groves of trees which he had seen set out. No one rode horseback any more. Where the cattle had roamed and the boys had raced the prairie wolves, fields of corn and oats waved. No open prairie could be found. Every quarter section, every acre, was ploughed. The wild flowers were gone. Tumbleweed, smartweed, pigweed, mayflower, and all the other plants of semi-civilization had taken the place of the wild asters, pea-vines, crow's-foot, sunflowers, snake-weed, sweet-williams, and tiger-lilies. The very air seemed tamed and set to work at the windmills which rose high above every barn, like great sunflowers."

With a nominal cost of seed, a range of two months for planting[,] it waits for the sick and the absent—may be harvested almost any time without expensive machinery, is almost indestructible, destroys worthless plants, gives about as much rough feed for all domestic animals, and is un-equalled for fattening purposes. The buxom girls and stalwart sons of the West deem it the staff of life when made into bread, and when made into whiskey many think it life itself. It supports the poor man's family, the rich man's flask and the merchant's trade. It is the basis of an immense trade in beef, the main pillar of our national prosperity, the golden fleece of America, the staple of the West . . .

—*Prairie Farmer*, 1864

Chapter 15

Prairie Corn

Farmers have grown corn in Iowa for a thousand years; it startles me to think of it. For the last ten centuries they have waited for spring soil to warm enough for seed and have eyed the summer storms coming from the west with fear of hail and wind. For nearly a thousand seasons, they have exalted in harvests, listened to dry corn leaves rattle in October winds, and cursed the droughts that made them hungry.

More than an arrowhead or the bones of an ancient slaughtered bison, I wish I could discover, along some creek bank, a stand of wiry little cornstalks, relics from cultures who lived and farmed here long before any surveyors came. They would be stunted and meager compared with the super-crossed hybrids of today, growing in long green rows across a thousand miles of the country. In my mind the image of short stalks and pickle-sized ears is a reminder of the human past of this region, a past that is far longer than we usually consider.

Corn is the human continuity in this landscape, the solid, dependable foodstuff of centuries; though early Euro-American settlers began with wheat, flax, and oats, they soon discovered that corn grew best here, something the old ones had known for a long time. Corn, or maize, is the right crop for Iowa, just as wheat is for Kansas. In any given year nearly half of the state is given over to rows of corn; the other half grows soybeans. Iowa has been called "The Hawkeye State," "The Land Between Two Rivers," and "Heartland of America," but no appellation could be more accurate than "The Tall Corn State."

The landscape in this part of Iowa undergoes a profound visual revolution through the cycle of a year, perhaps as complete and dramatic as anywhere this side of the sugarcane fields of Australia. Each spring, large machines go to work preparing the whole landscape for another crop; each summer, corn and soybeans turn countless square miles to brilliant green; each fall, the green dies back, is harvested, leaving soil for the snow and the next season. Whatever the visual change on the prairie of old through a season, the astonishing transformation through a year's cycle on agricultural land is akin to plowing under and replacing the prairie each year.

The economics and practices of agriculture altogether control the look of the land here today, just as they have for the last hundred years. The fact that barns, silos, fences, and entire farmsteads are disappearing, and that the towns are losing population, is clearly an effect of agricultural economics. So also is the obvious fact that woodland is asserting itself in hillside pastures in the region, and that large, metal-clad machine sheds have been going up on farms all over the region for the last twenty years.

The impulse on the part of farmers is, and always has been, to get the very most crop out of the fewest acres. Whatever the fluctuations of land value in past decades, good land has always been dear, and limited, meaning the successful farmer always works to get the most from the least. Farmers here, and everywhere else I've conversed with them, always use as the primary measure of success the yield of crop per square land measure; it is just as true for sunflowers in Wisconsin, rice on mountainsides in Nepal, rapeseed in Britain.

But here at least, unlike on steep terraced slopes in the Himalayas, yield-per-acre pressure does not mean that every available plot of land is pressed into service; there is considerable idle land at hand. Federal programs keep some land in the "soil bank," due to its erodibility and to prevent the overproduction of grain. Acres in reserve are common south of Peterson where the land slopes more; here, too, hay fields are more frequent because of the erodibility of the land. In this region farmers have planted some large fields semipermanently to brome grass. Some fields have been fallow long enough that a few prairie natives have begun to re-establish themselves.

But north of town, where the land is flatter and some farmers are still paying off the loans for the installation of miles of drainage tile, it is fence-to-fence, or, perhaps more accurately, ditch-to-ditch field crop. Farmers cultivate very little hay here and instead go hard at it with corn-soybean rotation year after year, with comparatively few acres set aside in government programs.

The cost of land is one factor in the look of the agricultural countryside, but so is the cost of fertilizer, herbicide, pesticide, fuel, and wear and tear on machinery. From first-rate land, farmers can easily recoup their investment in time and costly materials. On marginal land, it may not pay to invest the chemicals and time; hence poorer ground is most often left in hay or put in government set-aside programs. Any land that is farmed is farmed hard, while marginal acres are put in hay or left fallow.

Land altogether too rough to grow crops, like the hilly land along the river valley and in creek ravines, was once extensively used as pasture. In the days of my youth, every summer hillside had its pastoral herd of cows and calves, chewing thick grass and switching flies in the drowsy afternoon. The hills no longer have cattle, since it no longer pays to raise them this way, especially if it means maintaining miles of fence, up hill and down through rough country. Farmers' time is valuable, like that of everyone else, and the profit equations of raising stock cows have shifted in favor of the big operators.

With the disappearance of fences, cattle, and farmers, these pastures have reverted to a more wild state, but hardly to prairie. On open hillsides prairie grasses reassert themselves, like the bold stands of big bluestem encircling Peterson on the valley hillsides, but in ravines and anywhere else they get a start, trees and woody shrubs send up their shoots to fill in the understory, and, if left alone, make shady woods where there was once only prairie.

Despite abandoned pastures, and despite marginal ground left fallow, farming is intense here, as intense probably as anyplace in the country. This pressure for profits is best seen in the rapid accumulation of farmland into ever-larger farms. Each year the number of farms dwindles as those remaining accrue more acres. Iowa had its greatest number of farms in 1900; it has been a steady decline ever since. Rod Burgeson, for example, farms 650 acres, just over a square mile; 580 acres is planted in crops, the rest is pasture.

"This used to be considered a fair-sized operation," he told me one day, "but the trend is toward places of two or three thousand acres. The equipment is so expensive, and the profit margin is a lot smaller than it used to be."

Bob White says it another way: "Pretty soon we're going to wind up with one airline, one Iowa farmer, and one railroad to haul his grain."

The size of machinery, the size of planters particularly, tells the story. Back in the late 1960s, when I worked in my grandparents' John Deere dealership, I remember seeing a couple of two-row corn or soybean planters; most were four-row machines, but at least one or two stalwart operators still used old narrow equipment to get through their narrow gates to plant their small fields. Today, a dwindling number, including Bob White, still use four-row planters; most, like Rod Burgeson, use eight-row machines, and there is a growing number of twelve- and even sixteen-row units at work each spring. A neighbor of Bob's has a new, green sixteen-row planter. "Look at the size of that thing!" he exclaimed one day from the pickup. "And John Deere is talking about a twenty-four-row planter! Think of it!" Even the sixteen-row machine is big; any implement designed to cover sixteen rows has a span as great as the wingspan of a light aircraft.

Every other piece of farm equipment has grown accordingly. Big new tractors weigh a good ten times what an old John Deere B weighed, and many now have huge traction wheels at all four corners, and, of course, four-wheel drive. To navigate narrow gates in the dwindling number of places where fences remain and to be able to ply the county roads, planters, chisel plows, and multigang disk harrows all have hydraulically articulated units that pivot upward out of the way. Around Peterson they are a common sight as farmers with far-flung holdings make their way from place to place in the cabs of land behemoths. Even on wide, paved county roads, the operator must slow and pull clear to the side to allow a car to pass; motorists slow down as well, when they see how close they must pass to a ten-foot-high gang of slicing disk blades.

In 1900 several people were needed to farm a hundred and sixty acres; today, one family, even one operator without livestock and with the right equipment, can farm a thousand acres. As a result, half or more of the original farmsteads are gone in this part of Iowa; maybe half of those left are houseless or are marred by sagging, abandoned houses. People, mostly the young, have left the land, the countryside, the towns, the state, both because of the attractions of Houston, Phoenix, and Atlanta, and because of the lack of farm or other employment opportunities here.

While this whole region is justly considered the "Midwestern Farm Belt" or the "Corn Belt," geographers make some finer distinctions, and one of their regional boundary lines passes fairly close to Peterson. Unlike a state boundary or the shoreline of a lake, this line is indistinct. East of this line, which roughly follows the Bemis Moraine east of Peterson, the majority of farms are engaged in cash grain farming; to the west, a greater number are engaged in livestock production. Farmers to the east in the cash grain region, which coincides with the Des Moines Lobe of the Wisconsinan glacier, are more likely to sell their entire crop for cash. To the west in the western livestock region, they are more likely to feed a considerable part of it to their cattle and hogs.

In the central cash grain region, farms tend to be larger, as does the equipment that farms them, and a farmstead may have nary a fence of any sort, except perhaps the one around the dog kennel. On this ground, which is fairly level once past the hills of the Bemis Moraine, fields are large, and most are devoted year after year to corn and soybeans; there is very little hay or pasture. A complete modern farmstead may consist of a new ranch house, with satellite dish, a large metal-clad building for implement storage, and an elaborate system of driers, augers, and bins that can store more grain than some elevators in town. There will be no barns, chicken houses, silos, windmills—sometimes, no trees, even. Such places look more like factories than farms; in fact, they are factories more than farms.

To the west, where the land is more dissected by streams in the livestock-growing region, farm acreages tend to be smaller, as farmers give more of their time to raising cattle and hogs. The landscape is still devoted to corn and soybeans, but there is some hay here in places, especially on sloping ground, and there is still some land in pasture. Here, a few more of Iowa's old farm structures are likely to remain; while the barn may be in the process of falling down and the corncrib long disused with the advent of steel bins for shelled corn, there is a greater likelihood that a hog house or a cattle shed might still be in service.

Around Peterson the farms are a mix of the two. North of town, on the flatter land, farmers tend to raise more cash grain and less livestock, and there is a greater urge to tear out fences. South of town, where the land is more broken, I smell cattle and hogs more often.

Farmsteads—the relatively few that remain—all have personalities, and each has stories to tell a careful observer.

Like most any other place of intense human activity, farmsteads have undergone extensive evolution and adaptation to new roles. The mix of structures on any given farmstead is some indication of its history, present use, and possible future.

Houses in the area range from the small, 1880-era, two-story, gable-roofed home, to the 1980, single-level, triple-garage, ranch home with brick trim. Common still are the pre-turn-of-the-century, two-story, "upright and wing" homes that were built by the thousands everywhere across the agricultural landscape. Most went up before 1900. With a simple gable roof and only a single room wide, these houses were often the second ones constructed on a farmstead, nailed together right next to the soddie or shack, which was happily torn down when the new place was finished. The L or "wing" was often a kitchen and sometimes only a single story. Tucked in the corner made by the two wings is invariably a porch, usually home to a few cats and several pairs of muddy boots.

Built later, and no less common, is the "prairie four-square" or "corn belt house." Designed as a two-story cube, usually with a hip roof, it has four rooms downstairs and four rooms up. These became popular in part because furnaces began to replace coal or wood stoves; with radiators throughout the house, each room no longer needed its heating stove and therefore its proximity to a chimney. These, too, appeared in farm country by the thousands and were to a great extent built during the second boom in agricultural building, which peaked about 1920. Midwesterners loved their porches, and many of these four-square houses were constructed with porches around two and even three sides.

Modern farm homes, as they follow suburban trends, have taken a horizontal form. Split levels, flat ranches, and a good many double-wide mobile homes grace the landscape. While they run against traditional notions of farm home styles, they provide ample light and open space and reflect the shape of the land itself.

Farm homes, like homes everywhere, get remodeled time and again as new styles of living come and go. Residents enclose porches, knock out walls, build additions, add Tudor and Greek revival details—sometimes to the same house—or sheathe the whole thing in aluminum or vinyl siding as they get tired of painting it every couple of years.

Parallel with the evolution of homes is that of barns, although, unlike homes, barns are undergoing a great extinction. Since the departure of the horse from the farm, big barns have had little real function except as shelter for cattle or storage for hay and junk. Farm landscapes everywhere have fewer and fewer of them each year, and many of those that remain suffer from neglect or outright collapse.

The old-fashioned side-entry barns of Pennsylvania and upstate New York never made it this far west. There might be an example or two around of a barn with big doors on the sides, but by the time barns were being built here, several of the functions of the building had changed. Eastern barns had big side doors that gave access to the upper story. Often the building was set into a side hill, putting the second floor at grade level on one side; otherwise a soil ramp was built up to the door. On the lower floor was an area for livestock; on the second level, just inside the big doors, was a threshing floor for wheat. But by the 1870s, when the first barns went up in northwestern Iowa, wheat was being threshed in the fields, not in the barn, making this classic design obsolete.

Instead of a threshing floor on the second level, farmers in Iowa needed storage for hay and accordingly built barns similar to those in eastern farmlands but moved the bigger openings around to the ends, usually close beneath the gable. For decades common haying practice had farmers bring racks of loose hay to a spot beneath the high gable end doors, where hooks could be dropped down to the load and the hay lifted into the loft. Most of the barns in this region are hay barns of this basic sort.

There are finer distinctions, and they can be read by the shapes and angles of barn rooflines. The earliest barns in northwest Iowa, those built between about 1875 and 1895, are generally high and square and have simple, steep gable roofs, like those of farms further east. With the exception of door positions, these barns, of which there are very few left in northwest Iowa, could pass for common barns in upstate New York.

Around 1880, barns of similar dimensions began to appear with gambrel roofs, the classic Iowa barn multiangle roof. This simple adaptation allowed for greater headroom—or hay room—in the loft. These barns were built until the farm depression hit in the 1920s. Then, starting around 1940, a number of barns, built mostly to replace others lost to fire and wind, were put up using curved, laminated beams that gave the modern barn a distinctive curved roofline.

In regions and on particular farms that emphasized livestock raising, another type of barn was common. This structure also had a gable roof, but, unlike the others, the three-bay-gable barn was comparatively low and flat, often covering a substantially larger area than others. This barn provided hay storage above and usually had three large livestock bays beneath under the flatter and larger roof. Three-bay-gable barns were popular from about 1890 to the 1920s, about the same time as were gambrel-roofed barns. These barns were common in cattle regions farther west; I've seen examples in Nevada, Wyoming, and Washington.

There is a clear correlation between the general-purpose gambrel-roof barn and the prairie four-square house. Because they were popular at the same time, many farmsteads were built, or rebuilt, using these types between about 1880 and 1925.

These days it is hard to find a chicken coop on any Iowa farm, much less one inhabited by chickens. Likewise have gone hog houses, corncribs, and most of the other structures that made early farms such havens for cats, sparrows, wasps, and kids playing hide-and-seek. Most such buildings, no longer useful, are in the way; the old cattle shed gets pulled down not only because there are no longer any cattle, but also because it is too close to the new machine shed to get the new and larger riding mower between them.

Perhaps the only new buildings going up on farms today, with the possible exception of an occasional new home, are the metal-clad, general purpose shop and machinery storage buildings, being simply larger versions of Brown's Plumbing and Heating on Main Street in Peterson. Bob White has one and keeps his newer tractor, combine, corn head, field cultivator, planter, disk, two cultivators, and other machinery in the fifty-four-by-eighty-one-foot metal building. And, like many farmers, Bob has found just a little leftover space in the corners for his pickup camper and fishing boat.

Modern farming has brought other changes, and yet some parts of the life are the same as they were for my ancestor Anse Allbee. Farmers are a fidgety lot, and they always have been; they get nervous about a possible drop in prices just as a pen of hogs is ready for the market, or they worry about a sudden freeze just as the corn crop reaches maturity, or about the impending end of a farm program that leaves them without income they'd expected. Bob White, like most farmers, has difficulty tearing himself away from the farm. One reason is that he loves the work; another is daily livestock chores; another is his anxiousness about something happening while he is away. As a result, Bob's fishing boat and camper spend most of their time in the machine shed.

As they always have, farmers gamble with the weather, the markets, and their own decisions.

"That financial risk has always been there," says Bob. "You've got to know what you're doing. You can have a dry year or get hailed out—it's part of farming. We're the number one gamblers all right. You can just as well go out to Las Vegas and throw the old dice—it's the same growing or marketing a crop."

The difference between profit and loss for some operators is often only a couple of percentage points on the cost of borrowing operating money or a few cents on the price of corn. And any farmer with a few thousand bushels of corn in the bin is affected greatly by a few cents' rise or drop in the price. Consequently, they watch the markets carefully.

The markets have grown more complicated in years of late, but the basic structure, as it relates to Iowa farmers, has been the same since the railroad arrived. Today, paved roads and trucks haul a good percentage of the grain and livestock, especially from railroad-poor places like Peterson, but just like a hundred years ago, farmers ship what they produce to distant markets and watch the numbers on the Chicago Board of Trade with eager concern.

Bob White, like many, has a video terminal at home in his office just off the kitchen, an on-line terminal that gives him updated futures prices constantly. Bob checks it every time he walks by, more out of curiosity than anything, for the hour-to-hour changes won't affect him much. "Well, look at that!" he exclaims, as the Chicago corn futures drop a couple of cents in response to soaking rains moving in from the west, helping to ensure a good crop. He's a market junkie but knows that, like any sort of gambling, the addiction can be dangerous.

"Sometimes us little Iowa farmers decide to play with the big boys on the corn futures, buying and selling a little corn. If ten farmers play the board, eight will lose money, one will make money, and one will break even. I can't name anybody who's made big money playing the big board, but I can show you some who've lost farms over it. People think, boy, if I can just give her one more shot, I'll come out big."

Whatever the nature of their gambles, many farmers are increasingly interested in immediate information, and small dish antennas, like Bob's, aimed at a tower in Everly for continuous data transmission, are as common on farmsteads now as windmills once were.

The revolution in American farming, and most notably the greatly enhanced crop yields, is due to a combination of mechanical, chemical, and biological innovations. While the advantages of a four-wheel-drive tractor over a team of horses are evident to even the uninitiated, the advantages, and the dangers, of the widespread use of chemicals are less visible and sometimes less understood. Chemical usage has grown greatly in the last years to the point that a good crop seems at times to rely more on what farmers apply to the ground than the quality of the ground itself. Among other things, farmers apply broad-leaf herbicides, powerful insecticides, and nitrogen fertilizer in the form of anhydrous ammonia. While these chemicals have done astonishing things for crop yields, they have also contributed greatly to soil and groundwater pollution.

Nitrogen is one example. Although farmers have cut back on the amount of nitrogen they apply to the soil before they plant corn, the average amount applied per year is still high, and, according to some scientists, could be cut by another 30 percent and still be enough for the land to yield the same bushels per acre of corn. These days the average application in Iowa is around 127 pounds per acre, down from 145 pounds per acre in 1985, according to the U.S. Department of Agriculture. Of that amount, about a fifth winds up in the ears of corn; much of the rest stays in the stalk and the soil, but a certain percentage, a number hard to calculate, changes to nitrates and winds up in the groundwater and streams and thereby in water taps in the state. The effects of long-term nitrate consumption by humans are not clear, but many people are growing concerned.

Insecticides and herbicides are applied in smaller amounts but pose uncalculated risks as well. Some insecticides cost farmers as much as a hundred dollars per quart and are sufficiently concentrated that their containers are considered toxic waste and must be rinsed and returned to the manufacturer for proper disposal. They make Bob White nervous, and he uses as little of them as he feels he can get by with.

"We're really going to have to watch these insecticides and herbicides," worries Bob. "If we get out there and miscalculate our sprayers, all that extra stuff goes down in the field tiles, and it goes into the creeks, and into the rivers, then into everybody's water supply, oh boy, we've got a big problem."

Researchers are now even finding trace amounts of certain farm chemicals in the rainwater falling from the sky.

Soil erosion is another issue. On some steep, erodible pastureland around the area, one hundred percent of the topsoil has gone downstream, leaving nothing but harsh glacial till as a poor substratum for forage grass. On more gentle, but still erodible, cropland, smart farmers have installed field terraces. Rod Burgeson and his dad built three across the south end of the forty-four-acre cornfield. Rod has noticed how much less erosion there is now.

"Years ago we'd go out on that bare ground and plow like crazy in the fall, and it would get fine and loose, just like sugar. Then, in the winter, the wind would come up, and the fence rows, the snow in the ditches, they would turn just black. We put in those terraces, and boy, did they make a difference. We practice minimum tillage as well, and between the two, we lose a lot less soil."

Minimum tillage practices are now widely accepted in the area as farmers learned that fewer passes over the field save topsoil, moisture, and fuel. Where years ago farmers used to plow deep and then disk harrow a time or two each year to mix the soil, most farmers today make one or at most two passes across the field with implements that disturb the soil far less.

"The old moldboard plows are out, absolutely a thing of the past," says Rod.

In addition, by not plowing, farmers leave considerable plant material on the surface, which further reduces both wind and water erosion and moisture loss. As the stems and leaves of prior years' crops decay, their nutrients return to the soil.

At the extreme, minimum till is no-till. Some farmers are working with new planters that will plant crops amid the stubble of last year's, obviating the need for any field tillage at all.

"You know, I really think the no-till and minimum-till practices are a good thing," says Rod. "All that dirt that goes down the rivers has always upset me. It was just stupid the way we were doing it for so many years. If we leave enough of that trash, the cornstalks and all, on top, it really prevents washing. Everybody used to work the ground until it was fine as could be, then plant it, and along comes a gully washer and takes tons of soil downstream. That's what the Mississippi delta is made of—Iowa topsoil."

Because of hybridization and the use of chemicals, corn yields have risen from an average of 40 to 60 bushels per acre a hundred years ago to around 150 today; in a very good year on good ground, growers brag of 200 bushels to the acre.

Ever since Native Americans first domesticated corn several thousand years ago, humankind has experimented with crossbreeding to grow stronger, more reliable, better-yielding corn. The heavy-eared giants that grow around Peterson today are to ancient corn plants as a Boeing 747 is to the original Wright Flyer. Some estimate that a single kernel of today's corn contains as much energy as an entire ear of early corn. Originally a tropical plant, all wild varieties have long ago become extinct; without human hand to harvest seeds and plant them again the next season, corn, or *Zea mays*, would altogether disappear. The future of this species, it seems, is inexorably linked with that of our own.

To one unaccustomed to it, there is something inexpressibly lonely in the solitude of a prairie. The loneliness of a forest seems nothing to it. There the view is shut in by trees, and the imagination is left free to picture some livelier scene beyond. But here we have an immense extent of landscape without a sign of human existence. We have the consciousness of being far, far beyond the bounds of human habitation; we feel as if moving in the midst of a desert world.

—Washington Irving, *A Tour on the Prairies*, 1835

Chapter 16

Lost World

Take away all the houses and machine sheds, pull out what few fences are left, erase the section lines and the roads that follow them, the highways, the streets in town. Take out thousands of utility poles, sidewalks, ornamental shrubs, the flower gardens edged with little wire fences. Pull down the elevator, fill in the swimming pool and every basement, smooth over every place where humankind since Gust Kirchner and his family dug the first European garden in the area. Sift out all the brome grass, bluegrass, the crab, and the quack; take the scotch pine, hard maples, and clump birch; cut back even the native trees, the boxelder, the maple, and the bur oak, to the island tracts they covered when the fires still held them in check.

Smooth over every acre of crop land, mile upon mile of it; remove every furrow, and retrieve every grain of prairie soil washed downstream to enlarge Louisiana. Relocate the faint Indian trails that crossed these reaches of the earth; scatter bison, elk, deer, wolf, and even a few grizzly bear over the miles. And then replant one of the earth's great gardens—the tall grass prairie.

I never look to the horizon without thinking of the rolling grasslands that once fed bison here. I never walk through a pasture, along a fence line, across any waste piece of ground without looking for relict plants from that world; I never look at a cornfield without thinking of the other grasses that grew here once. And I never walk through a fragment of old prairie without wishing I'd been there to see it when it stretched for unending, light-filled miles.

I can barely grasp the former extent of this inland sea of grass. The great North American interior grasslands—tall, mixed, and short-grass prairie—extended from the heart of Saskatchewan some 1,500 miles south, almost to the Gulf coast of Texas, and west from the Indiana-Illinois border clear to the Rockies, covering nearly a third of the United States and making nearly a million square miles of deeply textured open country. In pre-horse days, a Native American with good legs and an exploring bent could begin at the edge of the boreal forest in the north and walk steadily south for three months and see few if any trees.

Iowa was the heart of tall-grass prairie, with more miles of high, coarse grass than any other state in the country. Prairie covered 85 percent of the state, some 47,000 square miles. The scattered scraps that remain amount to but a thousandth of the original; a few dozen fragments, some no bigger than a suburban lot, lie scattered across the state. Even if collected together, they would amount to only 47 square miles, a piece of ground slightly bigger than a township. And of this total, less than 8 square miles is found in state preserves where it is in any way protected.

The prairie was settled very quickly, though it must have seemed slow to the grasshopper- and depression-beleaguered pioneers in northwest Iowa during the 1870s. In Iowa alone, some thirty million acres of prairie land were turned by the plow in seventy years, at an average loss of four million acres per year. So quick and nearly complete was its disappearance that it is as if we'd drained Lake Michigan, and, as the very last gallons were swirling away, we had a pang of guilt and decided to keep a swimming pool of it to remind us what a big lake had been like.

Twelve miles southwest of Peterson, near the town of Larrabee, a tiny bit of the original raiment of the state thrives, much as it has for centuries. Steele Prairie, some 200 acres of ragged grass, wildflowers, badger mounds, now-unusual plants, birds, and tiny mammals, surrounded by fields, pastures, and farmsteads, has never felt the slice of the plow. Indian grass waves against the sky just as it has done for more years than even the Sioux could count. The vegetation here seems as old as the sky.

Steele Prairie is an anachronism. It is to modern Iowa farm life as an old pagan holiday is to modern Christianity; because we no longer quite understand it, the thing makes us a bit uneasy. But like Halloween, prairie is woven into our traditions and is a part of the past we cannot separate from our present. Whatever our misunderstanding, or even neglect, we can neither altogether ignore it nor erase it from our collective cultural memory.

For people around Peterson, the idea of prairie resides in tertiary memory, that part of the mind reserved for things that older people have told us were once important, things that the old people themselves never knew firsthand but heard about from the old people of their own day: great, square-rigged whalers, buffalo hunts of the Plains tribes, the Civil War, the tall-grass prairie.

What then explains the appeal of prairie? The word appears in countless contexts: Euro-American settlers here were prairie pioneers who came in prairie schooners and built their farms in the prairie states. We have Prairie Cities in Iowa and South Dakota, a scattering of Prairie Hills and Homes, and at least four Prairie Views, and two Prairie Counties, one in Montana and the other in Arkansas. We have an attachment to prairie that is as formless as its appearance to our non-prairie eyes.

Some scholars even think our proclivity for grassland reaches into our genetic past. John H. Falk, formerly of the Smithsonian, finds that people of many backgrounds exhibit a "deep, innate preference for a grass landscape." He believes that this preference may be a genetically based predisposition formed during the species' infancy on the savannas of East Africa.

We are drawn somehow to prairie, but few people know much about it. Farmers recognize big bluestem—turkey foot—and prairie cord grass as being prairie natives and sometimes a few other species as well, but not much else. There is no pressing reason to look for prairie and few places to look in anyway. Some people here know about and take interest in roadside wildflowers, but most such plants are woodland species and grow in deep valley shade. There are a few amateur botanists who can spot prairie grasses and other plants, and a couple of real experts, but for the majority, the word "prairie" refers to planiform landscape where corn and soybeans grow. To many people any grassy area is a prairie; shown a bit of shaggy pasture or even a government set-aside field planted to uniform brome grass, an imported pasture grass, they might wax wistful about the prairie of old and never understand that what they are viewing has no more in common with prairie than does the close-cropped green around the eighteenth hole.

An understanding of prairie—in aesthetic, botanical, or historical terms—requires more of us than the understanding of more easily read landscapes. The first difficulty with prairie stems from the fact that nearly all of it is gone; to understand prairie requires an exercise of imagination to reconstruct it from nothing. It is no more difficult to look at the open ocean and see the dry land of Atlantis.

And even when the willing student finds some real prairie, the job isn't finished. The allure of true prairie is subtle, requiring alacrity, insight, and patience, attributes not required for a basic appreciation of, say, the Grand Canyon. For a hike in the Smokies, all one needs are senses open to the beauty of the rounded mountains and variegated forests; for a hike in the prairie, one needs a willingness to collect a portrait of the place by means of the accumulation of myriad small details. Where the Rockies are concrete, prairie is abstract; where the meadows and mountains of Yellowstone have line and shape, prairie, apart from the single line of the horizon, has only texture; where the Lake Superior shoreline has focal point, prairie rolls away in formless sweeps. An understanding of prairie requires commitment.

But to some, these great grasslands were far from trackless. To eyes accustomed to grassland landmarks, the mental map was precise and detailed. Where Euro-American travelers sometimes had trouble finding their way across this grassy wildness, away from river valleys and established trails, Indians did not. People so used to forests, as were many of the white settlers of the mid-1800s, found themselves at a loss to identify the subtle landmarks that native inhabitants took for granted. Game and Indian trails were faint to Euro-Americans before they wore them in more deeply and plainly with wagons, and one prairie slough probably looked much like every other. Native Americans, familiar with many sloughs in the region, might identify a particular one by the subtleties of its shape or by a predominance of particular vegetation, clues invisible to anyone who expects more obvious signs.

George Temple's 1856 survey work in northwest Iowa reflects the Euro-American perception of tracklessness. His plat map of Clay Township, the township just north of Peterson Township, faithfully depicts all the section lines and quarter-section lines he made, complete with careful notations of acreage, but in this whole township he found but one physical feature worthy of notation: perhaps as an afterthought, he drew in a sketchy quarter mile of Willow Creek—in the wrong place. Except for this, the plat is nothing more that a series of empty squares, thirty-six square miles of blank territory. For forest-raised easterners, landmarks meant trees; in 1856, there were none in Clay Township.

Real prairie doesn't look like much when seen from a passing car; to the uninitiated, it is easily confused with a weedy hayfield. The difference lies not only in the kinds of plants growing there, but the number of species present. Where a pasture might contain a handful of plant species, true prairie will contain two hundred or more. Bohumil Shimek, Iowa's eminent naturalist, cataloged 265 species in the compendium of the state's prairie, seventy of them grasses and the rest forbs, meaning broad-leafed, flowering plants. Add to that a hundred mammal species ranging from bison to voles and an estimated three thousand insect species above ground alone, and a picture of a complex ecosystem emerges.

Not only is it complex, but it is closed as well. An undisturbed plot of prairie is very resistant to invasion by new seedlings. The ground surface is altogether shaded by thick grass, and so dense are the root systems of established plants that every drop of moisture that falls on the prairie either evaporates or is immediately soaked up by thirsty plants. But when a prairie plot is disturbed, opportunist invaders like thistles and brome grass find toeholds. Along the west edge of Steele Prairie, parallel to the section road, there is a wide area where smooth brome grass, an energetic invader, has crowded out much of the native grasses and forbs. For years, county crews sprayed the roadside ditches for weeds. Prairie natives, forbs and grasses alike, are very sensitive to weed killer; as the spray drifted across the first few yards of Steele Prairie, it apparently stunted prairie species and left an opportunity for spray-resistant brome grass.

Prairie made the topsoil here; everyone knows it. The entire economic and social structure of the region, its 175-bushel-to-the-acre corn yields, the intensive farming of the land, are all owed to the soil-building characteristics of the tall-grass prairie. Over a few thousand years, prairie has taken glacial drift—mostly clay, sand, and gravel—and made it into some of the best soil in the country, if not the world. In most cases, the darker a soil, the more humus, or decayed plant material, it contains; the more humus, the more fertile the soil will be. The forests of Ohio produced soil, and pretty good soil, but it literally pales in comparison with that of most of Iowa. In a forest environment, most plant material decays on the ground surface; leaves and branches rot where they fall, and their richness is never mixed into and incorporated with the mineral material of soil.

In a tall-grass prairie, a large percentage of the organic material is invested in the roots of grasses that thoroughly inform the upper layers of soil. In an endless cycle, these roots grow and extend themselves, then die in place, decaying to enrich the soil to a depth of several feet.

Says author and prairie expert John Madson: "A forest's richest soil may be little more than leaf-layer deep, while the basic fertility of balanced prairie is of uniform richness extending as deep as the root systems of the grasses, and beyond. The amount of true humus in a forest soil may vary from 20 to 50 tons per acre; an acre of nearby prairie may have 250 tons of humus."

In the early years of Euro-American settlement on the prairies, farmers were surprised by how well prairie soil seemed to grow trees. Many had assumed that prairie existed across the Midwest because the soil was too poor, or the rainfall too scant, to support trees; neither was true. No sooner had settlers built a new house and planted a couple of years' crops than trees—both those intentionally planted and those that simply arose out of the grass—flourished. And today, if not for the work of the plow, most of this landscape would become forest in a couple of generations. Prairie, it seems, required certain very specific conditions, and once these were altered, woodland arose.

There are several factors that are relevant for prairie, and different scholars rate different ones as being most important, but all agree that among the top factors is the evaporation rate. For prairie to remain prairie, an area must have a high ratio of evaporation compared to rainfall; that is, a high proportion of the precipitation that falls on a place must evaporate from the soil or plant cover and therefore not soak in to become groundwater. This makes for a drier soil environment than the mere measure of precipitation would indicate.

And what sort of environment has a high rate of evaporation compared to rainfall? Prairie, of course. Having grass instead of trees as ground cover means prairies are windy and sunny in the summer. The surface soil temperature is considerably hotter than that of a nearby woodland, increasing evaporation and reducing available soil moisture to the point that trees could not thrive. Odd, then, but prairie stays prairie in part because it *is* prairie. Northwest Iowa gets on average almost thirty inches of precipitation per year, more than enough for trees; yet, because so much of that moisture so quickly evaporated on the prairie, trees had little chance there.

In addition, those who study prairie and long-term climate have discovered a cause-and-effect relationship between the presence of prairie and a climate that has periodic droughts, droughts sometimes both severe and prolonged.

Prairie plant species are well adapted to water shortage, many of them having root systems of astonishing extent that allow them to gather water from great depths and distances. Grasses in particular are drought-resistant; their leaves are narrow, reducing their surface area and resultant transpiration.

Prairie is perpetuated as well by the grazing of large herbivores; the bison themselves were instrumental in maintaining prairie. Periodically they grazed through an area, browsing the leaves off shrubs and trees, killing them, and clipping grasses and forbs very close, exposing the ground to sun, and encouraging new prairie growth.

But most vital to any prairie is fire. A hot, fast prairie fire kills woody plants and burns off great masses of vegetation without harming the root systems of native plants. A fire returns nutrients to the soil and, when it occurs in the spring, allows warm sun to reach the ground, stimulating the early growth of lush summer grass. Prairie plants, by their nature, are fire-resistant, or more precisely fire-loving; they need periodic renewal of nutrients and sunlight to flourish.

For the entire century since the prairies were plowed under, scholars have debated the causes of the frequent fires of the past; were they natural, or were they set by humans? Some claim that a long history of Native American–set fires is essential to explain their number and their effect on prairie. Others claim that lightning, especially during harsh spring thunderstorms, is enough to explain fires sufficient to maintain prairie. Anyone who has observed at close range just how much electricity and wind, and, at times, how little extinguishing rain, some of these spring storms contain, can easily see that they alone were probably sufficient ignition for the prairie fires of the past.

Native Americans had long used fires to drive buffalo. They also set them in the spring to encourage good summer grass and thereby attract bison, so there is no mystery that fire was one of their tools. But they must also have used fire for protection. During spring and fall, any village set amid tall-grass prairie was by nature in danger. Prairie fires moved very quickly, often creating their own weather and wind as they went, and sometimes trapping even the fleetest with their rapid advance. And oddly, the only protection from them was fire itself. On calm and damp spring days, village dwellers must have set fires around their lodges to burn off extensive areas such that any big fire coming later over the horizon would be deprived of fuel in the vicinity of the village. How many of these backfires did Native Americans set, fires that smoldered for days, burned off downwind unnoticed, only to leap to life under a fresh wind?

There were trees on the prairie, of course; once in a great many miles a huge, fire-scarred, single tree would appear on the open grassland. They were known by travelers and provided shady camping spots in the summer and perhaps some deadfall branches for a fire. Their historical presence is suggested by the commonness of names like Lone Tree. Lone Tree Township in Clay County is named for a giant elm that stood alone along the Ocheyedan River until upstart woodland rose to surround it.

Clearly the prairies of northwest Iowa harbored fragments of true woodland as well. It probably was the ample woodland along the narrow stretch of the river valley that attracted the Mill Creek people to settle here; it certainly was the climax woodland at Peterson that caught the attention of the Kirchners. This bit of forested landscape looked familiar to anyone from the East and was indeed rare this far west. Temple reported bur oak, linden, walnut, and ash trees around Peterson; their progeny thrive here today.

This slip of thick timber amid endless grass owed its existence to topography. Woodland existed on the prairie only where fire could not advance. All of the originally timbered areas of northwest Iowa were inside river bends, in sharp ravines, or on valley sides protected from the prevailing winds and the fires they propelled. When the Kirchners arrived here, this timber extended from the south bank of the river up the south valley wall to the top. No doubt a few brave bur oaks peered cautiously out over the valley rim south across the flat plains. The timber was thus protected from prairie fire on all sides. Any wind-driven fire from the south or west, or even an unlikely fire from the east, would abruptly lose momentum dropping over the valley rim; and for any fire from the north, the river provided a good firebreak.

While prairie fire makes quick work of dry prairie grass, it stalls altogether when it reaches mature woodland. Whatever the topography, large trees slow the driving wind, and the wetter, more dense masses of leaves on the forest floor make poor fuel. Even when a fire can make headway through wooded areas, any prairie tree more than a few years of age will have developed thick, fire-resistant bark; the undergrowth and saplings may be killed off, leaving the larger trees unaffected.

While surveyors marked areas of timber on the original township plats of northwest Iowa, it is difficult to tell just what sort of woodland they saw. A few areas grew tall, dense, climax timber like that the Kirchners utilized, but many areas, especially along more open river bottoms, must have been brushy thickets with little heavy wood or were open savannas where prairie grew among widely spaced, fire-resistant trees.

Although they existed edge to edge, woodland and prairie environments shared very few characteristics. Prairie plants are adapted to sunlight, heat, and wind; those of the woodlands live in shady, cool, and relatively calm conditions. Hence, there is little overlap in species between the two. And not only does prairie tend to perpetuate itself, but so does woodland. Shade discourages prairie species and encourages woodland species, which then further increase shade, coolness, and moisture. Grasses of any sort are rare in forest.

If any tree can be considered a prairie tree, it is the bur oak. It was, and still is, one of the most successful trees of the prairie region. There are other oaks here, but in reduced numbers, both of species and of individual trees. In the eastern United States, great oaks of many varieties thrive, but as one travels west, through Iowa, they drop out one by one, until in western Iowa and eastern Nebraska, the bur oak is dominant and soon the only oak left. This tree is the only one that ever had a reasonable chance at establishing itself in unbroken prairie. In the struggle between prairie and woodland, bur oaks are among the front-line troops on the side of the woodland.

Bur oaks, individually and in great stands of similar-age trees, grace the river valley and creek ravines all around Peterson. They are thick in some places and altogether missing from others, suggesting something of their historical battle with prairie fires of the past. Certainly the most common oaks in the region, bur oaks have several characteristics that make them well adapted to a tree-hostile prairie environment.

A bur oak acorn, once germinated, sends an energetic taproot straight down to find moisture; it may plunge four or more feet in the first year. By the third year, at a time when the aboveground portion of the young tree is only three feet high, the root system may have developed enough to infiltrate a four-by-four-foot area around the tree to a depth of six feet. Such aggression gives even prairie grasses stiff competition.

Bur oaks also have useful protections against fire. A maturing bur oak grows thick, gnarled bark that insulates the tree from all but the hottest prairie fire. In addition, bur oaks create underground burls that once survived decades—or even centuries—of fires. Often when a sapling was burned back to the ground, the root system responded by forming a dense woody mass. These masses grew each time the young tree was burned, and they could store sufficient energy to send up shoots year after year. They were a special agony of settlers breaking prairie. Firmly anchored in the sod just below ground surface, burls broke plows and taught sodbusters an expressive new vocabulary as they sought to grub them out.

Bur oaks, while they are thick in protected places, don't extend very far out onto what was once flat prairie. No doubt this is a holdover from days of fire, when, despite their resources and protections, bur oaks made small progress colonizing completely open prairie. Around Peterson any grove of bur oaks on the flat will have its back to a ravine or the valley side; these groves do not form the classic oak openings so common on the open prairie of Illinois and Wisconsin.

The trees in such an oak grove will often appear to be about the same age, almost as if planted by the same hand at the same time. The explanation is simple: after the last prairie fire, or after the livestock was taken out of a pasture, all the burls sprouted at once, never to be burned or grazed off again, leading to groves of coeval trees.

While prairie could thrive as long as fire, grazing bison, and its own invasion-resistant nature maintained it, once turned, once erased, fire and bison gone with it, prairie probably no longer had, or has, the capability to come back of its own accord. Without fire to burn off the non-prairie species, prairie cannot reestablish itself; without fire, even preserved bits of prairie dwindle away to become something else, usually woodland. Today, without human-set fires to control the non-native grasses and forbs, and the trees, prairie doesn't stand a chance. Like corn, prairie has come to depend on the hand of humankind to survive.

During our time in Peterson, I spent a lot of time riding around with Clint Fraley, executive officer of the Clay County Conservation Board. He covers the county, looking after county parks, spearheading conservation projects, burning prairie, and practicing good public relations by calling on farmers. One day, out looking for prairie leftovers, he pulled the pickup to a stop along a gravel road in the valley east of Peterson.

"See that triangle of land there?" he asked. I looked where he pointed and spied a piece of land on the valley floor about two hundred feet on a side, fenced on all three sides, unused for some time. There was grass here, a bit of brush, and a good many young trees.

"Here's the change at work. There are no buffalo, no cattle, no fire—see the trees coming in? If we were to go out and age the trees today, we could tell just when this scrap of land was last grazed—I'd guess about eight or ten years ago. It's mostly brome grass with Chinese elm and boxelder coming up, all invaders into prairie. Leave it alone for a hundred years and it will grow up to be a jungle; but let fire happen again like it should, like it did, and it will come back as prairie."

Clint knows prairie, he knows woodland, and he probably knows everybody who lives in the county. He's a big, energetic man who talks easily and quickly, and he is a perpetual hit with schoolchildren when he brings his nature stuff to the classroom, or, better yet, the kids to the outdoors.

"I just want to get people excited," he says. "That's what I want to do any time I take anybody anywhere. Prairie hunting, fly-tying, anything else. You can't *force* anybody to get interested in *anything*, but if you once get them into it, get them out on the prairie or into the woods, they might take off on their own and might get really excited. Over time I've watched people, especially kids, get really fired up about all the natural stuff around them."

He dresses western and looks equally good in the front seat of a pickup or on a horse, though his perverse streak has him disdain horses and prefer mules. They're smarter, he says. He and his patient wife, Esta, live on the Fraley Mule Ranch in a perpetually unfinished house. Clint is always finding another project at work or at home: a trip to Wyoming, some prairie to burn, a boat ramp to build on the river, a few bushels of asparagus to pick, a saddle to make, a mule to break. Every time we'd stop by, he'd ask for our pocketknives. While we sat around the table, I'd tease him about not getting any more done on the house, and he'd put a razor edge on our dull blades. For the next month I would slice the bills to shreds just opening the envelopes.

Clint is the consummate outdoorsman, the woodsy observer always with stories to tell. Any trip by pickup or on foot with him is a series of illustrative tales, observations, riddles, wood lore, and an occasional outright lie thrown in to see if you're listening. Clint samples berries, listens for birds, feels winter twigs for incipient life, kicks at leaves, and looks under every rock for possible snakes, not out of fear, but out of scientific curiosity. The outdoors is a classroom to Clint, a limitless storehouse of activities, educational opportunities, and pure fun.

And while his curriculum is broad and his classroom limitless, he is foremost a collector of details, significant details. He once showed up at our door with a bucket of sand from western South Dakota; with no introduction, he handed it to us and told us to start looking—for what? Garnets. Scooped from an anthill near the Badlands, the smooth sand hid dozens if not hundreds of tiny red jewels. Now any bored kid visiting our house gets handed the sand bucket the instant he or she asks if we own a television. Start looking, we say.

For winter heat, Clint and Esta sometimes burn old utility poles. As he splits them for the stove, he looks for and often finds exotic stuff packed into the cracks and holes: bullets, unusual insect nests, odd debris blown in from everywhere. Clint misses little and never passes up an opportunity to share what he knows.

He observes people as well.

"I've got a guy in my fly-tying class; he's a retired farmer and must be seventy-two or -three. He comes every time with a Pioneer Seed Corn tablet with a spiral binding across the top, and a yellow #2 pencil; it's about four inches long, sharpened with a pocketknife. The tablet fits in his pocket, and every time I offer a little gem on fly-tying, he pulls it out and writes it down. Boy, is he motivated; he's the most exciting person I've been around all winter. Just seeing someone like him get involved makes it all worthwhile.

"Little things have always meant something to me," says Clint, "they just always have. I guess I don't know any different. Maybe it's because I was always the littlest one when I was young and didn't want anybody bigger to beat me up or eat me, so I was always on the lookout. I had to stay alert."

Clint watches over the woodlands and remaining prairie in the county and does whatever he can to preserve and protect them. "These little pockets of prairie are important for the same reason you care about what your grandparents were like; you just want to know. Is it critical to everybody?—No. Is it critical to me?—Yes. You hate to lose any more of these tiny pieces of the past because one day we won't have anything left to refer to, anything left to tell us what it was like.

"In Clay County there are only about forty acres of really good prairie left; in fairly good shape, maybe two hundred. Most of it is in little bitty pockets, an acre here, an acre there, but so much of that is being invaded by red cedar and other stuff."

One February day we stood looking out over the thickly wooded Little Sioux valley. "You're looking at a hundred-fold increase in timber compared to what there was when Europeans first settled in the area."

And indeed it is true. From where we stood, trees were thick everywhere the plow hadn't touched, agricultural herbicide hadn't reached, and cattle or hogs hadn't heavily grazed. That includes the valley sides and every creek ravine in the area. The Little Sioux valley sides in particular have in the last years grown in thick with eastern red cedar, an evergreen not seen at all in the wild by the naturalist Thomas Macbride at the turn of the century. Now, even on heat-soaked, south-facing slopes, cedars have filled in so thick in places they are hard to walk through.

"They're rough on prairie, but great habitat for dickeybirds," says Clint.

"Dickeybirds?"

"Yeah, that's a technical term for any non-game bird."

I've watched the process of trees filling in on the family farm. My grandmother recently placed a piece of ground in a conservation set-aside program for erodible land. Planted to uniform brome grass, the land is stabilized, but unlike prairie, a stand of brome grass is easily invaded by aggressive plants. Along the east fence, over where the field abuts a creek valley and the pasture, the set-aside acres are sprouting dozens of bur oaks, tiny trees with three or four leaves, still shorter than the surrounding grass. Along the fence and well into the field there are dozens of them that bear a distinct family resemblance to the big bur oaks across the fence.

At the opposite, southeast, corner of the field, green ash trees are doing an even better job. On that fence line is a mature green ash, a tree that has been there as long as I can remember. Downwind from it, far into the field, grow hundreds of little ash trees; in places they are dense enough to shade out the grass. The tallest are now about hood-high to the truck and will soon make driving through them difficult. If something isn't done with them quite soon, the land will have to be cleared with a chain saw before it can ever be farmed again.

The astonishing part of the story is the speed with which this has happened; the land was cornfield a mere two years ago.

Out of an impulse to return a hint of native vegetation to town, where it is especially lacking, Carol and I dug up a few of these little trees and planted them in the yard of the "Ida House," our home in Peterson. Long before my grandmother bought the place, I remember the corner lot deeply shaded by elms; today they are gone, leaving only hot lawn and the row of evergreens she planted recently. We dug and brought to town some eight native trees: a few green ash, an experimental bur oak, and one secreted cottonwood. Cottonwoods have earned a bad name among town dwellers in most places, for reasons that to me make little sense. Few trees express themselves as gracefully in their great, arching limbs and furrowed bark; few trees express so well their untamed nature. Someone someday will appreciate our choice.

We brought them to town in coffee cans; each of the tiny green things had about four leaves and was maybe eight inches high. We selected them with care, looking for straight little twig trunks that would grow arrow-true and behave themselves among the domesticated trees in town. While these are wild trees, native trees, they will be required to take up civilized city habits if they are to endure.

It struck me as I dug the first of the round holes into the dark soil of the lawn that we have little aesthetic appreciation for wild, uninhibited trees. We pay scant mind to the toppled riverbank suckers and the storm-broken giants in the old Kirchner timber. Perhaps we cast some favor on them because they provide homes for the owls we hear on winter nights, but we'd never call them beautiful. Allow them in the yard?—never. Trees are supposed to be symmetrical, ornamental, uniformly alive, and to grow with straight trunks, like those in the landscaping catalogs—attributes they manifest only under human guidance.

We see grass the same way, as our usual aesthetic urges run in quite the opposite direction from prairie. With grass, the greener, the smoother, the shorter, the better; in a perfect world, every lawn would be a putting green. Lawn grasses are never prairie grasses. Tastes run to fine and delicate Kentucky bluegrass, rye grass, and red fescue. Prairie is dangerous, and has something within it that cannot be civilized, cannot be tamed. Snakes, as everyone knows, can hide much more easily in prairie than in smooth lawn. Nevertheless, while I tolerate lawns, even mowing our own from time to time, my impulse is always to let it go, to see what would happen, what would come up, what creatures would live in the tall grass.

House yards in Peterson, and everywhere, are a strange composite of forest and prairie, an uneasy truce between opposing forces. Maintaining a balance between the two requires constant work to ensure that a lawn doesn't grow up to woods. We plant trees around our houses for shade, to slow the winds, to soften the harsh sky and earth, but we don't like the brush and matted leaves that forest shade brings, so we plant trees at greater distances than they grow naturally in forests, and distribute something faintly remindful of prairie to fill in between them. In order to keep the grass as grass, and not forest undergrowth, we mow and grub and reseed and fertilize; to our enduring chagrin, grasses shun the place to find the sun, while weeds and sprouting trees get their best start in the shade we've created.

Perhaps the single prototype for this collision of biomes is the oak opening, or oak savanna. To the east in Illinois and Wisconsin, groves of mature oak trees once held parts of the prairie, great stands of trees with individuals set at sufficient distance that thick prairie surrounded them all.

With care, and with fertilizer from Eddie at the hardware store, we planted our trees, our version of the African savanna from our species' childhood.

We planted some along the highway, a couple along the intersecting street, and the oak in the yard in front of the bay window. I've planted trees before, and every time I've done it I've been struck with the solemnity of the act.

If the tree lives to maturity, my decision as to the precise location for a tree will endure for several generations. It will form a great part of the character of a yard. I have sat under or looked through many trees and wondered who planted them and when. What was the planter thinking when he or she first pushed the shovel into the sod?

We watered and tended them all, but the oak died, as did a couple of the ash. I wasn't surprised the oak didn't make it; when digging it up out of the field, I had cut its taproot. Even though the tree was but a half a foot high, the young prairie tree had a central stem that plunged deeper than I could ever reach with a shovel. When I cut it, I hoped that it could overcome the stress. It could not, and within a week, the waxy leaves had shriveled and drooped to the stem.

Next in importance to the divine profusion of water, light, and air, those three great physical facts which render existence possible, may be reckoned the universal beneficence of grass. . . . Lying in the sunshine among the buttercups and dandelions of May, scarcely higher in intelligence than the minute tenants of that mimic wilderness, our earliest recollections are of grass; and when the fitful fever is ended, and the foolish wrangle of the market and forum is closed, grass heals over the scar which our descent into the bosom of the earth has made, and the carpet of the infant becomes the blanket of the dead.

—John James Ingalls, "In Praise of Blue Grass," *Kansas Magazine*, 1872

Chapter 17

Habits of the Grass

APRIL 10

At nine-thirty in the morning, I round the corner onto Main Street and am suddenly reminded of busy days of commerce in Peterson's past. There are twenty vehicles parked on Main, with most of them around the Senior Center and Sue's. Downtown looks busier than I've seen it in some time. It is a Wednesday, and there will be a congregate noon meal at the Senior Center, or "Dinner Date" as most call it, and already, at this early hour, card games are in full swing.

At Sue's, a double birthday is in full swing. The celebrants are Jordan Raveling and Wilda Wetherall, and they have pooled their resources to buy the house. People are coming and going, and there is hardly a seat in the place. Chatter is loud and easy. As I come in, Wilda sits with a group of women, a pile of birthday cards in front of her, with more arriving moment by moment. Even though it is his party, Jordan has already left to do field work. It is shaping up to be a good day to be in the field, one of the first of the season.

Sue has baked the cakes for this large crowd, but by the time I arrive, the chocolate is gone; Sue reads my disappointment and points out that the white cake has yogurt in it; maybe she thinks of it as a sort of health cake. With a big piece on a paper plate, I sit down at a table with Carl Brenner and Slim Wetherall, Wilda's husband. As usual, Carl wears a bow tie, blue today; Slim wears a new Garst Seed Company jacket and hat.

Carl offers, "Boy, getting together for coffee like this is really what keeps the town together, you know it? If we didn't have this place, why, I don't know what we'd do."

Slim points out how Linn Grove, seven miles east, has recently lost its coffee shop and how "you don't see many people in town anymore—they come in, go to the bank, and just leave." Slim himself is antsy to leave on this bright spring morning, though Wilda looks like she'll be staying for hours. "The farmers will be hittin' the fields hard today," he says, shifting in his seat. Slim has retired from farming, but the instincts are still strong.

Many farmers feel the pull today. An hour later, north of town, I find the machinery of spring farming on the move; chisel plows, disk harrows, fertilizer applicators, and farm pickups loaded down with bags of seed corn go about their tasks. The soil is drying out, and heat shimmers off the fields as implements dig in. Most farmers today work up the soil or apply fertilizer since it is still too early and the soil too cold for planting, though it won't be long now. For the first time since last fall, the sun again brings noticeable warmth. The high is predicted to be 55 today, with a good chance of rain or snow starting tonight, so farmers are eager to accomplish as much as they can. The forecasters are hedging their bets: if the low pressure system tracks a little south, we'll get snow; if it passes to the north, we'll have rain.

The cool season grasses—brome and bluegrass especially—are greening up quickly. Pastures, hillsides, the cemetery, the ball diamond, and lawns all over town are rich with the spinach-soup green that excites my eyes, so accustomed to the grays and browns of winter. The green stands in sharp contrast to still-drab trees, shrubs, and colorless fields. Many of the trees in farm groves are exhibiting the increased density, that spring fuzziness, that suggests leaves to follow, though their color has yet to change.

Other notices are posted for the return of spring. About eleven, a truck pulls up at Eddie's Hardware to unload the merchandise for his spring sale. Eddie, the driver, and I haul in new rakes, shovels, lawn sprinklers, sprayers, and paint. Last off the truck is a bundle of mailers imprinted with "Eddie's Hardware, Main Street, Peterson, Iowa," mailers that depict sale items amidst riotous spring flowers and Easter-green grass. I notice that Eddie has already set up his racks of spring seeds.

"I sold a bunch already today," he tells me.

Out on the uplands, the western meadowlarks have been back for a couple of weeks. Just now, the red-winged blackbirds are staking their loud claims to cattails around the county, and the turkey vultures are making their first appearances along the north rim of the valley. Warm weather the last two days has brought out a great explosion of Spring Beauties—the first woodland flower—in the woods along the river and an unusual hatch of moths and insects which besmirch my windshield as I drive the rural roads. The smell of warming soil perfumes the air.

Fertilizer arrives in town to enrich the soon-to-be-planted crops. In the afternoon, two semis arrive at the elevator loaded with potash from Rocanville, Saskatchewan. Only the license plates and the logos on the cabs identify these as foreign rigs, but they and the tired drivers have a distinctly foreign feel about them. Lyle Goettsch asks, "How's the weather up your way? Will you get home before the snow?" I find myself wondering what they think of this tiny town in a foreign country.

The elevator and scale office are busy today as fertilizer, seed oats, and livestock feed go out. A smattering of corn comes in, though it tapers off as more and more farmers put aside grain hauling to get into the warming fields.

The river, too, is busy as it pushes snowmelt downstream toward the Missouri, toward the Gulf. It runs higher than any time since last summer. Along the banks, green spikes of new reed canary grass poke through the dense mat of last year's crop.

South of town, in Rod Burgeson's cornfield, the soil waits. Except for a single pass along one edge with a disk to test soil readiness, Rod has done nothing here yet. Today he works on fields to the east as the fertilizer applicator makes the rounds nearby. Here black corncobs lie mixed with gray cottonwood leaves, molding between rows of bleached cornstalks still rooted in the coffee-colored earth. The time will soon come for this place.

On Steele Prairie, two townships west, on this April day, other spring rhythms are beginning to stir in the warming soil, and these signals of the coming season are ancient; like the territoriality of the red-winged blackbird, these rhythms are much older than sales on garden tools or the early greening of brome grass on the face of the Midwest.

On this April 10th, in stark contrast to the rich green of lawns and pastures around the county, Steele Prairie is still altogether brown. The palette runs the range from the silver-brown of a bit of prairie sage to the russet of last year's big bluestem. Mixed in is the khaki of the dormant clumps of little bluestem, the darker brown of great swaths of miscellaneous compacted plants, and the black punctuation of leftover coreopsis stems and coneflower heads waving on stiff dead stalks. On the prairie, early April is not a colorful time.

A breeze stirs the reddish brown stems of the big bluestem. This grand grass dominates the prairie here, just as it once did the entire prairie province. After the compacting effects of the winter's snows, the big blue is about all that remains erect. The four-foot stems lean to the northeast, slightly athwart the wind; I surmise the lean comes less from the wind today than from the first snowstorm of the season back in November; snow and wind from the southwest would push the tall grass into a permanent lean to the northeast. Beneath the tilted grass is the tangled mat of last year's growth: dry stems, leaves, seed heads, and plant material in all stages of decay.

Within Steele Prairie, but still unseen, there is a vernal angst as strong as that of Slim Wetherall and every other farmer in the state. Pulling back a big hunk of the prairie duff, I uncover a tiny forest of green grass spears and new leafy plants pushing upward toward the light. Some are pale, some are bright green. Most will be broad-leafed plants, but some will be grasses, and all are impossible for me to identify at this nascent stage. The ground is warm to the touch.

The month is right and the season is far enough along, but on my walk today I find no pasqueflower, the first spring bloomer on the prairie. No doubt it is here, but the flower is not very large, and its pastel petals blend in easily with the matted confusion.

To the Sioux peoples, the pasqueflower had great significance not only as a harbinger of spring, but as a guidepost of life. As the legend goes, upon seeing the first pasqueflower in the spring, a Sioux man is to fill his pipe, sit close to it, and in silence point the pipe toward the sky, the earth, then the four cardinal directions. He should then smoke the pipe, reflect on his own seasons of life, and consider his triumphs and failures and the unseen creators who guide his life and the world around him. He is then to pluck the bloom and take it to his family, singing the song of the pasqueflower as he goes:

I wish to encourage the children

Of other flower nations now appearing

All over the face of the earth;

So while they awaken from sleeping

And come up from the heart of the earth

I am standing here old and gray-headed.

Although this region is no longer prairie in any botanical sense, the area is still a grassland, even with the comprehensive impact of agriculture across the Midwest and the encroachment of woody plants. Grass grows everywhere that something else hasn't crowded it out. Pavement buries it, woodland shades it, and farm implements battle it every year as they edge close to field fences, but grass persists. Unlike parts of Utah, where bare rock and sagebrush form the predominant texture, or Vermont, where trees of all sizes are the baseline land cover, the Midwest is still deep in grass. In northwest Iowa native and imported grasses vie for every unused sunny place.

The grid lines and fields of the Midwest are appropriately but tiresomely described as a patchwork quilt. But perhaps the cliché has merit in a different sense than the usual. Grasses grow along the edges of most everything, along every stream, in every road ditch; they surround every farmstead and field. If the Midwest is a patchwork quilt, surely the grasses are the stitching that holds each piece to the next, the stitching that anchors the entire landscape. The tangled roots, rhizomes, runners, stems, and leaves of countless individual grasses bind the elements of the land into whole cloth.

The idea that the tendrils of grass hold things together here appeals to me greatly. By percent of ground cover, prairie was 60 percent grass; by weight, grasses accounted for nearly 90 percent of annual plant growth. Prairie grasses have root systems of astonishing dimensions and mass. The roots of prairie cord grass, for example, plunge as much as thirteen feet below the soil surface to find water in dry years. Many grasses send rhizomes, or runners, like relay racers, horizontally just beneath the soil surface to establish new stems and clumps, to colonize every crack, any bare spot of soil. Each rootlet and each runner holds a few crumbs of soil and therefore anchors a piece of the landscape against dislodgement.

J. E. Weaver, a patient Nebraska botanist, knew firsthand how grasses stitched the land together: "One exhaustive study of the binding network of roots showed that a strip of prairie sod 4 inches deep, 8 inches wide and 100 inches long was bound together with a tangled network of roots having a total length of more than 20 miles."

Grasses, perhaps more than any other plant, specialize in simplicity. They produce no showy flowers, develop no extraordinary foliage, and make no unusual demands on their environment. Most grasses, especially prairie natives, concentrate their efforts downward, sending roots to find water. A big bluestem seedling will have developed, after only seven or eight weeks, roots six to eight feet deep. In some grasses, 90 percent of the mass of the plant will be below ground to better gather and conserve both moisture and nutrients. Grasses are well adapted to drought. Supple stems support the leaves and bow easily with the wind, suiting them to the windy plains and prairie. In fact, grasses depend on the wind; they use it for pollen dispersal and therefore have no need for elaborate flowers to attract pollinating insects. Hence, their flowers are small, small enough to require a hand lens for study.

More than being the stitching for the landscape or merely forming a background texture to the land of the Midwest, different species of grass—quite apart from true prairie—have individual personalities. Around Peterson are clumps of native big bluestem, ruddy in the winter light of afternoon; a few sprigs of bottlebrush grass holding their own along a shady roadside through the old Kirchner woods; Indian grass on valley hillsides, Canada wild rye, reed canary grass, poverty grass and cheat grass; side oats grama on dry hills, with its pendant seeds like charms on a bracelet; witch grass and switch grass; prairie three-awn; and lawns full of Kentucky bluegrass and the hated crabgrass. Each has its habitat; each has a story. Some were here to tickle the bellies of the buffalo or even the woolly mammoth; others migrated from Europe just yesterday in seed bags brought by immigrants or as seeds in ship ballast.

Most compelling to me is big bluestem. More than any other plant, big bluestem symbolizes the vegetational history of the tall-grass prairie; the "tall" in tall-grass prairie refers to this grass. Just as it does today on Steele Prairie, big blue dominated the prairie in both size and distribution.

In terms of aggressiveness, big blue is to prairie as bur oaks are to woodland. I once planted a couple of clumps of big bluestem in the garden as an ornamental grass. They were small tufts, about teacup size, bought at a prairie-plant sale. I dug them in one day late in May and didn't expect much that first year. It rained a lot during June and July; the grass stayed green and healthy but didn't grow much at all until midsummer. Then, once it had established a strong root system, the grass went up like a rocket; by the last week of August, it bore no fewer than twenty heavy seed heads, the tallest being over six feet above the soil.

Scattered clumps of big bluestem today dot the valley hillsides around Peterson and announce their native status by turning a reddish brown every fall, and they provide a touch of color all winter against the dull straw tones of their domestic pasture cousins. Though they now stand in pasture, these great clumps remind me, each time I see them, that this was once all prairie.

Roadside grasses tell stories as well. Along most roads, especially along highways and improved county roads where herbicide has long kept native grasses and forbs in check, ditches and embankments have become uniform swaths of smooth brome, imported some years ago as a pasture grass. Brome is an aggressive grass that can outdo prairie natives unless fire is used to keep it in check. At times an uninterrupted stripe of brome will unroll for mile after mile alongside the car like an unpatterned hall runner. In such homogeneous stands, brome moves before the wind like ripened wheat, etching the eye with flickering lines as its pale stems move against the darker leaves. Individual brome plants are often as uniform as steel fence posts, making the stems, leaves, and seed heads look like pen strokes scribed as hatch marks onto a printing plate, each line exquisitely fine, each line distinct from, but formally identical to, the others.

Most pastures and fallow fields have been seeded to or colonized by smooth brome. It is good livestock forage, having nutritional value and the ability to withstand close grazing. It covers the majority of non-lawn grassy areas in this part of the world.

Brome, like Kentucky bluegrass and other popular pasture grasses, is a cool-season grass, meaning it greens up early in the spring, giving farmers extra weeks of grazing compared to most prairie natives that don't show much color or growth until the weather turns warm. On April 10, any swatches of green I see around the area are certain to be brome, or bluegrass, or cool-season lawn grasses; any place that is green today is not prairie.

Along the back roads, especially the section roads that have warning signs about "Level B maintenance," the story of grass changes. Here the old native grasses appear where they have been safe from road crews and spray trucks. Near Bob White's place is a wet tangle of native, frog-green, prairie cord grass where the ditch dips enough to hold a little water much of the time. The ancestors of this grass grew here in the prairie wet spots years ago; Velma Walrath, at about the same time she was discovering how afraid Gertrude Tolley was of storms, must have played here. The long, sawtooth-edged leaves of prairie cord grass earned it the name "rip gut" among pioneers, a name anyone walking through it would quickly endorse.

Here, too, are occasional clumps of little bluestem, switch grass, Indian grass, and a few great heaps of big bluestem with its graceful, tall stems. In the late summer at the top of each stem of big blue hang three heavy toes of seeds, reminding everyone of its name among the white settlers here: turkey foot. Then there is a thin run of side oats grama grass, a few oats washed from the field, and brome again, stitching in the spaces.

Leaving the post office one morning with the mail, I found myself wondering what, if any, elements of prairie still hid out in the feral corners of Peterson. Along my route and against the north side of the old Berg Jewelry store grew a few sprigs of grass, and I stopped to investigate. It occurred to me that if there were to be any hints of a lost world, I would find them in the persistent grasses, the grasses that had withstood centuries of drought, fire, hard grazing by bison, and later the assaults of humankind. In town, as in the country, the broadleaf forbs would long ago have been killed off by spray and eager weeding. But could native grasses survive the lawn mower and the sprayer attachment? The season was early, and a close look revealed that most of what grew along the building was in fact crab grass, brome, and common plantain, all aliens. Around Peterson, common plantain, which came from Europe and is not a grass at all, lives up to its name. It is found in sidewalk cracks and any disturbed place. Native Americans called it Whiteman's Foot; it sprung up wherever whites went.

We went looking for clues to prairie, Carol and I, in and around Peterson. This quarter section of land has been streets and yards for a hundred years; before that it had been a cornfield for a few; earlier it had been prairie for millennia. We scoured backyards for a rank holdout of big bluestem hugging a garage against the mower, a stem or two of side oats grama in the compost pile. We walked the back alleys and the perimeter of town looking for any signs. We searched near some old dog kennels; all we found was daisy fleabane, which is at least a native. We poked under farm machinery parked in a town lot; amid the protection of plows and disks we found nothing but bluegrass and quack grass. For several weeks we watched with interest the yard of an abandoned house as it grew up to thick grass and weeds. It was just high enough for the bluegrass to head up and seed out when some good citizen mowed it. A week or two longer and I might have found some old native grasses. But perhaps it was a false hope at that. In town a hundred years of human selection have canceled them out altogether. Our penchant for the fine texture, the tame, our quest for the orderliness of English prototype gardens doomed them.

Around the rough edges of town, the take was slightly better. Bottlebrush grass grows along the road through the woods south of town, and there are some stands of little bluestem on drier hillsides. In the arcs of the river, reed canary grass grows in sweeping, uniform stands. Some strains of this grass are native and have grown here since the glaciers left; others have been imported. I can't tell which this is, but Clint Fraley claims this strain is the aggressive invader.

Unquestionably native are the great bunches of big bluestem and the smaller bunches of Indian grass that surround the town on the hillsides where the trees haven't filled in to shade them out. Like sentries, they grow where they can watch over the town, waving in the wind of a former prairie.

And then we made a discovery, or at least it was a discovery for us. Up behind the schoolhouse, at the east end of the old football field, is what generations of kids have called the sledding hill. I hadn't been there for probably twenty-five years, and all I remembered of it was the rib-crushing dip at the bottom where the steep hill abruptly ended at the level football field. It was late summer, and the grasses everywhere were rank and heavy with seed. As we circled the school and our eyes fell on the vegetation of the hill, I noticed the characteristic russet color of prairie grasses, and spots of silver that suggested leadplant. Closer inspection revealed the sledding hill to be banked deep and undisturbed in fine prairie forbs and homespun grasses.

Here in profusion were Maximilian sunflower, wild garlic, stiff goldenrod, dotted gayfeather, purple prairie clover, prairie coreopsis, and leadplant, a good indicator of undisturbed prairie since livestock particularly like it. Shimmering above and through it all were wild grasses: big bluestem, little bluestem, Indian grass, side oats grama.

Here was a shred of real prairie, a few hundred square feet of what was once several hundred thousand square miles of biome. It lay unseen, as indigenous as a Sioux buffalo hunter and almost as rare, priceless to the eye and heart, and useless to anyone without a sled.

But why here? Why hadn't this scrap of land been put to some use like nearly every other square foot within a hundred miles? The hill is too steep to plow and too small to be worth fencing for livestock; besides, this land has been school property since shortly after the town was platted. Except for sledders and perhaps the browsing of an occasional pony tethered by a schoolchild years ago, this place has been altogether ignored since the bison left.

Carol and I are not the only people who know of the schoolhouse prairie. One of Peterson's elementary teachers knows all about this place, and has used it for several years as an outdoor classroom. She has brought second-graders out the school door, away from books and videos about important events and places, across the football field, to introduce them to something that is more a part of their past—and present livelihood—than any institution, structure, or idea in the region.

What better place could there be for a discussion about the bison, the Indians, Iowa's three-foot-thick topsoil, complex ecosystems, a lost world? But I was told that one of the kids was stung by a bee on a class trip to the prairie, and, because of the risk, elementary classes don't visit as often anymore.

It's funny what we think is important, what we seek to preserve. Even in so universally agricultural a community as Peterson, we see our significant past as being tied only to human endeavors; our history resides only in log forts, on the rusted share of a breaking plow, behind the plaque announcing the site of the first cabin in the county. The Christian Kirchner home in Peterson is not yet a hundred and fifty years old, and yet it is, and should be, carefully protected by Peterson Heritage and treasured by all who live in Peterson.

But these few square feet of original land cover represent something much deeper and older than mere human activity—of settlers and Indians alike—in the region. It may in fact be as old as the land itself. This ecosystem made not only the Kirchner house possible, but also the entire agricultural economy and social structure of the region, and yet we pay it little mind.

Within sight of this scrap of rare prairie, people tend their irises, weed their vegetable gardens, and fertilize their lawns; up on the sledding hill, each year the sumacs spread their shade a little further, overcoming just a bit more of the prairie, and recently someone looking for an easy source of fill dirt taxied in with a big loader and took out a few cubic feet.

First it was a dirt road, narrow between two hedges, with a car crawling along it dragging a tail of dust. Then the road turned off, but the line went straight ahead, now as a barbed wire fence through a large pasture. . . . Then the fence stopped, but now there was corn on one side of the line and something green on the other. Next it was a narrow dirt road again with farms on either side, and then suddenly, a broad highway came curving in, followed the line for a mile, and curved away again. For a short stretch it didn't consist of anything, but the grass, for some reason, was a little greener on one side and a little more yellow on the other. . . . Again it was a hedge until it broadened and became a road, dignified itself, and became for a few blocks the main street of a small town, filled with parked cars; people stepped out of stores to look up at me. Then it thinned out again. When I climbed away and resumed my course, I left it as a fence which had cows on one side and no cows on the other. That's a section line.

—Wolfgang Langewiesche, *I'll Take the High Road*

Chapter 18

Palimpsest

I walked one of the section lines that George Temple and his crew surveyed back in 1856. I walked it in late August, at about the time he made his survey. As a guide, I took along his brief survey notes.

Almost all of the section lines in this region are today gravel roads that cross level, former prairie; about these places he wrote very little, and today there is little to discover on a road running between corn and soybean fields. For this reason I chose a section line different from most; it does not carry a road, and it makes a sort of cross section of the characteristic terrains and environments of the area.

I went looking for the ancient, the new, the abandoned; I crossed a gravel road, the river, the former railroad, and the highway; I sought insight about former prairie, woodland, river, fields, steep valley hillsides, and flat uplands.

I began where George Temple began on September 18, 1856, as he and his crew ran the line that separates sections 33 and 34 of Peterson Township. Today the town of Peterson is half a mile northwest of this point. Temple, like all contract surveyors, was a busy fellow, constrained to making his notes with quill pen while surveying twelve miles per day on foot. His notes are brief, sometimes maddeningly brief, and not altogether accurate. In his haste he placed the Kirchner cabin in the wrong quarter section and often during his short days here slipped into the simple expedient of noting "Land gently rolling. Soil good 2nd Rate Prairie."

His notes for this section line begin: "Sept. 18, 1856. North between sections 33 and 34. Variation 11.30 E." The section corner where the crew began work that morning is just where it was all those years ago, but there is no longer any mound of earth, any notched post. It is instead marked by a stump, a rotted tree wrapped with several strands of rusted barbed wire. From here fences run south, west, and north, but they are old, long-abandoned fences; trees fallen across them have lain long enough to decay into rotten wood and soil.

Nor is this section corner amid prairie, as George Temple found it. We know this spot was prairie by the simple fact that Temple didn't record it as something else; he did record his entry into timber a few chains further north. Today this spot is in deep but immature woods; overlooked, unfenced, and unused, this place sees few people besides the occasional hunters of deer and mushrooms. There are maples, ash, walnut, hackberry—native species all. This is cut-over, disturbed woodland. There have been saws at work here ever since the trees were large enough to provide firewood and building material; hence, it has grown up to sub-climax woodland, with the average tree being a bit less than a foot in diameter.

There is a cottonwood close by the section corner, taller and straighter than other trees around. It stands perhaps sixty feet high, and its long, straight trunk suggests the tree grew in competition for sunlight with other tall trees that have been cut down. The surveyors found prairie here; subsequently the area grew up to forest, apparently dense, tall forest; then the mature trees were cut, probably in this century. The trees here now have been growing for as much as forty or fifty years and will themselves eventually be a mature forest.

From the section corner, I walked north with the fallen fence and the section line through woodland, underbrush, and a carpet of leaves. After a short rise, my walk took me sharply downhill toward the valley floor.

About two hundred feet north of the section corner, Temple noted that the line entered timber, and a short distance farther on my downhill trek, the line crossed a gravel county road cut into the hillside. Clearly, woodland is a good deal more common today than in Temple's time; from this point in almost any direction, timber is thick, if young. To the west is Wanata State Preserve, once the Kirchner woods, and to the northwest, within earshot, is Peterson.

Beyond the road, I crossed a sturdy fence and began a descent both steep and rough. Thomas Macbride was right; this part of the Little Sioux valley is indeed more of a canyon than a valley. The trace of the section line continues north and down as a broken fence, then as a sporadic row of fence posts. Whoever owns this ground owns the adjoining parts of both sections and pastures both sides of the section line. The tree cover is dense, and gooseberry bushes scratched at my feet and face as I walked. Grazing seems to have greatly increased the weedy undergrowth here; it is hard to see more than ten feet ahead. Soon the posts disappear, and so does the section line.

From here I ventured off to the east for a moment in hopes of finding the site of the Ambrose Mead cabin. Mead and his family came west with the Kirchners, and this long-gone cabin was the site of the first election in Clay County. Mead's cabin was here when Temple and the crew passed. He doesn't mention it in his notes for this section, but under his general comments for the township he locates it "on the S.W. 1/4 of section 34." From old maps I knew it must have been close by.

About eight hundred feet east of the section line, I came to a triangular patch of ground, about three hundred feet on a side, mostly clear of trees and quite level. Even on the topographic map it is easy to see that this is an ideal spot for a pioneer home. There is room for a cabin here, a garden, an ample enclosure for livestock, and a good-sized stable. The view north toward the river would have been beautiful a hundred years ago, before the trees grew up. This spot of land stands above the floodplain by about fifteen feet and is bordered on the northeast by a spring-fed creek. Behind, to the south, the slope of the valley rises sharply. There are no crumbling walls of logs here to signal a precise spot, no lines of foundation stones, only some places where the earth has been disturbed long ago. While no one today knows exactly where Ambrose Mead built his cabin, in all of section 34, there could be no better place.

I returned to the section line and continued northbound. Temple's notes mark a transition at seven chains, or 462 feet, north of the section corner: "7.00 Enter bottom."

The break from steep hillside to flat river bottom is dramatic, unexpected. Suddenly the dense undergrowth and tangled trees of the slopes fall away to become open stands of mature maples and cottonwoods scattered over a flat floodplain. The sky reaches into this open woodland through frequent gaps in the canopy, and most of the brushy growth is kept in check by the scouring action of occasional river floods. The bottomland is flat as far as the eye can see, deep in reed canary grass. Out of sight somewhere ahead through the trees is the Little Sioux River. The landscape behind me shows all the signs of alteration by humankind—fences, cut timber, a road, cattle—but the land ahead belongs to the river.

And there is no section line to be seen—no fence, no posts, and certainly no section road. With some irony I took my bearings from the position of the sun and set off to the north. In a region so bound by the land survey, where there are so few places that section lines do not control the entirety of human geography, here I was using the sun as my compass with absolutely no other clue as to cardinal directions.

Walking north, I tried to hold a true course as I stepped around horizontal logs protruding from the grass. There are no human landmarks here, nothing solid to use as a point of reference. Deadfall timber piles against the upstream sides of trees, many of which are twisted and distorted, and all of which bear high-water marks. That this landscape is swept clean by frequent floods is also a result of human intervention. Were it not for the turning of thousands of square miles of prairie to cropland, these floods would be ameliorated, throughout the entire drainage basin of the river, by the slowing effects of slough grasses, sluggish creeks, and the prairie itself.

I stopped for a moment to examine a toppled silver maple that must have fallen just this spring: great hunks of fresh black dirt still clung to the roots. The roots had worked loose in the waterlogged ground, and flood current finished the job. But the tree didn't die; it bore perhaps a dozen finger-sized shoots several feet long, thick with leaves, sprouting vertically from the now-horizontal trunk.

This sort of upended adaptation is common along the river, but they hardly look like trees as we know them. Botanist May Watts, writing of just such river snag silver maples, was unhappy to note that their ". . . many-trunked broad shape . . . seems to belong to the riverside fraternity always, and to the upland aristocracy not at all."

Soft maples and cottonwoods sprout easily on floodplains and are well adapted to such soft, unstable soil. They lean, topple, and spread their foliage wherever the sun shines; maples especially tend to send out runners and send up suckers on the slim chance that the floodwaters somehow will overlook them long enough for them to put firm roots deep into the sandy soil. Some seem to start from a central point and send out trunks horizontally in all directions, much like a clump of crabgrass. They draw sun from a great circle of the sky and grace the river bottom with angled limbs just right for sitting. The result is admirable as a symbol of persistent life in the face of shifting conditions.

It is quite possible that in 1856 timber was thicker here. To an extent the area was protected from fire, and since the river would have flooded far less often, saplings, suckers, and woodland forbs would have had an easier time getting established. George Temple considered this place woodland, but left us no idea of its density and character. Was it the open, near-savanna that it is now? A dense, climax river bottom woodland? Were parts of it open, wet prairie, thick with prairie cord grass that slashed the surveyors as they cut their line? There is no way to know.

This is not a place where people go. Peterson is nearby, and I heard trucks on the highway from time to time, but it felt as if no one had set foot here in years. The only obvious sign of human life I discovered was a five-gallon plastic bucket marked "Co-op," washed in sometime by the river in flood.

Walking north across the floodplain toward the yet-unseen river, I soon noticed that the land is not altogether flat. I stumbled several times in the deep grass as the ground fell away into former river channels beneath my steps. Crossing the third of a mile or so of floodplain to the river, I discovered no less than six abandoned, partially filled channels. All of them are about thirty to fifty feet wide and only a few feet deep. They are choked with grass and silt and occasionally homesteaded by large trees.

Temple's cryptic notes are helpful here. At twenty-five and a half chains, or 1,683 feet, from the starting point, Temple wrote in his field notebook:

"25.50   [chains] Little Sioux River runs west, banks high and sandy[,] bed 70 links wide and gravelly, gentle current, about one foot deep

"29.50   Little Sioux River runs North East

"35.00   Little Sioux River runs South West"

Perhaps the surveyors grumbled at the luck of having their line cross the river just where it meandered; they crossed the stream not once, but three times, in seven hundred feet. But if the day was hot, perhaps they were happy to go wading. And like all rivers free to find their way in alluvial soil, the Little Sioux has changed its course since 1856. On my walk, I cross the river but once.

Just which of the abandoned channels carried the river in 1856, I could not determine. They were impossible to sort out from among the many overlapping riverbeds that twist backward in time throughout the river's long history. These braided beds are testimony to the river's power and patience and ample evidence that, from time to time, the Little Sioux goes hunting for a new channel.

After walking a third of a mile across the flat river bottom, I saw the river itself appear, sprawling its way across the floodplain, moving slow and brown on a late summer day. Its course is just a few feet north of where the surveyors had found the northernmost loop of the river in their day.

I had reached the bank of the Little Sioux at the inside of a bend and quickly consulted the map to see if I had stayed anywhere close to the section line. I found that in my straggling across the unmarked floodplain, I had strayed only about 300 feet east of the section line.

As I approached the banks, I could see that the section line reasserts itself as a fence on the far side of the river. It runs as a distinct line across the remainder of the river bottom and up the north wall of the valley.

On the near side of the river, there were raccoon tracks in the sand and mud. The bank opposite is high, sheer, and crumbling as the outward-pushing water at the outside of the bend works its way north. The water was warm and slow and only a couple of feet deep.

George Temple recorded that he left timber behind when he and the crew crossed the river northbound; the same is true today.

The floodplain on the north side of the river is a good bit higher than that on the south, and the land for the first time along this section line became truly civilized; it became cropland. I crossed the river, and, walking north, I followed the section line as a fence, an old fence, with corn on the west side and beans on the east. The old river trees, the canary grass, the abandoned channels, all disappeared.

At forty chains, or 2,640 feet, or half a mile from the beginning point, Temple recorded that he "set quarter section post in mound." Today that point is near the north bank of the river and forms the corner for the bean field to the east.

Northbound with the fence, I found the character of the section line changes again a few hundred feet north of the river; the line runs through the middle of the Peterson sewage treatment lagoons. The section line between sections 33 and 34 follows the center of the berm separating the lagoons from one another. There are three bulldozer-built ponds; several ducks paddled about on the largest as I strolled through.

Immediately north of the lagoons the line crosses the former Chicago and North Western Railway right-of-way. There is little evidence of it today, but I remember it from summer hikes as a kid. The embankment has been taken out and the surface restored to smooth cropland. Tall Iowa corn now grows where conductors on westbound coaches once shouted "Peterson!—Next stop! Peterson!" and passengers stood up and gathered their bags for the coming station.

It is hard to find much evidence of the railroad anywhere around Peterson. There are a few old culverts, a scrap of right-of-way here and there, even a couple of telegraph poles. The depot is long gone, as are the telegraph line and the water tank, and with them all memory of scheduled train times at Peterson. There were six or even eight a day once, but now no one remembers when they came and went. It struck me as odd that the railroad, so important in the days of the last century, should disappear so abruptly and completely, while this section line, except for the one-third mile of it across the low river bottom, should persist.

Just north of the old rail bed, the section line tilts upward gently and begins to climb toward the north valley wall, and shortly crosses Highway 10. A power line lopes along the highway, paralleling road ditches green with brome grass. Immediately across the highway, the section line becomes a well-maintained barbed-wire fence and begins the sharp climb out of the valley. Temple and his crew found prairie here, not as thick as that on the bottomlands, but good prairie nonetheless, and they would have found no trees. Today the valley side is pasture on both sides of the fence. About half of the area stands in woodland that is anything from low scrub to fine stands of mature walnut and oak. A large oak stands astride the section line; so long has it supported wire that the fence is now part of the tree rather than the other way around. In open areas on the hillside, prairie grass easily outdoes the brome; big and little bluestem, switch grass, needle grass are all much more drought-tolerant than brome, useful on this dry, south-facing slope.

Abruptly the climb ended, and the earth went flat in all directions ahead as the view lengthened to a genuine horizon. Above the corn to the north I saw farm groves two miles away. The north wind was surprisingly strong; there had been hardly a stir in the valley, but on top it fairly whistled through the grass.

I turned and stood for a time looking back south whence I'd come, just as the surveyors might have done a hundred and thirty years earlier. I saw a valley as familiar to me as any anywhere. I put names to the farms scattered through the distance—Molgaard, Brees, Munger—and saw the slow river, fringed with trees, making its way west. There was not a scrap of prairie anywhere in sight.

It struck me as I stood there with the wind at my back that maybe I'd had the wrong idea about prairie. Certainly it began to disappear that day in 1856 when the Kirchners dug their garden into the sod, and certainly it was gone for good by 1900. But in a very human way, the disappearance of the wide and deep prairie should not be marked from the time that the last sod was turned; the actual end did not come until the death of the last person who remembered those miles of waving grass. The landscape of memory is very nearly as real as that of soil and grass, and as long as people lived who still recalled it, prairie could somehow still exist.

Nobody anywhere today remembers what it was like; no one can sit with you and tell stories of what it looked like when ten thousand square miles came into full summer flush, or what it felt like to be the tallest object for fifty miles as a summer storm came across a land uninhibited by tree, structure, or survey stake.

As I compared my view with that of George Temple, I wondered about the change and our roles in it. We are cast onto the landscape as observers and agents of change, but mostly we are observers. Our window on the landscape is of a certain size: it is the span of a life. Within that interval, a world of prairie was converted entirely to crops, farms, roads, and towns.

Likewise, in such an interval, taken at a different moment, fallow fields can spring into mature woodlands. An old farmer returning to farmland abandoned years ago may find tall ash and hackberries; he may stand deep in shade but still feel the plow in his hands, still see fresh soil under May sun. The inertia of memory seeks to preserve places, old haunts, purlieus, and as long as an old man still feels his grip on the plow handles, there will be wheat and oats here, and, in his memory, threshing days.

For the last five hundred feet, the section line between sections 33 and 34 runs level and true. A ragged fence leads to the section corner; it is fringed by large clumps of big bluestem mixed with brome. Owing to years of field erosion and the eolian soil trapped here by fence line grasses, the section line stands six inches above the fields on either side. If humankind were to leave today, and regardless of whether the landscape grew back to prairie or to woodland, the outlines of fields all across the region would persist for some centuries as discrete ridges.

The wooden fence post that once marked the section corner has toppled and is nearly rotted, and a volunteer plum tree a foot or so south of the actual corner has been pressed into informal service as a replacement. The trunk is about the size of the fence post, and several loops of barbed wire wrap around it with no apparent ill effect.

A collection of things common to field corners orbits the plum tree: a conical anthill, bare of all plant growth and teeming with red ants, broken pieces of barbed wire, chunks of wood that perhaps were fence posts once, rocks.

Piled at the foot of the plum tree are miscellaneous field cobbles—glacial erratics washed out of glacial drift. The Wisconsinan glacier brought them many miles from the north, maybe fifteen thousand years ago; farmers' tractors brought them the last several feet to the base of the tree in just the last few decades. They range from fist-sized to a bit larger than a human head; the biggest is about all a man could carry. Growing between them are clean blades of big bluestem and brome grass. Dark plums have dropped amid them and look out of place among stones.

Unwittingly, nature and humankind have joined to build and reinforce a monument to the grid, a monument to this corner, this junction among sections 27, 28, 33, and 34, Township 94 north, Range 38 west, Peterson Township. The plum tree and the stones mark a discrete point on the globe, a point that no one driving on the highway below ever sees. This is a point that can be described precisely and is memorable to me and perhaps others who have been here. Few would remember it for the stones or the anthill, but any farmer cutting the clover nearby on a warm summer day would remember it for the plums.

I tried to never wash clothes and bake bread the same day, but sometimes it happened. I would have to rush in the house and work the bread down and later make it into loaves and when they raised, get the oven hot and see to baking it.

Noon dinner had to be prepared, and much of the time we had a hired man during the crop season. So, get potatoes, meat, a vegetable and dessert of some kind.

—Velma Walrath, "A Farm Woman's Day in the 1920s"

Harold Kirchner of Lethbridge, Canada, was a visitor in the home of Mrs. Velma Walrath.

Harold is the son of the late Charles Kirchner, and grandson of Gust Kirchner. He enjoyed touring his grandfather's home now belonging to Peterson Heritage, Inc.

—*Peterson Patriot*, September 24, 1992

Chapter 19

Heritage

Carved in tan limestone at the top center of the old one-story building on Main Street is the single word "BANK." But inside, instead of a high counter and teller windows, there are several card tables and their complement of folding chairs. It is a small room—it was a small bank—but big enough for seventeen senior citizens to sit and talk while they await Lyle Mohror and their noon meal, brought hot from Spencer. An Iowa flag stands in one corner of the room; the U.S. flag has been taken outside and placed in its receptacle in the sidewalk, to make plain to all that the Senior Citizens' Center is open for business.

The place is pleasantly noisy as conversations circle the room. Topics range from the beauty of the irises this year to a death in Royal last night to ideas for what to use against the astonishing outbreak of mosquitoes and biting gnats.

On one wall is a series of photographs of past presidents of Peterson Senior Citizens. Many of them are dead, including my great-grandmother, Edna Johnson. On the opposite wall near the piano are a calendar and three framed prints.

Gesturing toward the three prints, one of the men tells me, "Your great-grandmother donated those pictures to Senior Citizens." None look in any way familiar to me.

All three show scenes of youth. One is of a boy and girl kissing; they wear traditional Scandinavian garb. Another is from Boy's Town, Nebraska, and depicts a young boy carrying his smaller brother. The last is a well-known modern photograph depicting two little boys in overalls, hands in pockets, standing in a farmyard, looking at the dust. The caption reads: "You been farming long?" An identical print hangs across the street in Sue's Diner.

The unsteady card tables are laid with place mats bearing official information regarding county and state social services; on top are neatly creased paper napkins, Styrofoam cups, and plastic plates. The flatware is mixed. Most of it is ordinary stainless steel, the sort one gets with coupons at the grocery store, but a few pieces are old, high-quality silver plate. Knives, forks, and spoons, now old and brassy, were heirlooms once. An old pattern from my own family amid the jumble of styles jogs my memory.

Velma Walrath sits across the table from me, dressed in an ultrabright purple floral blouse. Her hands are folded as she observes the scene, saying little. Nearly a hundred years old, she doesn't hear very well, and even with two hearing aids, she has trouble conversing in noisy places. She gets around with difficulty these days and was happy for the ride Carol and I offered her to Dinner Date. The one-block walk is a good deal beyond her range.

Velma is one of the two sages of Peterson; my grandmother Ione is the other. Velma enjoys the role, and although her memory is long and vivid, the years have piled up pretty deep. "Just because I'm the oldest person in town doesn't mean I know everything," she told me once.

Her picture is among those of past Senior Citizen presidents on the wall, and she was one of the founders of Peterson Heritage, the local historic preservation group. Soon after they organized in 1971, the group hit on a good idea for both recreation and fund-raising; the members bought a loom and began weaving rugs and place mats from old rags. Velma has been in charge of the operation since the beginning. She can still run a sewing machine and is even more able to use the phone. On any day, without warning, phones all over town ring, and without so much as a hello, Velma informs you that she'll be up at the Heritage House next Monday afternoon and sure would like you to come up to tear and sew rags. She doesn't ask if you'll come; she simply expects that you will.

Under Velma's sometimes stern direction, members gather old clothes, tear them into strips, sew them into long strands, and weave them into folksy and inexpensive rag rugs, place mats, and even "mug rugs," recipe-card-sized drink coasters. Our house sports a good selection. On rag day, Velma runs the show, gathering scraps of similar colors and directing the sorting, sewing, and weaving. The sound of tearing fabric mixes with spurts of action from ancient sewing machines; the bang of hand-operated looms adds percussion. Were it not for the coffee, desserts, and easy conversation, one could be forgiven for mistaking this basement operation for a sweatshop.

Velma knows what sells, and she takes special orders. Someone restoring a home in Pennsylvania recently ordered a thirty-foot stair runner, and Velma had members in an uproar until it was finished. Her front porch is the warehouse for the finished weaving. Surprisingly, the stock makes only small piles on a table; despite the output of several volunteers, supplies sell pretty quickly—"except for the green; nobody likes it anymore," Velma told me. Any friends who visited us in Peterson were dutifully taken to Velma's to meet her and see the rugs and place mats. Most took home an armful, not because of Velma's stern sales ability, which is considerable, but because of the quality and price of the goods.

"We've got rugs and place mats in thirty-three states and eight foreign countries," she told me a couple of months ago. "Those men from China who were here to speak a few years back, they had never seen anything like them."

A few minutes before noon, Lyle pulls up and parks his van in front of the Senior Citizens' Center. Though many of the seniors present cannot walk very far, and though there are numerous cars parked on Main Street today, the spot directly in front of the center has been left vacant for Lyle's arrival. It is an unspoken rule that on Wednesday—congregate-meal day—the parking space immediately in front of the door is reserved for the van that brings the dinner. Someone from out of town who didn't know the fact, and unwittingly parked here, might leave town perplexed by the cold demeanor of the older people of Peterson.

The most able among us quickly unload the food, and, after a short prayer, several of the women swing into action to get the big insulated carriers set up on the serving table. Sensing the eagerness of the crowd, and noticing that we apparently don't know the rules, Florence Krause informs Carol and me that as guests we are to go first. The rest of the group, many with canes, fall immediately into line behind us. For $1.75, we are served minute steak, boiled potatoes, green beans, bread and butter, a little cup of cherries, a lemon bar, and coffee.

Peterson Heritage has done a lot more than simply sell place mats and rugs. Since its organization, the volunteer group has restored the Christian and Magdalena Kirchner house and the nearby Gust and Rachel Kirchner house. Heritage, as it is known, restored the Peterson fort blockhouse as well, and put up a museum for farm machinery. Almost every autumn, with the help of the local churches, businesses, and service clubs, Peterson Heritage sponsors a very popular tour of homes. Members spearheaded the publishing of two large volumes of local history and are now at work to microfilm all existing copies of the *Peterson Patriot.*

Both of the Kirchner houses, surprisingly, had remained relatively unchanged from their original configurations, and Peterson Heritage members worked long months to put them back in good condition and furnish them with period furnishings. Though very few furnishings and appointments are original, they do reflect the nineteenth-century past of the town and some sense of life here then.

For Velma and other members, it is hard to put into words why preserving local history is important. Most people, including my grandmother Ione and her husband, Art, both founders of and active in Peterson Heritage, find it a lot easier to answer questions about when and how things were restored and who helped out. Answers to *why* are difficult to pin down. One day over coffee, I pressed my grandmother and Art about the reasons it was so important to preserve these homes.

"People who go through the old houses—the Christian Kirchner house and the Gust Kirchner house—think it's wonderful to see how life used to be," said my grandmother.

Art added, "It does give the younger generation a view of how people lived years ago, how they cooked, how they farmed. There has been such a change in farming in just my lifetime."

Said my grandmother: "I think every town should have a restoration group. Many places have them now, more and more all the time, but for some it's too late. We had buildings on our own Main Street that we should have saved and restored—the old White Front Store, for example, would have been beautiful as a museum."

They both worry about the town and about the future of Peterson Heritage, and they hope that the historic group can help keep the Peterson of today alive by rekindling a sense of the past. My grandmother is concerned: "It worries us what would happen without Peterson Heritage. We've worked so hard to restore and preserve some of the history in Peterson. There is so much history here, and now we're down to twenty-five or thirty members. We need younger people to join."

Peterson, a town regarded by many as having at best an uncertain future, has an understandable fixation on the past.

Over our plates of minute steak at the Senior Center, Velma looks me up and down, and says: "Say, that shirt would make nice place mats—any chance you'd give it up? I had some brown and white ones like that and they sold right away."

Those at tables around us laugh and make protective gestures toward their own clothing; Velma smiles at her own joke.

In a loud voice I ask her if she remembers when this building was a bank. She hears me and so does everyone else; there is a chorus of affirmative replies from around the room. A couple of people gesture to indicate where the counter was and where the president's desk stood, next to the window. Others count on their fingers and name the officers and employees who worked here long ago.

"You know it was the post office after the bank closed," says someone nearby.

Tora Tigges sits with her back to the open vault door. Above her head in faded gilt paint are the words "Peterson Bank"; above that hovers a cast-iron gargoyle watching over the long-vanished hoard of a failed bank.

"It failed sometime after the crash in twenty-nine," Tora reports between bites.

"Nineteen thirty-three," someone offers.

With the detachment and lack of remorse common in older people, Tora says, "I was a young working girl, had all my money here, and lost every dime I'd saved." Musing a moment, she smiles and continues, "Gee, maybe I ought to look around in the vault to see if any of it got left behind."

Pasted just inside the vault door are old inspection stickers that indicate periodic maintenance of the lock's time clock. The last one is dated in a careful hand and with a fountain pen: "July 9, 32." The time clock stares silently, motionless for decades. Opposite the inspection stickers is pasted a brittle and faded list of names and what appear to be safety deposit box numbers. Some of the names sound familiar to me; they evoke a glimmer of recognition, but no faces, no voices, no personalities, no web of meaning.

The vault is now a closet. It holds a vacuum cleaner and supplies, extra chairs, boxes. The safety deposit boxes are gone, and in their slots are light bulbs, envelopes, electrical parts, a forgotten certificate of appreciation.

Conversations fall back to a murmur as people eat their dinners and discuss who worked in the bank.

There is a feeling here of alliance against the common enemy of old age. People seem to know a lot about one another's lives and health and are quick with sympathy and support for anyone who is having a rough go of it. There is a feeling of leisure among these seniors, of being done with work, but not with life. Laughter and conversation, the bonds of community and life-long friendship, are freely exchanged.

Velma, who seldom misses a senior dinner date, has deeper roots in this place than anyone else alive. She was born Velma Tillinghast on her parents' farm, four miles north of town, in 1894, into a world that would change more in the century of her life than it had in the prior several. She grew up on a farm in the days of horses and hand labor, before electricity, not long after prairie had all but disappeared.

"When I was a kid, there was some land a half a mile west that had never been cultivated. There were flowers that grew there that we didn't see anywhere else. I don't know who plowed it up finally, but it's been gone now for years. It was maybe twenty acres. As I think back, it's a shame that more land wasn't left as prairie—there's so little of it left now."

When her parents retired from the farm to town, Velma and her husband, Carl Walrath, took over the operation. They farmed the level prairie for twenty years and raised four kids in the process. Later, they retired to town, where Velma still lives on Main Street. But Velma never retired; no longer having any bread to bake and no threshing crews to cook for, Velma turned to other work, including housekeeping for my grandparents, and taking care of me as a small child. In later years she began her work in the rug business for Peterson Heritage. She now has eleven grand-children and eighteen great-grandchildren and still owns the farm where she was born; Bob White farms this century farm.

"There were thirteen buildings on the farmstead when I was a girl; let's see, there was the house, and of course a privy, three chicken houses, a granary, a corncrib, barn, hog house, tank house, washhouse, calf shed, and wood house—that's thirteen, isn't it?"

All of them are long gone; the only buildings on the place today are a newer corncrib and a machine shed.

"I remember when they burned the house. My son had started to tear it down—he hoped to reuse some of the lumber—but it was mostly old cottonwood boards and wasn't worth a thing, so they burned it and filled in the cistern and well. My daughter and I went out to watch, and she cried and cried—she was born there, too, you know. But I was glad to see it go—there's nothing I hate worse than seeing an old house rot and fall down. It looks so sad, so terrible. I'd rather see the green grass.

"Sometimes my son drives me out there, and when we turn in the yard, I can hardly believe it's the same place I grew up on—I hardly recognize a thing. There were once so many buildings. Warner, he keeps the place mowed like a park. The only thing left from the old place is some pie plant—some rhubarb."

The senior diners are finished with their coffee and dessert now, and the women are washing up the dishes in the kitchen. Conversations taper off as people leave one by one. With the efficiency of long habit, tables are scrubbed and utensils put away, and the place is returned to a state of preparedness for the next event.

"Well, that's it for this week," Velma says, and we help her up to leave. Dinner Date is over; most of the seniors have left, and Velma, slowly but steadily, cane in one hand, my hand in the other, makes her way out and down the steps.

The ancestors of Peterson gaze at me from the walls of the Senior Center, smile down at me from decades of graduating class photographs hung in the upstairs hall of the Peterson school, stare up at me from drawers of loose photographs at my grandmother's house, and look at me, unblinking, from the pages of the two volumes of Peterson's local history.

In these two large books, there are Braunschweigs and Plagmans, Chattertons, Johnsons, Gangers and Langfords, Tibbets, Brockschinks, Pingels, Reeds, Kirchners, and a thousand more. There are young faces and old faces of every era and age. Modern, grainy snapshots, done with no regard to light, angle, or attire, mingle with smooth wedding portraits of crisp men in uniform beaming beside their young brides. I find bearded and stern preachers with set lips and tiny glasses, startled babes thrust before the electronic flash, and a pair of young brothers in agony with smallpox; Victorian portraits of starched families posed stiffly in front of painted-on columns and tassel drapes; and tiny Hazel Pansy Strait Kirchner Hagerty. She is perhaps four in this turn-of-the-century portrait and stands before the camera in a new dress and sunbonnet, clutching a handful of flowers, cooperative but wary, and coaxed to her uneasy smile by off-camera parents.

When I look at the face of this tiny girl, I remember the same face as that of a tiny old woman. I knew Hazel as an old woman, and she was the adopted child of Phillip and Ann Kirchner; Phillip was brother to Gust and Charlotte and was twelve when the family came to Iowa in 1856. I can hear her voice still, a lovely old woman's voice that broke often into unrestrained laughter. For me, Hazel is a bridge between the Peterson of earliest times and the Peterson of my own. For decades I heard the rumor that there was a relic of the old fort, the end of a corner post or something, buried in her backyard, but no one ever found anything.

The faces in these pictures bear the weight of unending farm and family labor; stern eyes speak of temperance; children express barely contained glee at the joy of playing with cousins at a family reunion; some faces radiate pain and some the joy of life lived well.

In these history books there are pictures of Gust and Rachel Kirchner, and one of Gust in particular draws me back. It is an informal photograph, a snapshot from the first years of simple Kodak cameras. He is a round old man standing by the back step, caught in his work clothes, with stooped shoulders and a cane in one hand; he smiles gently, as he does in every photograph I've ever seen of him. Gust's ample girth is covered by a cardigan sweater—which, obviously and comically, is misbuttoned.

Gust lived out his years in Peterson; his traveling days were finished the moment he felled the first log for the family cabin in 1856. He and Rachel watched over the town from their comfortable house on Fourth Street. If the photographs in the two volumes of Peterson's local history are representative, Gust enjoyed a comfortable old age as the father figure in the family; several photographs depict his easy smile as he sits at the center of large family gatherings. Rachel and Gust are buried in Oakland Cemetery at the top of the hill, on what was once Kirchner land.

Like her brother, Charlotte Kirchner had some traveling to do before she settled down. She left Peterson and attended college at Grinnell and Iowa City, then taught school for a time back in the Peterson and Cherokee area. In the Peterson Heritage books there is a photograph of her as a young woman: serious, intent, but not stern. In 1880 she married Moreau S. Butler, a Cherokee physician; after his death fifteen years later, Charlotte became dean of women at Lake Forest College in Illinois and afterward traveled through a bit of the world before returning to Peterson in 1907, where she lived until her death in 1932. Her adopted granddaughter, Julia Booth, spends part of each year in the family place northwest of Peterson.

There are plenty of Kirchners in the books, but it's odd; there seem to be only two descendants of the Christian and Magdalena Kirchner family living in Peterson today. Many of Gust and Charlotte's brothers and sisters stayed in the area, but the following generations found their opportunities elsewhere and scattered to such places as Montana, Sioux City, Alberta, Fort Dodge. It seems that the family, once in motion, had trouble settling down.

Paging through the Peterson books, I often stop at the photograph of an elderly Anna Fonley; her clear eyes arrest me every time the page passes. They suggest something deeper, and more painful, about lives here. She sits dressed in black with her hair pulled back tightly, emphasizing weary Norwegian eyes that have seen more than their share of hardship. The brief text begins beneath the photograph: "Anna Fonley was born in 1845 in Norway, died in 1927 at Linn Grove, Iowa, and is buried in Barnes Township Cemetery. She was one to rise very early in the morning, dress and start a fire in the cook stove, then sit by the stove drinking very, very black coffee."

According to the text, Anna's husband, Halvor, went one day to town for a load of lumber. While he was standing atop the loaded wagon, perhaps to secure it for the trip home, something spooked the horses; Halvor was thrown to the ground and died of a broken neck. What did Anna's gentle eyes see that day when the grim reaper, dressed as a neighbor or the minister, rode into her yard with the worst news possible?

Her son, Ole, married Matilda Larson, a fine Norwegian woman, in 1901; their wedding portrait is on the same page as the portrait of Anna. The wedding took place at his mother's home. In the picture Ole sits and looks straight at the camera, hair freshly combed, expressing confidence with his clear gaze and strong hands. Matilda stands at his side, dressed as a Norwegian bride, flowers and ribbons woven into her long braids. She looks off camera; there is fear in her face, fear of something just outside the photograph's frame or outside the photograph's moment.

In seven years Matilda would give birth to six children. The first was stillborn; the second child lived; the third was stillborn; the fourth lived; the fifth survived twenty days; and on September 26, 1908, the last child died at birth and claimed Matilda's life with its own. They were buried together. The slim lines of text report that Grandmother Anna raised Herman and Agnes, the two children who survived; we learn nothing more of Ole except that he died in 1935. I can see Anna Fonley sitting alone and silent next to her warming cookstove in pre-dawn prairie hours. That she sipped her coffee very, very black doesn't surprise me.

The text devoted to these events amounts to just forty-three lines of spare prose in a pair of books that run 850 pages. Line after line, page after page, these two books spin the thin and scattered threads of lives past, lives that are picked clean of all but the most salient facts. What is left out of a life that is condensed to fifteen lines?

"They lived there for several years, and all four children were born there."

"She ended her years at Emily's home in 1922 aged 92. She had had no illness, no wasting away. She probably just felt that she had done all there was to do."

"His step-grandfather married another woman who did not take kindly to Art, and the next years were very unhappy."

"Her life as a pioneer woman included planting trees, sewing, removing rocks from the fields, driving teams of horses, cooking meals for 20 hungry men, washing clothes in the iron kettle, and rearing five children."

"He clerked in the Commercial House, Peterson's hotel, and enjoyed the stories the salesmen would tell of their trips around the country."

"There is a story about 'Dad' Leslie about when he ran a dray line in Peterson. He trained the horses to return to the railroad depot for another load of items without him being at the lines. As they went through the streets, 'Dad' would turn cartwheels and hand springs in the empty wagon. [One day] the new doctor observed the antics of the drayman from his second story office window with astonishment and asked his office girl who that crazy old man could be, only to have her say, 'That's my father.'"

These streets, woods, and fields murmur with the presence of those who came before us.

In my own family there are Johnsons, Barrys, Allbees, Gaffneys, Mungers, and Hokansons. Most of them arrived here well before the turn of the century, coming from Ireland, Wisconsin, Denmark, Canada, New York, and Vermont. The Hokanson end, in the form of my maternal grandfather, didn't land in the country from Sweden until 1911 and didn't arrive in Peterson until 1943. As I look at the slim paragraphs about my own family in the Peterson history volumes, and as I talk with my grandmother Ione, who wrote the entries for the family, it becomes clear to me just what role chance events play in the fact that I, or anyone else, ever came to exist at all.

It strikes me, as I consider my own family history, that my family tree, like most, more closely resembles a twisted, river-bottom maple or a storm-shattered cottonwood than any classic oak. When I look across the generations—what few I can see from here—I am struck by the turns, dead ends, and interruptions, the accidents of fate that steer the course of any family. Like soft maples on the river bottom, families grow lopsided as branches are shorn off by wind and ice, premature death, disease, accident. A trunk is split by lightning as a brother leaves Sweden for America, never to see again those left behind. As branches grow upward from split trunks, younger family members in the States lose contact with those in Sweden, leaving to some future genealogist the task of retracing the path.

There are dead limbs in families, and certainly deadwood, and strong branches that angle off to seek sunlight where another has died; there are great, central trunks that lead upward and maintain their lofty straightness as the two hundred descendants of so-and-so gather every five years to compare pictures of all the great-great-great-grandchildren.

Except when it came to "her people," as she referred to them, my great-grandmother Edna Johnson wasn't much interested in history, in things of the past; she wanted everything new and up to date. Dishes, wallpaper, recipes, cars, and furnishings all went out the door as newer, better things came along. Frozen pie crusts and canned filling worked fine for her—"They make just as good a pie!" she'd say.

My mother, Mona Beck, is by and large indifferent to the artifacts of the past; if something old works better, that's fine, but she'd never put up with an unreliable toaster just because it was old and looked interesting. Her appreciation of the past stems from its connection to the present. She and Eddie happily share their house with the ghosts of ancestors; Anson and Helen Allbee built the place when they retired from the farm north of town. Hanging today in the living room is a fine domed-glass portrait of Anse as a young man in his Civil War uniform, a portrait that may well have hung here before. "Anse lives here, too," says Mother.

It is my grandmother Ione Johnson, the daughter and mother between, who attracts artifacts and stories of the past—especially Peterson's past—like a magnet attracts paper clips. The fragmentary history of Peterson, some of it no doubt adjusted a little, inevitably finds its place in her mind and in her house, like birds collecting on a winter feeder. In her memory are countless tiny stories that connect people and events to this place and countless artifacts that prompt the stories.

She tells stories in a different way than I do. Beginning with a cast of characters, she parcels out a bit of the narrative but will often halt partway to connect additional characters—not to the narrative, but to the original characters. She will parse family trees and farm neighborhoods, church circles and war buddies, connecting their places to people who live on those places today, and embroider a set of characters to the point where the narrative is overcome by crowds of names that, for me, have no faces. What she constructs is much less a story than a framework of kin and neighbor, of bonds that hold now-dead people together in eternal association. Unlike some Indian tribes, who refused to speak the names of the dead, my grandmother utters them to keep others—and herself—alive.

Stashed around her place are cottonwood boards from the first courthouse in the county, pews from country churches torn down long ago, a captain's chair from the front porch of the old Commercial Hotel; give-away crockery, old calendars, framed pictures, bread knives, letter openers, ash trays, dish scrapers, key chains, and outdoor thermometers all lettered with the names of every business that ever opened and closed its doors in Peterson. Mixed in are family artifacts of greater and lesser import, including dining-room tables, photographs, railroad lanterns, ancient magazines, and a thirty-pound box of salty and corroded pennies that is the accumulated take from the peanut machine at the John Deere shop over the course of a dozen years.

But clocks are the best example of her deep historical accumulation.

The house, where she and her husband Art live, is peaceful with the heartlike rhythm of pendulum clocks ticking away the last years of the century. Their sound is restful background to every other activity and reminds me not of the passage of time today, but of the passage of past time. Clocks, in my grandmother's house, not only keep time, but maintain concrete links with people and events now gone; I find something comforting in knowing that my ancestors, and Peterson's ancestors, marked time to some of these same instruments.

In the basement hangs the Regulator clock that once graced the John Deere shop. For years it kept time in the back room right where "Batch" Batcheler first hung it, when the place was a Ford Garage. It kept time for mechanics repairing Model T's and was sold with the shop when my family bought it in 1938; for its last years there, its pendulum swung to the sound of modern diesel tractors. I barely recognize it now in its refinished glory; they used to paint tractors nearby, and I always thought the clock was supposed to be John Deere green.

Upstairs in the den is a bright kitchen clock with ornate woodwork. Uncounted years ago, it was a gift to my great-great-great-grandparents; it clangs out the hour and half-hour just as it has for a hundred years.

And in the basement stairway hangs the large-faced Waterbury wall clock that was once on the wall of Halver Berg's jewelry store. On the glass below the dial is painted "H. H. Berg, Watchmaker and Jeweler." Inside the case are four keys that must have found their way to this spot while it still hung in the jewelry shop. When Halver Berg died and his sons cleaned out the old store, they gave my grandmother his old clock; even then, over thirty years ago, history had a way of finding my grandmother. For the years of my childhood, the clock hung in the hall of my grandparents' house and ticked away the hours right near the telephone.

"Nellie Berg, Halver's widow, would call me sometimes," says my grandmother. "We'd talk a while about things around town, and after a while, she'd get quiet, and she'd say 'Well, I can hear old Halver.'"

It is quiet at my grandmother's house; the television is seldom on and the radio only at mealtimes, which correspond with news and weather times, so the only sounds here are the gentle sounds of daily life in an old house—footsteps, squeaking doors, water running, cooking sounds, an occasional ringing telephone, soft voices, and the murmur of clocks.

Spring was blowing through Iowa searching for the vanished prairie. It found no broad, grassy, open spaces over which to waft the cry of the wild-fowl, the soft altohorn note of the grouse, the fragrant smoke of the burning grasses, the scent of the millions of wild-flowers of the springtime of old. Yet, it carried the new smell of the turned furrow to become accustomed to which it had had only a mere half-century; it bore the low of cattle and the crow of the cock, the scent of the crushed corn-stalks of last year's fields as the harrows ground them up over the newly-sown oats, it was filled with the rustle of the leaves of the high groves which made the roads shady and filled the horizon with the upstart beauties of a new woodland. And it brought to human hearts the same thrill that spring has always brought, since the time when it summoned us from our caves in the rocks to a summer of sunshine on the outskirts of the herds of mammoth.

—Herbert Quick, *Invisible Woman*, 1924

Chapter 20

Coda

On May 24, 1991, Rod Burgeson plants forty-four acres of soybeans in the field south of the old cottonwoods, completing one year's cycle and beginning another. Rod has worked this field and others in days of late, disk harrowing at a slight angle to the rows of last year's corn stubble, breaking up the old roots and the now-soft clods of spring. Today Rod's eyes are dark, his face dirty. He's been disking and planting—first corn, now soybeans—for the last several weeks nonstop and doing his livestock chores morning and night. "I'm good and tired; I wish it would rain," he admits. He has about a hundred and twenty acres of soybeans left before he can put the planter in the shed for the year.

The season is well along, and rapidly turning toward summer. Yards in town and in the country are brilliant with irises of every color, and the spirea are just now exploding into white blossoms. The cottonwoods by the road are dense with dark leaves.

A year has passed since Rod last put the planter to work in this field, and, in that time, changes both minor and profound have come to the Peterson area. There have been births and deaths. Like all fields, this one has lost a bit more topsoil. A couple of miles away, the loops of the Little Sioux River have grown a tiny part more acute as the river gradually shifts its course. The trees in the area grew a little taller and thicker, and a few more prairie plants were pushed out by brome grass and shade. A year ago, in May 1990, Sioux Valley High School graduated its last class; there were twelve students. Since then the Sioux Valley School District has combined with Sioux Rapids–Rembrandt to the east to become Sioux Central. The Sioux Valley Soos have become the Sioux Central Rebels. On Main Street in the past year, the old Tumler and Fedderson building was torn down, leaving another vacant lot. During the year, two businesses closed on Main Street: the Dairy Cafe and the Peterson Mercantile; one, Eddie's Hardware, opened.

Today Rod starts planting at the northwest corner of the field, just across the road from the cottonwoods. After first planting the "end rows," along the east and west margins of the field, he turns ninety degrees to plant the main rows of the field. His first pass takes him westbound along the road and fence at the north end of the field; at the far end, he promptly swings around, lines up facing east, drops the planter to the soil, and returns eastbound, twenty-four feet farther south.

The planter is an International 400 Air Planter; it plants eight rows at a pass, and he pulls it with a well-worn International tractor. It is hot and noisy inside the cab, so Rod props open all the windows for maximum breeze. The rows are set thirty-six inches apart, and at a steady five and a half miles per hour with no turns, the machine could plant exactly sixteen acres per hour. But nobody has rows five and a half miles long, and in this field the machine must be turned every quarter mile. Add frequent replenishment of seed—and the inevitable breakdowns—and Rod says that planting sixty acres is a good day's work.

From time to time he stops and dumps seed soybeans out of fifty-pound bags into a central hopper that feeds the eight planter units. Each bag holds 115,000 shiny kernels; a bag will plant about three-fourths of an acre.

The red planter bears a certain resemblance to an octopus. The hopper on top is the oversized head, and eight black hoses protrude from it, reaching out to each of the planter units. On the front of the hopper, facing the tractor, is an oblong window that allows Rod to monitor the level of seed in the hopper. Next to the window is an air-pressure gauge; it holds steady at 10 p.s.i. As he works his way across the field and their level drops, the spherical beans frequently readjust themselves against the window in curious geometric fashion. They are uniform enough to be tiny marbles, or ball bearings, and form surprisingly regular patterns against the glass.

Agricultural planters work by various methods, but the goal of each is to place one seed—and only one—carefully in the ground at an exact depth in a precise line at a precise distance from its neighbors along the line—and to do so at a fast trot. At five and a half miles per hour, and at a seed spacing of ten per foot, each planting unit plants 4,840 seeds a minute; this number times eight rows is nearly 40,000 seeds planted for every minute the planter rolls through the soil. Soybeans, being spherical, are easier to handle than corn, but both require mechanisms of considerable complexity and complete reliability to place the seeds in the ground precisely and one at a time at such speeds. Farmers take special care of their planters; since the last act of the planter as it passes is to gently cover the seed with soil, the success or failure of the job is not evident until weeks later when the crop comes up—or fails to.

Farmers tell stories, mostly apocryphal, of other farmers who forgot to fill their planters with seed, planted eighty acres, or the whole farm, and were flabbergasted and humiliated when no crop came up. More common and more likely are the errors where a single planter unit planting a single row skips for a distance or quits altogether. As I've flown over the Midwest I've often seen farmers' errors from a few thousand feet. Farmers tell me they like it best when mistakes happen away from the road where only light-plane pilots—and not their neighbors—ever see them.

The main mechanism of Rod's machine makes use of a perforated drum and an air blower. The drum sits behind and below the seed hopper and is ringed by eight circles of small holes. It closely resembles the inner drum of a washing machine, but tipped on its side to rotate like a Ferris wheel. Each hole in the drum is a bit smaller than a soybean. The air blower pressurizes the drum slightly; there is a tiny draft of air from each hole when the machine stands at idle. As the planter moves across the ground, the drum rotates on its horizontal axis as soybeans dribble into the drum from the hopper above. Seeds fall into the holes Chinese-checker fashion and are held, one to a hole, by the air pressure as the rotating drum carries them around and upward. Soybeans that haven't found a hole fall back to the bottom of the drum. The seeds are thereby regulated: taken from a status of disorder to one of rhythmic linearity and readied for their regular placement in the ground.

Each bean in each hole, as it reaches the top of the drum's rotation, passes over the open end of one of the eight tubes that lead to the eight planter units. Here a roller comes in contact with the outside of the drum, and as it crosses each hole-cum-soybean, the bean is pushed downward from the hole, breaking its air seal, and it falls into the open tube, making its way to the planter units, to the ground.

Even more than the legs of a octopus, these long black hoses remind me of Fallopian tubes. Each of the eight hoses runs from the drum and hopper, the ovary, to a planting unit; each seed, each egg of a new plant, is carried invisibly to the womb of the warming soil.

Rod often looks back to check the general operation of the planter as we cross and recross the field, though he knows he can see only major breakdowns from where he sits. His system is modern and more foolproof than many. He relies on a monitor on the dashboard of the tractor; connected to light sensors in each planter tube, the device will sound an alarm whenever there is an interruption in the flow of seeds.

East, then west, and east again he plants, moving twenty-four feet farther south with each pass, back and forth in an age-old pattern. There is a name for this motion: boustrophedonic; it means "as the oxen plow."

The steering on this tractor, like most that have been in service as many seasons as this one, is a bit loose, and the field is somewhat rough, and Rod skillfully works the wheel in broad arcs to ensure straight rows when the crop is up.

"Some farmers don't much care about straight rows; their rows just go every which way. They say you can get more seed in a longer, crooked row," smiles Rod above the noise. "You'll always get some crooks and bends now and then, but what you have to do is try to work them out every time you come back by; otherwise they will just get worse and worse and you'll have a big bend by the time you plant the whole field."

The eight planting units roll across the ground, each independently bobbing over lumps, following the terrain, each planting a row. All the efforts of the planter units are focused downward, into the soil, and focused on the exact spot where a seed enters the earth. First in line on each unit are the trash whips, a pair of serrated disks set at an angle to shove aside cornstalks and any bigger clods that would interfere with the delicate act of planting; then follow two polished, sharp disks, side by side; set into the earth, they cut a precise and shallow groove in the soil surface. Between these disks is the open bottom end of the black tube, the exact point where the seed enters the ground. Here is where the attention of the whole operation is directed, yet the actual planting of the seed is invisible; the disks closely shield the operation to ensure that each seed falls into the groove and isn't displaced by Iowa's spring winds.

Immediately after the seed drops, there are two smaller disks, set at an angle, to push soil over the seeds, filling the groove. Finally comes a roller that gently packs the soil in place.

Rod, like all farmers I've ever been around at planting time, concentrates hard on his efforts, checking and rechecking his work, indulging in habits that reward him later with straight, unbroken rows and uniform fields.

Once, after stopping to refill the seed hopper with soybeans, Rod begins another pass, but stops after only a hundred feet.

"Guess we'll have a look," he says.

Down out of the tractor cab, Rod walks back to the fresh line of gently packed earth that marks one of the eight just-planted rows. Under the blue Iowa sky, he puts one knee in the dirt, bends down over the row, and removes his work gloves. The smell of warm soil rises to fill the air. Gently, so as not to disturb the seedbed, Rod brushes back the dirt, uncovering a foot or so of the narrow and shallow groove in the ground. Softly, after two or three passes with his bare hand, he reveals a straight and even row of tiny, spherical soybeans, sharp in the sun, bright and smooth against dark, clumped soil.

Here are small but significant facts, lying close to the surface, that suggest larger truths more deeply buried. They matter somehow, not just for planting, not just for a successful crop, but in the understanding of a place and people's lives here. Details buried just below the surface hint at the underlying structures of a place, the unseen characteristics, the paleolandscape hidden beneath windblown soil.

These particular seeds don't matter much; they'll produce a cup or two of soybeans and represent about a dozen seeds in some 6,700,000 that Rod will plant in this field today. In one sense all their presence here tells us is that this unit of the planter is working, but they also echo the presence of seeds that have been planted all across the region in the last weeks and the seeds that have been planted in this region for centuries. They suggest hope, and a continuing cycle.

Rod looks at each one as the tractor idles in the background, his fingers unconsciously breaking up a clod of dirt. His eye follows the row, measuring the soybeans' separation, their depth in the soil.

They are compelling, these details, memorable and mysterious. The four keys left in Mr. Berg's clock, a crooked section line, bright pottery fragments from a Mill Creek site, a town name with no story, a slip of prairie behind the school, the wait between lightning and thunder, and twelve soybeans laid out one after another, glowing under a May sun.

"Well, we're making progress," says Rod. He smooths the soil back over the soybeans, pulls on his gloves, and returns to work.

Epilogue

Since 1990 and 1991, when the events of this book took place, time has not stood still in Peterson, and its passage has affected the individuals and locations detailed herein.

Velma Walrath no longer goes to senior Dinner Date; she died in January 1994, just as the book was going to press.

Meanwhile, Rod Burgeson was burned in a tractor fire in 1993 and is recovering well at home. Janet Anderson no longer works at the city scale office; because of city budget cuts, her job was eliminated, and the duty of weighing grain haulers is now done by elevator personnel. The old Methodist church was torn down in 1992, and a modern structure now takes its place. On Main Street, the Sundberg veterinary office has closed, and one window of the old storefront is now covered with plywood.

Meanwhile, Peterson Heritage is working diligently to copy to microfilm all extant copies of the *Peterson Patriot*, a job being done in the back room at Eddie's Hardware. And thanks to the tree-planting efforts of several community leaders, including Eddie Beck, Peterson has earned official designation as a "Tree City, USA."

But some things haven't changed; Sue still does birthday coffees at the diner, the farmers still talk of weather and grain prices, and the clocks all keep good time at the Johnson house.

Bibliography

AGRICULTURE

Bogue, Allan G. *From Prairie to Corn Belt.* Chicago: University of Chicago Press, 1963.

Coffin, L. S. "Breaking Prairie." *Annals of Iowa* 5, no. 6 (third series), July 1902.

Oschwald, W. R., et al. *Principal Soils of Iowa.* Ames: Iowa State University Cooperative Extension Service, 1965.

Soike, Lowell. "Viewing Iowa's Farmsteads." Robert Sayre (ed.). *Take This Exit: Rediscovering the Iowa Landscape.* Ames: Iowa State University Press, 1989.

United States Department of Agriculture. *Soil Survey: Buena Vista County, Iowa.* Washington, D.C.: U.S. Government Printing Office, 1977.

———. *Soil Survey: Clay County, Iowa.* Washington, D.C.: U.S. Government Printing Office, 1969.

ARCHAEOLOGY

Alex, Lynn Marie. *Exploring Iowa's Past: A Guide to Prehistoric Archaeology.* Iowa City: University of Iowa, 1980.

Anderson, Duane. "Ioway Ethnohistory: A Review, Part I." *Annals of Iowa* 41, no. 8, Spring 1973.

———. "Mill Creek Culture: A Review." *Plains Anthropologist* 14, no. 44, May 1969.

———. *Western Iowa Prehistory.* Ames: Iowa State University Press, 1975.

Henning, Dale R., ed. "Climatic Change and the Mill Creek Culture of Iowa." *Journal of the Iowa Archaeological Society* 15, 1968.

Lawver, Clinton. "Notes on a Mill Creek Site in Buena Vista County, Iowa." *Journal of the Iowa Archaeological Society* 1, no. 2, January 1952.

Tiffany, Joseph A. *Chan-ya-ta: A Mill Creek Village.* Report 15. Iowa City: Office of the State Archaeologist, 1982.

Vis, Robert B., and Dale R. Henning. "A Local Sequence for Mill Creek Sites in the Little Sioux River Valley." *Plains Anthropologist* 14, no. 46, November 1969.

ATLASES AND MAPS

Andreas, A. T. *Illustrated Historical Atlas of the State of Iowa, 1875.* Chicago: Andreas Atlas Company, 1875.

Clay County Farm Directory 1959. Algona, Iowa: Northern Iowa Directory Service.

Plat Book of Clay County, Iowa. Philadelphia: Inter State Publishing, 1887.

Historical Maps

Gray's New Map of Iowa, 1881.
Rand McNally Map of Iowa, 1890.
Mast, Crowell and Kirkpatrick Iowa Map, 1892.

United States Geological Survey Maps

Peterson quadrangle, 7 1/2 minute.
Sioux Rapids quadrangle, 7 1/2 minute.
Sutherland quadrangle, 7 1/2 minute.
Fort Dodge, 1:250,000.
Fairmont, 1:250,000.

GEOGRAPHY

Garland, John H., ed. *The North American Midwest: A Regional Geography.* New York: John Wiley and Sons, 1955.

Hart, John F. *The Look of the Land.* Englewood Cliffs, N.J.: Prentice-Hall, 1975.

Jackson, John Brinckerhoff. *Discovering the Vernacular Landscape.* New Haven: Yale University Press, 1984.

———. *Necessity for Ruins and Other Topics.* Amherst: University of Massachusetts Press, 1980.

Lewis, Peirce F. "Small Town in Pennsylvania." *Annals of the Association of American Geographers* 62, no. 2, June 1972.

———. "Axioms for Reading the Landscape." D. W. Meinig

(ed.). *The Interpretation of Ordinary Landscapes.* New York: Oxford University Press, 1979.

Plowden, David. *Commonplace.* New York: Dutton, 1974.

Zube, Ervin H. *Landscapes: Selected Writings of J. B. Jackson.* Amherst: University of Massachusetts Press, 1970.

GEOMORPHOLOGY

Carman, J. Ernest. "Further Studies on the Pleistocene Geology of Northwestern Iowa." *Iowa Geological Survey Annual Report* 35, 1929.

———. "Pleistocene Geology of Northwestern Iowa." *Iowa Geological Survey Annual Report* 26, 1915.

Hoyer, Bernard E. *Geomorphic History of the Little Sioux River Valley.* Booklet for GSI Fall Field Trip #34. Iowa City: Iowa Geological Survey, 1980.

Macbride, Thomas H. "Geology of Clay and O'Brien Counties." *Iowa Geological Survey Annual Report* 11, 1900.

Prior, Jean Cutler. *Landforms of Iowa.* Iowa City: University of Iowa Press, 1991.

Thornbury, William D. *Principles of Geomorphology,* 2d ed. New York: John Wiley & Sons, 1969.

———. *Regional Geomorphology of the United States.* New York: John Wiley & Sons, 1965.

HISTORY

Allen, Arthur F., ed. *Northwestern Iowa: Its History and Traditions, 1804–1926,* Vols. I–III. Chicago: S. J. Clarke, 1927.

Brown, Dee. *Hear that Lonesome Whistle Blow.* New York: Holt Rinehart Winston, 1977.

Bryant, Ray L. "A Preliminary Guide to Iowa Railroads, 1850–1972." Manuscript, 1984.

Casey, Robert J., and W. A. S. Douglas. *Pioneer Railroad: The Story of the Chicago and North Western System.* New York: McGraw-Hill, 1948.

Cooper, Clare C. "The Role of Railroads in the Settlement of Iowa: A Study in Historical Geography." M.A. thesis. Lincoln: University of Nebraska, 1958.

Copp, Henry N. *The American Settler's Guide.* Washington, D.C.: Private printing, 1882.

Gilbreath, W. C. *The History of Clay County, Iowa.* Dubuque: Private printing, 1889.

History of Clay County. Chicago: S. J. Clarke Co., 1909.

A History of the Settlement, Development and Present Advantages of Clay County, Iowa. Supplement to the *Clay County News,* April 1892.

Hokanson, Anthony Drake. "The Geometry of Landscape in a Small Iowa Town." M.A. thesis. Iowa City: University of Iowa, 1988.

Iowa Board of Immigration. *Iowa: The Home for Immigrants.* 1870. Reprint, Iowa City: State Historical Society of Iowa, 1970.

Levering, N. "Recollections of the Early Settlement of Northwestern Iowa." *Annals of Iowa,* Various volumes, 1869–1872.

Lokken, Roscoe L. *Iowa Public Land Disposal.* Iowa City: State Historical Society, 1942.

McKusick, Marshall. *The Iowa Northern Border Brigade.* Iowa City: Office of the State Archaeologist, 1975.

Peterson. 2 vols. Marceline, Mo.: Walsworth Publishing, 1980–1983.

Wall, Joseph F. *Iowa: A History.* New York: W. W. Norton, 1978.

Williams, Maj. William. "History of Webster County, Iowa." *Annals of Iowa* 7 (1st series), 1869.

LAND SURVEY

Agnew, Dwight L. "The Government Land Surveyor as Pioneer." *Mississippi Valley Historical Review* 28, 1941.

Cook, Ira. "Government Surveying in Early Iowa." *Annals of Iowa* 2 (3rd Series), 1895–1897.

Dodds, John S. *Original Instructions Governing Public Land Surveys of Iowa.* Ames: Iowa Engineering Society, 1943.

Gillespie, William M. *A Treatise on Land-surveying.* New York: D. Appleton, 1883.

Johnson, Hildegard B. *Order Upon the Land.* New York: Oxford University Press, 1976.

Kastelle, Russell. "Fence Lines, Title Lines and Property Lines." *Technical Papers.* Falls Church, Va.: American Congress on Surveying and Mapping/American Society for Photogrammetry and Remote Sensing, 1985.

Pattison, William D. *The Beginnings of the American Rectangular*

Land Survey System, 1784–1800. New York: Arno Press, 1979.

Secretary of State (Iowa). Land Survey Records, Meridian 5 West, Range 38, Townships 93–96. Volume 256, microfilm roll #25.

———. Original plats of Iowa. Microfilm roll #2.

Stewart, Lowell O. *Public Land Surveys: History, Instructions, Methods.* Ames: Collegiate Press, 1935.

White, C. Albert. *A History of the Rectangular Survey System.* Washington, D.C.: U.S. Government Printing Office, 1983.

LITERATURE

Dondore, Dorothy A. *The Prairie and the Making of Middle America.* Cedar Rapids: Torch Press, 1926.

Garland, Hamlin. *Boy Life on the Prairie.* New York: Harper and Brothers, 1899.

———. *A Son of the Middle Border.* New York: Collier and Son, 1917.

Herron, Ima H. *The Small Town in American Literature.* Durham: Duke University Press, 1939.

Lewis, Sinclair. *Main Street.* New York: Harcourt Brace, 1920.

Morris, Wright. *The Inhabitants.* New York: Da Capo Press, 1972.

Quick, Herbert. *The Hawkeye.* Brooklyn: Curtis Publishing, 1923.

———. *Invisible Woman.* Brooklyn: Curtis Publishing, 1924.

———. *One Man's Life.* Indianapolis: Bobbs-Merrill, 1925.

———. *Vandemark's Folly.* Brooklyn: Curtis Publishing, 1922. Reissued: Iowa City: University of Iowa Press, 1987.

METEOROLOGY

Anderson, Bette Roda. *Weather in the West.* Palo Alto: American West Publishing, 1975.

Battan, Louis J. *The Nature of Violent Storms.* Garden City, N.Y.: Anchor, 1961.

Eagleman, Joe R. *Severe and Unusual Weather.* New York: Van Nostrand, 1983.

Ludlum, David M. *The American Weather Book.* Boston: Houghton Mifflin, 1982.

Lydolph, Paul E. *Weather and Climate.* Totowa, N.J.: Rowman and Allanheld, 1985.

Schaefer, Vincent H., and John A. Day. *A Field Guide to the Atmosphere.* Boston: Houghton Mifflin, 1981.

NATIVE AMERICANS

Bataille, Gretchen M., David M. Gradwohl, and Charles L. P. Silet. *The Worlds Between Two Rivers: Perspectives on American Indians in Iowa.* Ames: Iowa State University Press, 1978.

Blaine, Martha Royce. *The Ioway Indians.* Norman: University of Oklahoma Press, 1979.

Bunge, Robert. "Indian Iowa." Robert Sayre (ed.). *Take This Exit: Rediscovering the Iowa Landscape.* Ames: Iowa State University Press, 1989.

Hassrick, Royal B. *The Sioux.* Norman: University of Oklahoma Press, 1964.

Hoover, Herbert T. *The Yankton Sioux.* New York: Chelsea, 1988.

Mott, Mildred. "The Relation of Historic Indian Tribes to Archaeological Manifestations in Iowa." *Iowa Journal of History and Politics* 36, no. 3, July 1938.

Utley, Robert M. *The Indian Frontier of the American West 1846–1890.* Albuquerque: University of New Mexico Press, 1984.

NATURAL HISTORY

Brown, Lauren. *Grasses: An Identification Guide.* Boston: Houghton Mifflin, 1979.

———. *Grasslands.* New York: A. A. Knopf, n.d.

Costello, David. *The Prairie World.* Minneapolis: University of Minnesota Press, 1969.

Gleason, Henry Allan. "The Vegetational History of the Middle West." *Annals of the Association of American Geographers* 12, 1922.

Madson, John. *Where the Sky Began: Land of the Tallgrass Prairie.* San Francisco: Sierra Club, 1985.

Pohl, Richard W. *How to Know the Grasses.* Dubuque: William C. Brown, 1968.

Runkel, Sylvan T., and Dean M. Roosa. *Wildflowers of the Tallgrass Prairie: The Upper Midwest.* Ames: Iowa State University Press, 1989.

Thompson, Janette R. *Prairies, Forests and Wetlands: The*

Restoration of Natural Landscape Communities in Iowa. Iowa City: University of Iowa Press, 1992.

Thomson, Betty Flanders. *The Shaping of America's Heartland.* Boston: Houghton Mifflin, 1977.

Tjernagel, N. "Prairie Fires Menaced Settlers." *Annals of Iowa* 32, 1953.

United States Department of Agriculture. *Grass: The Yearbook of Agriculture, 1948.* Washington, D.C.: U.S. Government Printing Office, 1948.

Weaver, John E. *Native Vegetation of Nebraska.* Lincoln: University of Nebraska Press, 1965.

———. *North American Prairie.* Lincoln: Johnson Publishing, 1954.

TOWNBUILDING

Atherton, Lewis. *Main Street on the Middle Border.* Bloomington: Indiana University Press, 1984.

Hudson, John C. *Plains Country Towns.* Minneapolis: University of Minnesota Press, 1985.

———. "Towns of the Western Railroads." *Great Plains Quarterly* 2, no. 1, 1982.

Jakle, John A. *The American Small Town: Twentieth-Century Place Images.* Hamden: Archon, 1982.

Lingemann, Richard. *Small Town America.* New York: Putnam's, 1980.

Index

The American Land and Life Series

Bachelor Bess: The Homesteading Letters of Elizabeth Corey, 1909–1919
    Edited by Philip L. Gerber

Edge Effects: Notes from an Oregon Forest
    By Chris Anderson

Exploring the Beloved Country: Geographic Forays into American Society and Culture
    By Wilbur Zelinsky

Great Lakes Lumber on the Great Plains: The Laird, Norton Lumber Company in South Dakota
    By John N. Vogel

Hard Places: Reading the Landscape of America's Historic Mining Districts
    By Richard V. Francaviglia

Living in the Depot: The Two-Story Railroad Station
    By H. Roger Grant

Mapping American Culture
    Edited by Wayne Franklin and Michael C. Steiner

Mapping the Invisible Landscape: Folklore, Writing, and the Sense of Place
    By Kent C. Ryden

Pilots' Directions: The Transcontinental Airway and Its History
    Edited by William M. Leary

Reflecting a Prairie Town: A Year in Peterson
    Text and photographs by Drake Hokanson

A Rural Carpenter's World: The Craft in a Nineteenth-Century New York Township
    By Wayne Franklin